A R C H I T E

T H E   S T O R Y   O F

The MIT Press
Cambridge, Massachusetts
London, England

ARCHITECTURE:

THE STORY OF PRACTICE

DANA CUFF

This book was set in Univers and Trump Medieval by DEKR Corporation and printed and bound in the United States of America.

Library of Congress Cataloging-in-Publication Data

Cuff, Dana, 1953–
    Architecture: the story of practice / Dana Cuff.
       p.   cm.
    Includes bibliographical references.
    ISBN 0-262-03175-2
    1. Architectural practice—United States.   2. Architects—United States—Interviews.
3. Architecture and society—United States.   I. Title.
NA1996.C84   1991
720′.68—dc20   90-42960
                                                       CIP

To my Mother and Father, and to Kevin and Amelia

CONTENTS

ACKNOWLEDGMENTS

It seems now that this book was inevitable. I have always been attracted to contradictions, so architecture school was fertile ground for me. It was not long before the profession's janus-faced aspect appeared: on one side were the unscathed heroes looming large—among them Corbu, Aalto, Kahn, and Wright—while on the other were the battle-scarred practitioners I had recently befriended, who told tales of demanding clients and disabling planning boards. Somewhere, the lofty aspirations of us students were bound to overlap with the experiences of those just a few years our senior. While still in school, I got my first job, and the shape of architecture's contradictions (and of this book) grew visible.

That was over a decade ago. The intervening story is recounted in the pages that follow. Here, I want to acknowledge the many individuals who have helped guide my interpretation of what is going on in architectural practice. Probably the most significant advisers have been the many architects who participated in this project. In formal interviews and structured observations, along with casual get-togethers and informal conversations, these architects generously shared their worlds with me. At times I was fed the party line, when someone wanted me to believe what ought to be rather than something less presentable. But more often, when asked point-blank about problems in their practices, the architects reacted with candor. It is my hope that the practitioners who contributed will recognize their masked selves in these pages and feel that they have been fairly presented. In particular, I want to thank the three offices that opened their doors to me when this project was in its nascent phase. The good friends I made in those firms deserve much credit for their patience and thoughtfulness as the ideas in these pages struggled to take form. There was enough curiosity about what I was learning to make me think that this book may partially repay the vast debt I accrued.

Another important group of individuals participated in the beginning stages of this work—my advisers in graduate school at the University of California, Berkeley. Jean-Pierre Protzen, Russ Ellis, and Ken Craik supplied early critical reviews that got me started on the right foot. Parts of the work were also informed by the insights of other faculty members, including Roger Montgomery, Joe Esherick, Galen Cranz, Marc Treib, and the late Don Appleyard. Berkeley was probably the only institution in America that could have provided the breadth and depth of faculty to support my undertaking, and I feel fortunate to be one of its graduates. As the work evolved, Russ Ellis again gave it direction through his reading of the entire manuscript.

Throughout this work, I have had one mentor and friend who has provided the model for how to analyze architectural practice, and to whom I am intellectually indebted—that is, Bob Gutman. From our first meeting, when I was still a graduate student and he took me aside to discuss a conference presentation I had made, to our collaborative projects at present, Bob has been a strong, steady influence on my thinking. His constant challenges to the theories, research methods, and facts pertaining to the architectural profession have inspired my studies.

A series of professional gatherings helped forge this analysis of practice, through arguments and alliances among those of us who attended them. The American Institute of Architects has held numerous seminars and workshops that included David Haviland, Mary Dolden, Bob Shibley, Jim Franklin, Weld Coxe, Bob Gutman, and myself, among others. The AIA's support has been crucial to this study from the beginning, encouraging Mike Joroff, Bill Ronco, Marv Adelson, and me to apply for the National Endowment for the Arts grant we received, which led, in part, to the study on design excellence reported in chapter 6. Through Gutman, Princeton University hosted several key meetings on the profession of architecture. Donald Schon at MIT invited me to present early versions of this work at symposia about designing. In these collective settings I have fielded questions from some astute listeners, and my book is the better for it.

I have also had significant support during this decade of work from the three universities that have employed me: the University of Colorado, Boulder, Rice University in Houston, and the University of Southern California, Los Angeles. In all three schools, administrators, colleagues, and students have contributed in important ways. In particular, I want to thank Mike Martin, Jack Mitchell, Bob Harris, and Alan Kreditor, the deans at these institutions. At USC, Anastasia Loukaitou-Sideris helped with the bibliography and Ken Beck worked on the diagrams. Michael Dear and Jennifer Wolch gave many helpful impromptu critiques of my ideas. The text benefited from Jeff Chusid's close reading of each chapter. Special thanks are due to Roger Conover at MIT Press for his backing, frankness, and gentle prodding.

Another group of people played a crucial role in shaping this book, making it more coherent and well-stated. These women read versions of each chaper over and over again, offering critical assessments at each pass. Diane Favro, who plunged into architecture with me at Berkeley, has consistently asked the right questions and offered historical insights about the profession. Anne Fougeron's reflections on her own practice were extremely helpful. Caroline Hinkley enriched my thinking through conversations about the book's central ideas. Beth Robertson always managed to put her finger on the weak spots while offering ways to strengthen them at the same time. Most of all, Gerda Norvig was my persistent and incisive companion during the writing of the manuscript. From her generous encouragement of the roughest early draft to her intelligent evaluation of my arguments in later versions, she helped me bring this book into existence.

Finally, I thank my parents, Ruth and Charles Cuff, for bringing me up in the way they did—with challenges and support, in the confidence that I could do whatever I set out to do. Their love and encouragement have been the rudder that brought me back on course more times than I can remember. My husband, Kevin Daly, has urged me steadily onward over the past decade. His perspective on architectural practice has balanced my own, informing and sharpening my understanding. He has been partner and compatriot, with whom I have shared every detail. In the final weeks before the manuscript was completed, we gave birth to our daughter, Amelia. Last but not least, I thank her for her sweet spirit that not only brings such joy, but also left just enough room for me to finish this book.

ARCHITECTURE:

THE STORY OF PRACTICE

As I neared the end of my architectural studies in graduate school, I looked out upon a San Francisco skyline completely transformed from the one I'd seen when I started school. It wasn't the new buildings. Taking in the view four years earlier, I had been struck by the genius of architects, by the power that resulted from carrying their intentions into practice, and by the potential of new ideas (maybe my own) to improve the urban scene. Four years later, I wondered who actually *had* created this scape; what hordes of politicians, planners, clients, bankers, engineers, civic groups, corporate executives—as well as architects—had struggled to get a given building built in its final form. I wondered what their initial intentions were and how those had been transformed into what I was seeing. I marveled at those few buildings where some integrity of design, some conceptual coherence, persisted.

Like other novice students and much of the public at large, I was under the impression that architects, in their artist-like studios, worked in relative isolation, making drawings of buildings. While this is certainly an important part of architectural work, it captures neither the range of activities nor the people involved. Where did this innocent vision come from? Chiefly, perhaps, from Howard Roark, hero of Ayn Rand's novel *The Fountainhead*, who pursues at all costs his personal vision in the face of society's mediocrity. With this myth of the autonomous architect-hero in mind, I was caught off guard by my early ventures out of the university into the realm of actual architectural practice. What, I kept asking myself, is going on here? I felt as though I had awakened in a foreign culture with a coherent yet invisible system governing its behavior, a system that seemed only vaguely familiar.

At one level, what goes on is quite simple: architectural practice is the everyday world of work where architecture takes shape. It transpires both inside and outside the office and involves numerous individuals who perform the various tasks required to build buildings. But in actuality, what goes on is not at all simple. In the course of my studies I found small and large warehouses literally filled with young men and (some) women who sat at drawing boards writing memos, talking to others around them, filing, and drafting. There were architects who did nothing but make models and others who seemed only to talk on the phone. Their bosses usually had offices that looked more bureaucratic than artistic, for even those with drawing boards

1.1 Architect Howard Roark
(from Ayn Rand's *The Fountainhead*) burns drawings of
creative masterpieces, never
built because they were too innovative for conservative
clients.

1.2 This meeting is more typical of architectural practice
than Howard Roark's isolation. Among the architects
and clients discussing the
Connecticut General Project
by Skidmore, Owings and
Merrill are SOM's Gordon
Bunshaft (with arm raised) and
Connecticut General's chairman Frazier Wilde (in jacket),
circa 1955.

WHY STUDY THE CULTURE OF PRACTICE?

kept them covered in paperwork. Their clients were even more startling; often they were committees, actively involved in the design enterprise and apparently in charge of it. When the architects and clients got together, it was hard to follow the thread of their conversation; they left meetings with no more decisions made than at the outset.

Was I naive? Of course. But my expectations were representative of the outsider's vision of architectural practice. This contradiction between what I believed to be true about architecture and what I observed in action sparked a decade of research, culminating in this book.

What initially appeared to me as the natural manifestations of an architect's work at the drawing board—the buildings on San Francisco's skyline, for instance—now reverberates with so much complex activity that it is difficult to keep the architect in focus. As with the deflation of any myth, this adjustment to reality was both a disappointment and a revelation. Disappointing because architecture can be so pure, so elegant, when a single architect creates without outside interference, and because the opportunities to do so are virtually nonexistent. Yet there was also the intuition that architecture both relies upon and exceeds individual creativity. History insists that buildings are part of our cultural heritage, reflecting our collective concerns, yet historians are typically reluctant to suggest that buildings might have been born from a collective conception. This book examines how buildings may be collectively conceived; that is, it considers architecture as a social construction. It is my hope that such an understanding, along with the attempt to work more effectively in the collective endeavor of architecture, will guide us toward making better environments.

WHAT IS PRACTICE? To study practice requires a working definition of the term. In general, practice is an action or performance, but the term also implies a method of action, in the sense of habitual, customary, or routine. A professional practice, then, is the customary performance of professional activities. This definition suggests two lines of inquiry that can help clarify the nature of architectural practice: what are architecture's professional activities and how are they customarily performed? A partial answer is that architectural practice emerges through complex interactions among interested parties, from which the documents for a future building emerge. This I never learned in school.

The idea of routinely performed activities suggests that the actions stem from routine knowledge and that they mean something within a specified context. Practice is the embodiment, indeed the expression, of the practitioner's everyday knowledge. In practice, the architect does not refer to textbooks or procedures manuals to determine how best to behave. Only when stumped, say by a financial or legal problem, might the architect revert to a textbook solution, or, when inspiration is needed, an architect will seek out appropriate images. By contrast, routine activities based on commonplace experience are awkward to explicate. The architect finds it difficult to explain how to persuade a client, recognize an acceptable compromise, work within the budget—these are things you "just do." Such routine actions, which undergo continuous development, are meaningful components within the particular setting of architectural practice. But they are exactly the elements of which outsiders have no inkling and so develop distorted images of architects and their work.

Customary actions, as they evolve, weave webs of meaning among a group of participants; these form the very basis of culture according to some definitions.[1] In this book, I recount the story of the architect's work in terms of what I call a culture of practice. Use of the concept of culture fosters a certain kind of analysis, one that looks closely at people's everyday lives, their situated actions, as well as what they say and the meanings they construct. I want to make clear, however, that to consider the practice of architecture as a cultural system does not imply that the profession or its members constitute a culture. If a culture must have some coherence, some shared meanings, routines, knowledge, and values, then the architectural profession as a whole is a far more dispersed entity for analysis than an architectural office. As I will elaborate later (chapter 5), a firm's characterisitcs correspond neatly to cultural constructs, which led me to focus upon the culture of architectural practice rather than the culture of architecture.

A NOTE ON THEORY AND METHODS

When anthropologists undertake a study of an unfamiliar culture, they typically write an ethnography. Although the legitimate contents of an ethnography are always being debated, most current ethnographic studies look at the patterns of interpretation that members of a cultural group invoke as they go about their daily lives. Into the general knot of making sense of the world, an ethnography ties ideas about the group's knowledge, its beliefs, its social organization, how it reproduces itself, and the material world in which it exists.[2] These guidelines for studying "unfamiliar" cultures apply equally well to those communities that we encounter every day, be they work groups, ethnic groups, or social networks. Semantic ethnography has been especially helpful to me in analyzing the present case studies and interviews with architects. Semantic ethnography provides an insider's interpretation of the scene by emphasizing close observation of the actors' terms and structured categories that reflect the sense they make of their world. As speakers describe any part of their work world, a second, unself-conscious work world is being exposed in the way they tell the story.

Two important lessons can be learned from contemporary cultural studies: that the group's story should be told from its members' point of view, and that ethnographers should step into the scene and "write themselves into their accounts" (Traweek 1988:ix). I begin and end this work with vignettes from my own experience in architectural practice, which instigated the present study. My own career in architecture, as a teacher and consultant, provides rich data to augment what I have learned about others in the field and makes me an "indigenous ethnographer" (see Clifford 1986).

Although ethnography is the best single description of this study of architectural practice, other theoretical precursors and philosophical allegiances point its fundamental orientation. In particular, ethnomethodologists provide conceptual guidance for the examination of everyday sense making and the social construction of reality. Ethnomethodology, like phenomenology (on which it is based), focuses upon interaction and its explicit practices of talk and action.[3] In addition, as the quotidian practices of a group unfold, an observer can pay special attention to the dilemmas confronted. Many of the findings in this work are readings of the dilemmas practitioners face, and how they resolve them, only to create new dilemmas.[4] The theory that has directed my way of understanding what is going on in architectural practice stems primarily from specialized fields of cultural and social analysis. Philosophically, what I value in these perspectives is their rejection of positivist notions of the social world, embracing interpretation, meaning in context, interaction, and the quality of the commonplace.

Most architects find that their everyday life is invisible except when it is problematic: a client sues, the building department sends plans back for revisions, the contractor goes bankrupt. War stories are readily recounted when architects describe their practice, as are tales of great success, but it is difficult to hear about the commonplace (cf. Clifford 1986). If we are to offer sound advice about how architectural practice *ought* to function, we must know more about how it functions now. I therefore emphasize descriptive analysis, but overstep the bounds of ethnography by offering some prescriptions as well. The primary goal for this book is to achieve a better understanding of architectural practice, relying on "thick description" (Geertz 1973) and cultural analysis that digs deeply into the significance of any actions, in their ongoing context of intricately interlocked meanings. The focus is on rich stories with high internal validity—stories that will ring true to insiders—and a careful examination of the meaning and significance of those stories.

The goal of thick description led me to conduct case studies and interviews and to assemble the resulting in-depth, qualitative data. Issues intimate to insiders but unknown to outsiders can only be grasped if the actors' own viewpoints are carefully unearthed. To complicate matters, what architects say and what they do are often two very different systems (see Argyris and Schon 1974). Thus, a description of practice based solely on architects' own reports will not necessarily capture their commonplace activities. Under such conditions, valid, reliable research requires a balance between the insider's self-report and an outsider's observation. Coupled with participant observation, ethnographic methods can reveal the sophistication and intricacy concealed in the apparent disorder of everyday life.

THE ARCHITECTS AND FIRMS

My first step in understanding architectural practice was to get into it. This proved to be a difficult task. In 1980, on the advice of a number of architects and scholars, I sought entry in firms representing a range of types of practice. Of the seven firms approached, three granted my request to observe, first hand, their quotidian worlds.[5] I spent the next six months in the midst of those three offices, located in different parts of the San Francisco Bay Area. Because they form the bedrock for all my subsequent research, I will describe these firms in some detail. They vary in orientation, management style, organizational structure, market for services, quality of work, and size. This latter factor is a magnet for many characteristics of a practice (Blau 1984), yet the number of office members fluctuates enough that most principals cannot accurately state how many people work for them. The three firms produced very different buildings and rarely competed with each other for work.

The first firm, situated in a bustling garment district, occupied a narrow slot of warehouse space that left the office with little natural light. Brick walls, wood columns, a Persian rug in the conference room, and a roof deck with jacuzzi (not often used) together created a casual atmosphere. Of the twelve to fourteen members four were partners, one of whom was the firm's founder and inspirational leader. Relative to other firms in the area, the ethnic and gender mix at all staff and management levels was considerable, and management was generous with responsibility as well as salaries. The office's work was varied but small-scale (generally under 15,000 square feet), consisting mainly of private residences, small institutional projects, developer office buildings, and some retainer work for a local agency. They won local awards for their projects and had a local market for clients.

The second firm was somewhat smaller, headed by a single partner who was aggressively trying to develop the firm. He was an entrepreneurial type who traveled often, read *Business Commerce Daily*, and went after government work because it mandated the hiring of minority-owned businesses like his own. Labor was specialized in this six- to ten-person firm, which consisted of the partner, usually two project architects, one designer, one business manager/marketer, one accountant, one secretary, and two drafters. The majority of their work was multifamily housing, both private and public, and small-scale developer office buildings. The firm was located just off a run-down commercial street leading into downtown, above an automotive repair shop. Inside, the recently remodeled office was all glass and white stucco with a cool, high-tech ambiance.

The last office had three partners, about six associates, and another 30 employees including a business manager, the total varying between 38 and 45 people during my time there. This office occupied the ground floor of a large warehouse building with big industrial windows on all four sides. All the work stations were open, allowing the space to be filled with light, activity, and noise. Since the firm was large enough in size, it had more facilities than the others, including a well-stocked reading and materials library, an employee lunch area, and a model shop. An established firm, its founder was scaling back his participation while a younger partner assumed a greater leadership role. The office had local, national, and international markets, with projects ranging from single and multifamily residential, to retail, to relatively large-scale institutional buildings (but little office or industrial). This firm won local as well as national awards for its work.

In general, the firms, like the profession, were homogeneous in terms of race and gender. Of the eight principals, there was only one woman (who held responsibilities more traditionally associated with women's work in the design fields: interior design and accounting). The office staffs were approximately 20 percent female, primarily at the lowest levels, which reflects not only the difficulties women have with advancement but also the larger numbers of women entering the profession in recent years.[6] There was a high proportion of Asian architects working at all levels (for example, three of the seven principals), but Hispanics and blacks were underrepresented (none were principals, and among approximately 60 nonprincipals in the study, there were only three Hispanics and one black.)[7]

During my six months of observation, I rotated among the firms on different days of the week, setting up a work area in each where I would read project files and take notes on the activities in my immediate vicinity. Since I was engaged in the sophisticated anthropological activity called "hanging out," I welcomed frequent interruptions, and so spent a good part of every day observing meetings, interviewing firm members, or casually conversing with anyone available. I made myself useful, which helped me gain access to the parts of practice I needed to see, by doing some drafting, photography, proposal writing, and model making. My most fruitful contribution was copious note-taking at meetings, where I scribbled furiously for my own purposes. The architects soon discovered that these meeting notes were useful for office records and memos. The notetaking gained me invitations to more meetings, and at the same time, offered an explanation for my presence to clients and consultants. Besides my primary activity of attending meetings, I took part in many special occasions and informal get-togethers: a weekend retreat for the entire office, potluck dinners, Friday afternoon picnics, movies, lectures, meals out, drinks—casual situations in which the most candid conversations took place. My activities, as those of the architects I was studying, varied dramatically from day to day: one day I flew in a private airplane to attend a client meeting, the next day I went with several architects to help run electrical wiring out to the secretary's garage, the next day I drove with a partner for three hours to do a site inspection, and on the weekend, I went on a camp-out to Yosemite with a group of partners and staff.

After six months' research in the offices, my contact with two of the offices continued on other bases. I became close friends with the partner of one firm, and another firm hired me to lead bimonthly office meetings on topics ranging from improving design quality to increasing employee satisfaction. Both continuing contacts were important forums for discussing my evolving analysis of the field work.

During the field work, I accumulated more than 600 pages of field notes, observed about 70 meetings, conducted 25 interviews with firm members, and read office files on 10 separate projects. Since that time, a range of additional studies have developed and refined my early work (see appendix A). Over the past several years, I have conducted formal and informal research in San Francisco, Los Angeles, Houston, Memphis, New York, Princeton, and Tampa. Between the first in situ observations in California and another case in Houston four years later, I have formally interviewed 77 people, including 50 architects (see appendix B), 20 clients, and several business developers and programming specialists. I have also observed or facilitated five roundtable discussions about practice that engaged 52 architects. Four of these group discussions were organized by the American Institute of Architects specifically to gather a national sampling of their members' problems in practice. All together, 244 individuals participated in the various studies, representing 80 different firms. There have also been infinite opportunities for informal observation and data gathering in the sphere of architects with whom I teach, work, and associate. In this book, nearly all sources have been masked for confidentiality, but in the retelling of the stories, I have preserved enough of the truth so that the actors will be able to recognize themselves.

The vast amount of data I collected from various architects, clients, offices, and regions was necessary in order to overcome certain built-in biases, that may still lurk in spite of my efforts to eradicate them. In the self-reports of architects and clients I interviewed, both typically represent their labors in the best possible light, but architects have an added incentive to exaggerate since all interviews are publicity opportunities. Such self-promotion would constitute a serious bias in the study were it not for the controls of my own observations and the numerous intimate conversations, relatively unguarded, that I had with architectural associates. The level of generalization I use in the book is also somewhat arguable. While case studies by no means constitute a sample, the three initial cases have been augmented by many further studies that allow me to draw broader conclusions. Nevertheless, I have missed some important differences among architects and firms, thus distorting the collective portrait I have drawn.[8] Finally, I have spent far more time with architects than with their coparticipants, including clients and consultants. This is the architect's story; it is the tale of architectural practice from the architect's point of view.

Because, as critical theorists and contemporary anthropologists argue, good interpretation should admit its own biases, I will admit mine. My training in both the social sciences and architecture has given me the ability to examine the gap between the two. I have taught as a social scientist among architects, and as an architect among social scientists. Straddling this chasm has enabled me to borrow without license from diverse disciplines, neither supported nor inhibited by a tight-fitting paradigm. My main concern, however, is the quality of the built environment. In my own experiences in architectural practice, I have been frustrated by how difficult it is to create buildings and cities that both are aesthetically pleasing *and* meet the needs and desires of clients and inhabitants. Over time, the complexities of this task have become more apparent to me. This book explains my current understanding of how architects handle the task, and describes the model of design that addresses those complexities: design as social construction, or design as negotiation.

I expect that architects' responses to this work will be mixed, ranging with the three types of reporting it contains. First, there are descriptive elements, primarily stories and dialogue drawn from immediate practice that enable readers to examine my data and formulate their own judgments. In addition, a major portion of the text describes practice through organized summaries of great masses of field notes. The second kind of reporting is analytic; here I structure and interpret the descriptive element according to both theory and observation. The third type is evaluative, contained in the final two chapters. I examine the evolution of works of architecture acknowledged for their excellence and study their collaborative origins. To conclude the book, I formulate some recommendations for bringing architecture's principal institutions more into line with the culture of practice. I expect that architects will recognize their everyday life in the descriptive part of the work, that the evaluative portion will expand their way of thinking about the field, and that the analytic or interpretive aspects of the study will be controversial.

ISSUES AND FINDINGS

In the course of my research, I have found that the view of practice as a series of dialectical dualities is an apt model. Analysis of the data has led me to the conclusion that the profession tends to favor one component of each duality while neglecting the other, thus creating an imbalance that can lead to certain problems. The neglected domain is the territory of practice itself, which is why I focus on bringing practice back into the balance, back into dialectic tension with the profession. I raise several important issues or dualities in nearly every chapter in order to explore central themes from various perspectives and to delineate their several aspects. The first duality counterposes the individual with the collective, tapping into the contrast between architecture's fundamental respect for the autonomous artist and its use of teams of professionals to do the actual work for any project. The individual/collective issue is at the root of much of the analysis. A second dilemma counterposes design against business or art against management in the architectural office. While practitioners recognize the inescapable links between the two, it is by no means a happy marriage. Third, I raise the debate about design as decision making versus design as making sense of a situation. The way architectural problems are construed as well as how they are resolved ties into this theme. Last, an underlying question posed throughout is whether architecture is best created by a mosaic of specialists or is inherently the comprehensive task of qualified generalists.

All four issues come into focus when we turn our attention to architects and clients, since the different expectations they bring to a project make that contrast more explicit. The issues also arise in comparisons between schooling and office practice, because these are the primary social settings for practitioners, where the bulk of professional ideology is developed. The umbrella under which all these dilemmas collect is a broader contrast between beliefs and practice, or ideology and action. That discrepancy, which every architectural student confronts in her or his first job, persists within the culture of practice. The concern with ideology and practice brings the discussion back to

1.3 An early view of the MIT
Department of Architecture
(1902). Such life drawing
classes were intended to
develop the young architects'
artistic faculties.

analyses of professionalism, in the contrasting light of the actualities of the building industry and the myths that enshroud it.

The fundamental point is a simple one: the design of our built environment emerges from collective action. Typically design is believed to be an individual's creative effort, conjuring up images of late nights at the drawing board. Indeed, this is a significant part of making buildings, but it is not sufficient to explain the design process. Those who argue that the individual architect determines *what* the building will be, and all such issues of practice, clients, and collective action concern *how* the design will be implemented, are simply separating content from method, form from means, while overlooking the integral balance necessarily struck between them.

An inverse relation is generally supposed to exist between design quality and degree of participation by nonarchitects. We know that great buildings, and many great unbuilt proposals, have come from creative architects. But in what context? With what assistance and contributions? Even these architects were assisted by sympathetic allies, if not promoters—people who paid for the construction, denounced established standards in favor of new ideas, or helped the architect financially (see Becker 1982). For example, Monsieur Frugès, the client for the Pessac housing project, wanted Le Corbusier to consider the entire district his laboratory, to abandon convention, and to carry his ideas to their extreme conclusions. Many of the innovations at Pessac were possible because of Frugès's patronage, and some of the failures were due to the fact that Corbu had not designed the collection of individuals and agencies needed to complete the project successfully.[9]

To develop any design proposal so that it can become architecture requires knowledge of aesthetics, siting, function, structures, mechanical systems, graphic conventions, and perhaps even "the theory of the heavens."[10] Theory and skill in these areas are taught in school, but to build the design proposal an architect needs further expertise. She or he must be able to nurture the scheme through its stages of development in the everyday life of an architectural project without compromising its quality. That everyday life has an economic, an interactive, and a political component, all of which falls under the rubric of what I call the social dimension of architecture. If good design is to emerge from groups, we must acknowledge the situation and learn as much as we can about it in order to work together effectively.

The artifacts of practice, buildings, are socially constructed by the hands of individual architects, their coworkers, the organizations they work within, the array of contributors from clients to consultants and their colleagues, and by larger socioeconomic forces that affect the profession. Direct observation of architecture's everyday world dis-

1.4 Building the Tower of Babel. This fifteenth-century illumination portrays building methods of Gothic times, with numerous craftsmen coordinated by overseers. Visible at left in the distance is a mason's lodge, which functioned in part as a meeting place for these craftsmen. By the thirteenth century, these builders had attained something like professional status.

plays the interaction of these characters and permits context-based interpretation. Such observations, however, have been difficult to come by and studies of architectural practice from the inside are virtually nonexistent, since professions tend to isolate themselves from outside scrutiny. The oversight is also due to architectural researchers who have focused all their attention on the professional product—buildings and places. The *process* of design has only in recent years received empirical attention as well. This book is the first to report extensive empirical data from observations within architectural practice, and as such, should interest two principal groups of readers. It should be of value to social scientists interested in the nature of work, practice, and the construction of social reality, who have heretofore been denied access to architecture. But the book is written primarily for all participants in the design process: architects, clients, politicians, engineers, citizen design boards, and planners. To those who do the work of shaping our physical environment, I hope this study fosters a new understanding that will assist the social construction of architecture.

Not long ago, a prominent architect who works almost entirely on immense projects—urban design commissions and complexes of buildings usually hedged in by regulations, committees, and developers—told me his analogy for the design process. He likened architectural creation to the process a potter must go through when she has a kiln that distorts as it dries. Each pot must be shaped with that distortion in mind, or the potter will never achieve her aesthetic objectives: "When you put in a pot that is tall and fat, you have to know it's going to come out short and skinny." Based on past experience, this architect broaches the design process by factoring in future distortions produced by the kiln of committees, regulations, and clients. His early designs include numerous ideas intended to "burn off" as the scheme is developed, so that the final result has the qualities he seeks. That kiln distortion is the very negotiation process discussed in this book. Unlike the kiln, however, the culture of practice does not lock out the artist once the object has been created, but is a creative context in its own right. In a way, this book is about how to take the heat.

OVERVIEW OF THE CHAPTERS

The chapters in this book are structured around vignettes from practice, in order to give the reader a tangible feel for the architects and firms in the study, and the problems they face. These tales of practice act as springboards from which to leap into an analysis of practice's underlying patterns. The chapters are intended to stand as interconnected yet somewhat independent essays woven together by the general themes described above. Each chapter covers a different component of the cultural system of architectural practice: chapter 2 provides historical and demographic background; chapter 3 examines the differences between design problems in practice, the academy, and as construed by the professional organization; chapter 4 explores the metamorphosis of layperson into architect, and chapter 5 looks at the architect's social milieu, and the office and the client in particular. These four chapters incorporate description and analysis, comprising the interpretive body of the book because they view architectural practice in a new way. Chapters 6 and 7 are the evaluative components, sparked by that new vision. In chapter 6, design quality is defined and studied in relation to the notion of architecture as a social art. The conclusion, chapter 7, takes a step further into the realm of "should" and "ought"[11] to project how the profession, and particularly the schools, might respond to this revisioning of architectural practice.

THE PARTNER: Really, we should call this place a studio, not an office. Basically, we've gathered around us people who like to work with us, and sometimes they would rather sit and draw in peace, but that's not the way we work. We work together closely on projects. This is the way we began working with Robert [the founding partner]. We never used to talk about design—we came to an understanding by doing it. Robert set our way of working.

Now we bring in lots of young people and we have to give them a sense of the way we work. It's really a ritual of making buildings—that's what our process is. But when people haven't worked with us for long, they don't understand. Now I have to say "We don't do things like that" and they don't know what I'm talking about, I can't spend the time to lead each person through the office philosophy. I have to take command. I'm not ashamed to say that's how the office runs now. We can have academic discussions and question the program, the design, and all that. But at some point, I'm going to say, "We'll do it this way." And then the argument should end and we should draw it up.

THE PROJECT ARCHITECT: An office like this, that had a way of working—informal, but based on a philosophy of design—when it grows, the problem is how to carry on the ethic. There must be some critical ratio between old and new people, a threshold. But now, new people are less committed to the office than to their own personal careers. Among the new people, it's an ethos of transience for personal growth.

THE DRAFTSPERSON: It's been really frustrating, coming to this office from the strong formal design training I had at Princeton. But I came here because I wanted to learn about wood construction and how buildings are put together—to follow a project from design through working drawings, so buildings are buildings and not just pictures. Then, I need to do the same for steel construction and detailing. And I want to learn to do working drawings. At the same time, I always want to keep something going on the outside, you know, [my own] little projects. Eventually I'll start my own office, maybe a cooperative with a few others if we share the same attitude toward design but bring in different expertise. I'd like to get the chance to run a job though an office before I go out on my own, so I'll do this for a while longer, but I can't imagine working for someone else after about five more years of this.

In these three independent interviews, an oldtimer, a rising firm member, and a recent recruit tell their versions of the way their office runs. The three describe how to make sense of what goes on in their everyday work environment. They explain the reasons why they and others do as they do. Somehow, these three people with all their theories about ongoing activities, along with clients, consultants, and all the other office members (and all their theories), find a way to design buildings in a coordinated fashion. To understand design practice, we must explore how participants such as these make sense of their worlds, and how that sense making functions in the social construction of architecture.

Each of these three individuals—the partner, the project architect, and the draftsperson—takes a different view of what is going on in their office. The partner begins with his vision of the practice, of what it has been and ought to be. His model is based on the office's early days, when a small group of associates worked closely with a strong, charismatic designer. But he recognizes that this model is difficult to reproduce as new employees come and go with little time to accumulate a sense of the office's design process. In fact, he has changed his way of working to cope with these circumstances. The project architect, who shares some of both the partner's and the draftsperson's attitudes, interprets the circumstances as a two-part problem. First, the office has grown and perhaps passed the critical threshold where novices outnumber veterans. Second, these novices have no allegiance to the office, but rather a commitment to their own careers. The draftsperson's comments link those of the partner and the project architect. She wants to gain knowledge and skills that she intends to use for her own, not the office's, purposes. Her actions and attitude toward the job embody the contemporary ethos that the other two describe. Yet her vision of her own small office matches the partner's nostalgic image, and thus the three statements come full circle. At the same time, all three circuitously consider the discrepancy between their beliefs or ideals and the realities of practice.

The three architects raise a variety of themes that I will analyze in this chapter and those that follow. They express ideas about training in schools and in offices, and about the differences between the two. They insinuate the tremendous importance placed on design in their work, and the desire for voice and authority to control it. The small office—the studio—is recalled and aspired to as the setting where one can be directly involved in good design. By contrast, the large office presents problems of management. The emphasis is on the individual designer, who tries to find a way of working within a collective. At the same time, the partner and project architect acknowledge that the collective organization is a kind of culture, which has its own heritage and rituals and which continues to evolve or deteriorate. Above all, each conceives of architectural practice in time, as a dynamic relation between past, present, and future.

The raison d'être of this chapter is twofold. The first purpose is to view the architectural profession as a dynamic organization, operating within a larger social structure that is itself continually evolving. The

2.1 Architect Greg Walsh
(seated), who has worked with
Frank Gehry for over thirty
years, with newer firm members. Collaboration across
office "generations" is one
means to pass along values, attitudes, and beliefs in the firm.
Walsh's litany "I just want to
get it right" sets a standard for
junior office members.

second is to critically analyze architectural professionalism, to reveal links and disjunctures between ideology and everyday architectural work. Key components of professionalism are scrutinized: the evolution of the profession, its distinctive relation to art and patrons, professional knowledge and values, the role of education, the workplace, the work itself, the employees, and clients, the ultimate employers. Together, these sections provide a frame for understanding architectural practice.

WORDS AND DEEDS

When architects explain and justify their actions, they are presenting what is called espoused theory. According to Argyris and Schon (1974) in their study of professional effectiveness, practitioners flounder in the proverbial contrast between what they say or believe and what they do. They recount "espoused theory" to explain and justify their actions, but employ a "theory-in-use" to actually guide their actions. In the vignette above, the partner outlines his idea, or theory, that design is a kind of ritual that a novice learns over time by working closely with an experienced designer. Yet, espoused theory is not a sufficient explanation of what is going on. What architects want us to hear about design practice often tells us more about beliefs and ideals than about the principles that guide action, or theories-in-use. The implied strategy the partner *uses* is more akin to unilateral control than ritual initiation: it is authoritative and, he hopes, efficient. Contradictions between espoused theories and theories-in-use are not uncommon, but such contradictions reduce professional effectiveness until the practitioner becomes aware of the dilemma.

Practice is the embodiment of professional ethos bound to circumstance. We want to know why architects hold certain beliefs and ideals, but we also must explore how these function in practice. Why does the partner believe his firm should be called a studio rather than an office? Why does the draftsperson hold the ideal of having her own firm? How do these notions affect office operations? What are the consequences, if any?

In architectural practice, the reasons why architects act and believe as they do are framed fundamentally by the architectural profession. The context set by the profession promotes and discourages certain ways of rationalizing practice's daily events. The partner invokes the studio analogy from architecture's heritage as a profession allied with the fine arts. When he describes actions that he feels contradict the studio model ("I have to take command") he is responding to changing demands confronting the profession—for example, that offices must often grow in order to offer the services clients demand. For present purposes, I will consider architects' explanations of their own actions and beliefs authentic, without making any assumptions about their truth. The task of social research, then, is to critically examine the justification of belief while respecting its authenticity (Giddens 1979). I suggest that certain attitudes and actions are tacitly justified by a system of professional beliefs—an ethos—that is rarely challenged. This can create problems in architectural practice, when the ethos no longer responds effectively to everyday circumstances. The project architect and partner grasp one such problem when they conclude that the office's ritualistic way of working is difficult to inculcate as the office grows bigger and its personnel more transient.

The problematic aspects of professional beliefs are most apparent when intended and unintended consequences are taken into consideration—that is, when we see how an ethos functions in practice. In the example above, the partner explains that he exerts more control over projects and employees because he cannot effect the old way of doing design. Among his intended consequences are probably design control, consistency among the projects undertaken by his office, and an efficient use of time. There are also unintended consequences: feeling of a detachment among employees who bear little responsibility, and a related increase in management activities, including the creation and maintenance of company policy. The more the partner acts, therefore, the less the office resembles a studio and the more bureaucratic it becomes. In Argyris and Schon's terms, the partner's theory-in-use (that he must exert control over the uninitiated) creates a self-fulfilling prophecy thwarting the espoused studio model. A novice cannot follow the tacit in-use principles, thus behaving in a manner that frustrates the oldtimers. It is only with experience that the ritual is absorbed, but this takes time and close proximity to a mentor. As the office grows, however, novices are less likely to have a relationship with the partner that resembles the partner's relationship with his mentor Robert, which assisted in passing the rituals along. Likewise, when novices are granted little voice and responsibility, they are less likely to develop an allegiance to the office and more likely to change jobs, so that they do not spend sufficient time to absorb the culture of practice.

Architecture's professional ethos tends to constrict the behavior of the partner and employees, particularly by assigning to design the status of a "master value," as sociologist Judith Blau (1984) explains in her extensive study of architects and firms. Architects are trained to assume responsibility for design; their professional identity depends on it. Yet design is a scarce resource in practice which those in charge tend to hoard, prompting others to seek a situation where they, too, can be in charge.

A critical examination of the professional ethos is valuable for several reasons. First, architects are not always able to see how their own actions may create undesirable consequences for their work. Long-standing and perhaps obsolete beliefs go unchallenged. Most important, the conditions that frame the ways architects make sense of their practice tend to get submerged by the routine of actual practice itself. The sociocultural approach I take to the interpretation of everyday architectural practice augments the more popular psychological approach evident among the office members I interviewed in the above case, who explained the partner's and the draftsperson's views as the result of personality characteristics and background: the partner, they said, was an autocrat who for many years was frustrated by his senior partner's dominance; the draftsperson had no useful architectural experience but was nonetheless self-impressed with her degree from Princeton. While an autocratic personality (or a creative genius for that matter) may be extremely influential in an office's practice, the prevalence of individual psychological theories have limited our understanding of how buildings are made. Even architectural geniuses act within a social context, about which we still know very little.

To characterize architecture as a social activity requires drawing upon a range of existing studies. The principal constructs for an analysis of architecture derive primarily from sociologists who study professionalism and the production of art and architecture.[1] The architectural historians Kostof and Saint have set precedents for a study of design practice.[2] More recently, Robert Gutman's *Architectural Practice* (1988) presents an outstanding critical analysis of changes within the profession and the building industry in America. Chris Argyris and Donald Schon's (1974) work with a wide range of professionals set forth the concepts of espoused and in-use theories, and explores the significance of unintended consequences for professional effectiveness. Their work does not, however, explore the larger socio-economic or ideological systems that frame professionals' words and deeds. Finally, the management of architectural practice is a rapidly growing field in itself. Much of the literature amounts to how-to books, explaining, for example, how to achieve financial objectives or avoid liability problems. With few exceptions, these works lack historical or critical perspectives, and since they tend to be written by people with legal or business backgrounds, they remain somewhat removed from the architect's realm of experience. Moreover, the management literature emphasizes how practice should be run rather than how practice actually functions on an everyday basis.

DEFINING PROFESSIONS

A profession, because it exists as a collection of practitioners, must be conceived as a dynamic, continuously reconstituted organization of colleagues. It is by nature a social entity: "Since there is no literal professional body, all contacts with the profession are in the form of interactions with other professionals" (Blankenship 1977:10). Yet contacts with the profession also exist in the form of principles, policy, and procedures issued by the professional organization. While a profession is not a coherent, unified entity, it retains a continuity that its members must struggle to maintain if they are to remain part of it.

Professions are special occupations because they impart knowledge and skills related to tasks of high social value. Defining a profession, in order to distinguish it from an occupation, is the subject of much debate. One definition enumerates the characteristics that an established profession typically exhibits:(1) it is a full time occupation; (2) it has its own training schools; (3) it has a professional organization; (4) it has a licensing component and community recognition; (5) it has a code of ethics and the right of self-governance (Blankenship 1977).

Descriptions of professions as sets of characteristics, however, fail to explain why these characteristics may have been worth acquiring and how they function in professional practice.[3] Such descriptions also tend to deny the dynamic quality of an enterprise, since professions evolve from occupations striving for autonomy, social status, and control over a market for their labor. Cullen (1978, 1983) argues in his study of professionalism that any occupation can be evaluated as to its *degree* of professionalization, and that those occupations we call professions show a high degree of development in certain dimensions. He locates five of these: complex relationships with people, degree of organization, length of training, licensure status, and prestige.

In America, the age of professionalization arose between the Civil War and about 1920; by then architecture, along with other select occupations, had developed its distinctive professional cast. Sociologist Magali Larson (1977) proposes an explanation for this professionalization of occupations. She suggests that in the early evolutionary phases of professionalization, a primary link is established between a standardized expertise and a market for services. In architecture, individual practitioners such as Richard Morris Hunt, Charles McKim, and Henry Hobson Richardson tried to institute a particular type of architectural education at a time when architectural training and practice were completely unregulated (in the second half of the nineteenth century). In this preprofessional stage, practitioners are semi-autonomous agents.[4] By standardizing expertise through education, educated practitioners can justify their competence over the unschooled. And the professional degree provides the public with a simple index by which to evaluate a rather esoteric expertise. Ideologically, professions are bound in a social contract with the public: they retain certain rights and privileges in society in return for bearing certain responsibilities. For example, the architectural profession determines its own standards for training and licensure, but must bear the legal responsibility for professional competence.

The link between education, expertise, and the market sets a model for the profession, which persists even as social and economic conditions change. Larson maintains that the model is transformed in contemporary society into ideology. Ideology serves an inspirational function for what are no longer semi-autonomous practitioners, but wage earners and salaried specialists. In other words, as architects move further from their idealized professional role, the ideal becomes more important for role maintenance. According to Larson, ideology also obscures the real social relations that obtain within a profession. My use of the term *professional belief system* refers to this dual ideological function of inspiration and obfuscation. The duality, and paradox, is transparent in the case of draftspersons running prints in offices across the country for minimum wages while espousing the glories of architecture as an artistic endeavor. It is in just such examples that we find the contradictions between espoused and in-use theory. Although the recognition of such contradictions can be unsettling, no contemporary practitioner can fully escape the dilemma it presents. If the contradictions between the exigencies of architectural work and its persistent ideology are to be uncovered, it must be done within the sphere of professional practice where they are most apparent. It is important to acknowledge these contradictions so that they can inform the task of shaping our future.

THE METAMORPHOSIS OF ARCHITECTURE

In the nineteenth century, American architecture began to develop nearly all the features of a full-fledged profession. The American Institute of Architects (AIA) was formed in 1857. The first architecture school opened at MIT in 1865, and a total of eleven schools had been established by the turn of the century (Draper 1977). By 1912, their academic programs were being coordinated through the umbrella organization that still fills the same role: the Association of Collegiate Schools of Architecture. In 1897, Illinois became the first state to require licensure for architects. In 1909, the first formal code of ethics was adopted. But what was actually going on during this fifty-year period when architecture leaped into professional status? To answer that question, we must inquire into the preceding century.

During the 1700s, it was not uncommon for wealthy Americans to send their sons (though not their daughters) to Europe for study and the grand tour. This was also the case for would-be professionals, who might first study in one of the colonial colleges before going abroad.[5] While in all the professions the majority of practitioners had no formal education, only the aristocracy was able to go to college in America and abroad, and thus the educated elite became the professionals of

2.2 This is the earliest known
photograph of an AIA convention, taken at the meeting in
Providence, Rhode Island, in
1883. The first convention
took place in 1867, and thereafter annual meetings were
held (lapsing only during war
and depression) in order to
make decisions that would
affect the membership as a
whole.

BELIEFS AND PRACTICE

highest distinction. When the elite returned home after foreign training, they tried to establish similar professional education in America. The most established professions (law, medicine, and the clergy) clearly followed this pattern, while in architecture men were still able to rise to social distinction out of apprenticeship in the skilled crafts. Even so, all professions in colonial and postrevolutionary America, including medicine and law, were highly disorganized, heterogeneous, and unregulated (Larson 1977).

Perhaps because then as now law and medicine were considered more essential services, architecture was slower to find its way to the European universities. Throughout the nineteenth century, thousands of men and eventually some women called themselves architects and practiced their craft at whatever level they chose. For example, there were over 10,500 individuals who called themselves architects in the 1900 census, yet less than 400 students were attending architecture schools in 1898 (Draper 1977). All but a few practitioners, therefore, acquired their training in apprenticeships, the length and content of which varied on an individual basis. Architectural practices at the time were small, centered around a principal, and rarely survived after that individual's death (Boyle 1977). The disorganization and growth of architecture in the mid-nineteenth century prepared the ground for professionalization.

Up until the late 1860s, architecture as an occupation proceeded virtually without standards, regulations, or organization. At the same time, the American city and the building industry were undergoing dramatic change: massive immigration, the development of efficient transportation systems, manufacture of new building materials, and urban growth. American society, including its architects, tried to come to grips with these changes, particularly in the period following the Civil War. New bureaucracies, like those undertaking large-scale public works and transportation projects, spawned the emergence of engineering specialties.[6] These institutions promoted the rise of professionalism through their need for guarantees of competence and technical expertise. For example, city officials in New York in 1867 adopted the first minimum housing standards, which, though ineffective as a building code (Mayer 1978), perhaps served as an effective warning that architecture would have to meet certain standards.

The movement to professionalize architecture gained momentum and coherence with the return to America of Richard Morris Hunt, the first American architect to study at the Ecole des Beaux Arts in Paris. Hunt attended the Ecole between 1845 and 1853, followed by numerous other American practitioners, mostly notably H. H. Richardson, Charles McKim, John Galen Howard, Louis Sullivan, Bernard Maybeck, and Julia Morgan.[7] When Hunt and Richardson returned from

2.3 Richard Morris Hunt in 1883. Graduate of the Ecole des Beaux-Arts, Hunt is dressed as the painter Cimabue, evidence of the architect's strong identification with the artist.

the Ecole, they established American ateliers (in 1857 and 1866 respectively) soon considered centers of architectural education (Boyle 1977). Their emphasis on art, intellect, and theory stood in sharp contrast to the ad hoc training in skills and construction acquired by less aristocratic practitioners of the time.

The Americans who ventured to Paris and the Ecole were struck by the atelier system, in which a student-run studio undertook competition projects under the direction of an atelier master or *patron* who critiqued the students' projects. The patron was typically an established architect who practiced out of another office. Joan Draper, in her study of the Ecole and its influence in America (1977:223) describes the ambiance of the ateliers:

Whichever atelier they chose, Americans were greatly impressed by the atmosphere they found there. Tales of rowdy parties, mad *charrettes*, and lively traditions filled their reminiscences. The key ingredient of atelier spirit was group loyalty. The *patron*'s little band pulled together to defend its honor against the other studios. Everyone, from the greenest *nouveau* to the most advanced *ancien*, helped one another, at the same time maintaining a friendly internecine rivalry. The *anciens* criticised the work of the the *nouveaux*, and the *nouveaux* pitched in to help the *anciens* render plates for a big competition. This atmosphere of cooperation and the personal guidance of the *patron* were as important as the more formal aspects of the program.

While Hunt followed the French model, keeping his architectural practice separate from his atelier, Richardson combined the two. The latter atelier-practice model is still regarded as an ideal form of architectural practice, as we saw in the opening interviews, where the partner stated his preference for the term *studio* over *office*. On the other hand, the atelier separated from practice has become the model for academic architectural training, the core of which is the design studio led by an architect-teacher. It is not surprising that the first architecture school, MIT, was founded by a student of Richard Morris Hunt.

Although American society changed rapidly during this period, Americans were reluctant to leave behind the traditional order of things, which included a layered, class-based society. For architects as for other professionals, the emphasis on academic training, particularly foreign education, was a means of preserving professional activity for those of social status. Two forces operated in tandem: educational movements were established to raise the status of the profession, and professional activity was kept in the hands of those of status.

PATRONAGE AND THE ARTISTIC DISTINCTION

The social and economic conditions that helped shape the architectural profession in the nineteenth and early twentieth centuries were accompanied by a constellation of beliefs and ideals. The strongest among these were architecture's alliance with the fine arts and its dis-

ÉCOLE NATIONALE DES BEAUX-ARTS — Architecture Atelier Pascal

2.4 The Atelier Pascal, Paris,
circa 1905. This postcard captures some of the camaraderie
of the atelier and its members,
who worked closely together
and felt strong loyalty to their
group.

2.5 Henry Hobson Richard-
son's assistants in his private
study and library, circa 1886.
Richardson's office (which was
attached to his house) was a
model at the time, borrowing
qualities of the atelier and
serving as a training ground
for young architects.

sociation from crafts. Schools of architecture have had a powerful influence on professional unity and control not only because of their more centralized, coordinated structure (as opposed to professional practice's dispersion), but because they further the profession's distance from crafts-based training.

Perhaps because engineering was evolving into a profession in its own right, architects were unable to claim sole proprietorship over the technical aspects of building.[8] The architect's primary expertise, as it was brought home from the Ecole, was design-as-art. This has created a legacy for architecture distinct from other professions, and partially explains why medicine and law are more fully developed. Art, or design as conceptual work, has been a difficult commodity to sell in America's pragmatic marketplace. Since at least the late nineteenth century, architects have decried the public's ambivalence toward aesthetic concerns. C. Francis Osborne, (1891–92:281) for example, wrote in the first volume of *Architectural Record*: "The public knows little and cares less about the canons which underlie the art of building. Evidently, then, it is high time some serious attempts were made to awaken such an interest by an appeal to the good sense of our 'employers' which is not wanting when they are concerned with other matters than those relating to art." The different paths of each profession have been significantly influenced by the fact that art has less "market appeal" than medical or legal services. Compounding the problem, architects are more tightly bound to clients and to a local market for services when compared to artists (Blau 1987). The emphasis on art also presents dilemmas about professional training. In 1934, for example, the eminent architect and teacher Paul Cret wrote, "All education in the Fine arts [including architecture] . . . has for its main object the development of the artist's personality."[9] The larger professional project—to achieve unity and standards—was contradicted by curricula intended for personal, nonstandardized, artistic development. Whether architectural training belonged in a university at all, and if so, in what form, were questions that would be debated ad infinitum.

In a study of the historical definition of the architect's role, Larson (1983) points out that architects have been unable to monopolize a market for their services because "cultural plurality is admissable in the arts." Doctors and engineers whose expertise resides in science (and lawyers in the law) offer services that are less readily challenged in our particular cultural milieu. Larson goes on to suggest that the public may reject architectural products because they are not functionally distinct from nonarchitectural ones. This argument is valid to a point. It is true that builders, engineers, and contractors, as well as Sears, *Sunset* magazine, and mobile home manufacturers can deliver plans for a building that will accommodate one's needs, stand up, and keep the rain out. That the result may be unappealing is not nearly as persuasive as the results of other professionals' neglect, which can be fatal or incarcerating. Architects' products *do* differ functionally from the work of competing professionals when they are tailored to the specific needs of the client, yet this form of architectural service is limited to a small segment of the market—the wealthiest clients and their homes, office buildings, or commercial establishments. In mass housing and speculative office or retail space, architects have less clearly distinguished themselves from the rest of the pack. Presently, there is a growing body of literature about user needs in housing and in the workplace that is making it possible to design buildings that function markedly better.[10] If this research becomes more fully integrated into design education, architectural products may become functionally superior to nonarchitectural ones.

Another problem arises in architecture when we compare it to the other arts. What architects create are highly specific, costly, immovable objects. While some sculpture or painting may also have these qualities, the other arts are generally not defined by characteristics that so neatly defy commodification. A building may be considered valuable to its owners, to its inhabitants, to real estate speculators, or to its locale, but it is specific to its site and program. And while a building is a highly public product, much of its evaluation remains private and nongeneralizable—to the client, the building is a good one for highly specific reasons.

Architecture, like other arts, produces "cultural capital" (Bourdieu 1984) by which people display their upper-class status through their tastes and possessions. One can hardly consume more conspicuously than through architecture, by the very fact that buildings are large, public, and permanent. Moreover, the architect's services alone do not produce the product, the work of art. Many other actors intervene between the design of a building and its occupation. Poor work on the part of landscape architects or contractors, for example, can greatly reduce the perceived quality of the overall project (see Vischer and Cooper Marcus 1986). Some professionals have developed new "two-party" firms to regain control of the product. Like the popular architecture and engineering combination, new practices merge architect and developer (à la John Portman, who has spearheaded the design and development of many urban centers) or architect and builder (design-build firms). This is a more formalized version of architectural firms that develop partnerships between individuals with complementary expertise (for example, a business partner and a design partner) and with consultants like engineers, landscape architects, and interior designers that are hired repeatedly. Because architects' intentions are more apparent in drawings than in buildings, however, drawings have become an important object of architectural study. There are also architects today who produce "paper architecture," and there are galleries emerging across the country to distribute these works. These architects have found a form of architecture that is more like other art forms and can be marketed as such.

Larson (1983) makes an additional distinction between architecture and other professions, that being the relationship between patron and practitioner. While all professions depend on the power and wealth of sponsors, architecture has been unable to make use of this necessary initial condition to achieve its own autonomy. Architects, more than other professionals, remain tied to their patrons. Since doctors and lawyers, for example, have made their services indispensible to nearly all economic groups except the very poorest, they are less dependent on elite patronage. Architects, however, depend on the powerful and monied, who are likely to play a forceful role in their dealings with professionals. For architects, that can mean less autonomy in their work. Examples of this type of architect-client dynamic are sprinkled throughout the book.

Clients, be they state, public, church, corporate, or private, provide the function of a building, thereby placing a critical dimension of the architectural product under the client's control. By contrast, clients of medicine and law do not control their illnesses and legal problems to the same extent (in part because the architect receives less credit for diagnostics). That clients own the building's function and thus control a part of the professional product has led to an interesting set of responses in the architect-client liaison. Some architects include diagnostic services such as extensive programming as part of their work.[11] Of course, other professionals, such as environment-behavior researchers, have also taken over this job. In some buildings, the architect is no longer involved with day-to-day functioning, which is designed by specialists such as space planners, laboratory consultants, or manufacturing specialists. The architect's task in such cases is limited to the building's skin. Another development in this area is the increasing importance of the developer, who has to some extent commodified architecture through the creation of speculative commercial, residential, and industrial buildings, thus removing a degree of specificity from the product.

Architects, acting as translators, employ design—the art of architecture—to mediate between function and the final form. Since art is a pluralistic domain, even among architects, it would seem that additional expertise for the translator might strengthen the professional project. I suggest that there is a role that architects have always played

2.6 This fourteenth-century
illustration shows St. Denis at
the upper left with his two
legendary companions giving
instructions for the building of
the cathedral. The church was,
at the time, the primary patron of architecture.

(since the split of *techne* and *telos*, as Larson puts it) but have rarely cultivated, which is translation as a social art. That clients, planners, consultants, building departments, draftspersons, and designers must together arrive at some agreement is a key element of the architect's role, and could be better developed and marketed.

It should be clear by this point that architecture, while sharing characteristics with other professions, also distinguishes itself in terms of its relation to art and its relation to sponsors. The interaction of professionalism and the contemporary situation in architecture can now be examined with these distinctive features in mind. Here, contradictions become apparent between achieving the status of a powerful profession and working within the particular realm of architecture. Those contradictions are most obvious when the profession suffers the consequences of its own ideals: downplaying the importance of profit creates minimum-wage workers; professional autonomy is reflected in public disinterest; emphasis on design allows other necessary skills to fall to other specialists promoting the emergence of new professions. Individual architects do not consciously forsake their own interests in order to live up to professional ideals, but I suspect that undesirable consequences tend to get dissociated from the beliefs and conditions that foster them and thus the situation goes unchallenged.

Contradictions between beliefs and practice are inherent to designer's task, as C. Wright Mills noted in his 1958 essay on the American designer as a cultural workman: "His art is a business, but his business is art and curious things have been happening both to the art and to the business—and so to him" (374). The relationship between art and business captures a significant share of the distinctions between ethos and circumstance. Art and business exist as a dialectic in architecture that has created a dilemma for the profession since its earliest days. I will argue that the client stands at the center of this dilemma.

Professionals, in general, promote individualism and the intrinsic value of their work, espousing antimarket principles and downplaying the profit motive (Larson 1977). Architects follow this model; "design quality" is named as the profession's top problem (23.7%), yet adequate compensation is second on the list, not far behind (16.6%).[12] Professionals attempt to maintain a "service ideal" wherein the profession's function and the intrinsic value of the work are advanced. At the same time the profession remains more or less independent from those it serves. This is a delicate balance, since too much autonomy can eliminate the market for services, while too much service may reduce the architect's power. Architecture has been accused of not taking a service model to heart, thus fostering public antagonism and lack of understanding (Sawyier 1983).

The primary means by which professions establish a degree of autonomy from other members of society is to claim a particular knowledge territory as distinctly their own (see Freidson 1986). In all professions, the knowledge base is to some extent definable and to some extent mysterious. By some definitions the very distinction between a profession and an occupation concerns a profession's non-rule-governed criteria of success or qualification—criteria such as virtue, creativity, persona, talent, or imagination (Larson 1977). In nineteenth-century England, for example, architectural registration was opposed on the basis that design ability could not be tested since it was not a "practical" subject (Jenkins 1961). There are of course advantages to registration laws, for they allow legitimation and entry into the profession to rest with collegial rather than public evaluation. The expertise of any profession is based on a core of relatively well-accepted knowledge among practitioners, and a periphery of more esoteric knowledge, which in architecture might include historic preservation, codes and regulations, computers, and so on. Among nonexperts, the professional's knowledge of both core and peripheral knowledge is the source of power. But within the professional firm, where core knowledge is shared, mastery of a more peripheral area links expertise to power over an area of uncertainty (see Blau 1979).

The tacit or ill-defined aspects of profession's knowledge, skills, and talents provide a kind of secrecy about the profession, which in turn contributes to the profession's ability to remain self-regulated and self-evaluated. In a sociohistorical analysis of higher education in America, Jencks and Riesman (1968) make some interestiang observations about professions they characterize as occupations that are relatively colleague-oriented rather than client-oriented. The professional's values in this case are not based on a concern for laypeople, but for fellow practitioners—their opinions, judgments, evaluations.

Since clients may not always be satisifed with a professional's service, it is to a profession's advantage to keep evaluation within its own circle. Institutions and events are established for collegial recognition (in architecture these include the American Institute of Architects, the professional journals and their annual design awards, and so on) while the clients' judgments are relegated to a secondary status. Everett Hughes (1958:141), the noted sociologist of work, makes this point: "The essence of the matter appears, however, to be that the client is not in a position to judge for himself the quality of the service he receives. . . . Thus the public is to be protected from its own impossible demands in that "quacks"—who might exploit them—will not be allowed to practice." Hughes goes on to say that "quacks" are defined in functional terms, as exactly those professionals who continually please their clients but not their colleagues.

Professions generally reserve the right of peer evaluation, which they prefer to conduct secretly since their criteria may be far removed from the clients' interests (for example, a malpractice suit in the death of a patient). The service ideal is upheld by arcane peer review. In architecture, however, these discussions are not always secretive, but they are inaccessible when couched in the sacrosanct terms of art. It has been claimed that the public's two basic criticisms of architects are leveled against their arrogance and ignorance (Sawyier 1983), charges that would be exacerbated in the minds of most consumers by the placement of aesthetics over accommodation. Comments from the juries for design awards usually display a lack of concern for clients, the building's technical systems, or the accommodation of human activity. Published in the professional journals, these conversations are not intended for public dissemination. In general, one finds little or no mention of the client, as in the following deliberation among three well-known architects about Michael Graves's entry for the 1980 *Progressive Architecture* awards (1980:98):

JAHN: They [the buildings] only address themselves, however, to a particular element of architecture which is the aesthetic, cultural side, and not . . . with the problems of getting buildings built. . . .

STERN: The aesthetic is the only important thing about building. . . . The only buildings that we are finally interested in are the ones that speak to us from an aesthetic point of view. . . .

GEHRY: I'm interested in architecture as a work of art, and whether it will hold up as art.

The issue of art coming between clients and their architects is addressed in an insightful and exploratory dissertation by Boughey (1968), who interviewed fifty architects about their intentions to influence social action through design. He discovered what he calls the "art defense," in which architects assume an artist's role as a means to retain autonomy and escape judgment: "In the role of the artist, the architect has a right to deal in mystery, in subjective truth. He has the artist's right to complete autonomy, to change his mind at whim, to be free of anyone's judgment but his own inner lights" (Boughey 1968:92). This is the kind of "ideological safeguard" described by Larson (1977) that professionals can bring to bear if threatened by client dissatisfaction or if trying to suppress client demands for some right of review.

Mysteriously based knowledge and the profession's control of its own evaluation help establish the exclusive (exclusionary) nature of the profession and the primacy of the autonomous architect. But perhaps architecture has carried this project too far. Its strong link to elite

2.7 Frank Lloyd Wright with
Solomon R. Guggenheim
(right), the client for the Guggenheim Museum, and Hilla
Rebay, an artist who was also
curator of Guggenheim's collection before the museum
was built. She was the driving
force behind finding an architect and a permanent home for
the collection.

patronage may have fostered some resentment against professionals that has had the unintended consequence of alienating the general public. The current slow-growth/no-growth grassroots activism in neighborhoods across the country testifies to communities' dissatisfaction with the way professionals have planned their environments.

One definition of professions appears particularly astute: they are occupations "whose indeterminacy/technicality ratio, intrinsic to the system of production, is generally high" (Jamous and Peloille 1970). In other words, a profession involves some objective information, but there is always *more* that cannot explicitly be known. Although professions try to establish and protect a technical, objective knowledge base to counterbalance their indeterminacy, architecture has been relatively unsuccessful. One of architecture's peculiarities is that, unlike other fields, it has failed to develop a set of hypotheses that can be advanced or refuted (Rittel 1976), escalating the indeterminacy/technicality ratio for architecture. High indeterminacy is partially the result of architectural problems themselves, which defy clear definition and solution.[13] Another component of architecture's high indeterminacy is the professions' unusual tendency to slough off constitutive skill areas, which subsequently become professions in their own right—for example, civil engineering, structural engineering, interior design, site planning, and urban design (Rittel 1976). These related professions then compete with architecture. According to some analyses, engineers are claiming a larger share of the building design and construction fees, while the architect's portion shrinks (Ventre 1982). Reviewing Bureau of Census figures, Ventre suggests that today's information-based, energy-pressed society is demanding the technical expertise that only engineers are prepared to provide.[14]

In the negotiations between architects and their clients, as in any negotiation, an underlying consideration is control over knowledge and information. Parties communicate only what they want each other to take into account, manipulating the extent and accuracy of the information contributed (Zartman 1976). Just as clients keep their actual bank balance private, so architects employ mysterious justifications like the art defense and scientific justifications like the analogous structural defense[15] as means to withhold information from clients. Indeed, architects can and do capitalize on clients' lack of knowledge, particularly technical knowledge about structure, materials, codes, and building systems, as well as the significant but ambiguous knowledge based on "experience." Since architectural decisions are inherently negotiable, this protects the architect's decision-making authority—design control (see Cuff 1982a). Technical knowledge and experience offer protective shelters where clients' challenges can be rebuffed.

In architect-client relations, the respective weights each party will have as to decision authority will be established in their interaction. Hughes (1958) asserts that the strongest influence on the role assumed by actors is their association with a reference group. While the client's reference group is typically powerful in its own right, in the design context the client's power is more ambiguous than that of the architect, giving the latter some advantage and helping to balance power in their exchanges. The architect as manager of all participants can define the appropriate relations among actors in complex architectural negotiations more easily than his or her alter ego, the artist-architect. While most architects admit they perform a managerial function, however, they do not see it as their primary role. The stereotypical artist is not a coordinator, even though, as Becker (1974, 1982) points out in his study of social networks in the arts, all artists work at the hub of a large web of people whose cooperation is essential to the final product. And there are artistic role models involving creative collaboration—musical conductors or film directors, for example—that are appropriate to architects.

In terms of relationships between parties and the role the professional will be *able* to assume, the client and the role that he or she assumes is the key counterbalancing factor. At the outset, client and professional are dependent upon one another. Without clients there is no architecture. Very often, the architects' clients are an intimidating lot: they are powerful, wealthy, and able to go elsewhere for service. Striking a balance with members of this group and gaining their respect is an art in itself, leading some architects to use their own form of intimidation. Van Renssalaer, writing in 1890, disavows the architect's dependence on clients, saying that client participation is the real problem: "And if what you get is not quite all you want, or exactly what you think it ought to be, why, be thankful still; for the chances are (nay, the certainty is) that had you interfered, the result would have been more unsatisfactory still" (cited in Mumford 1952:202). More recently, architects Roland Coate and Peter Eisenman took up the same theme in a *Newsweek* interview (in Davis 1976:66, 69):

COATE: With most big public commissions you are concerned with nothing but safety, budget and function. That's boring.

EISENMANN: None of my houses is shaped for client's needs. They are designed to shake them out of those needs. . . . If you believe, as I do, that architecture can change culture, you don't make architecture to please a rich client.

But often such stances create the self-fulfilling prophecies that Schon and Argyris warn against: the intimidating architect alienates the client. Architects such as these establish a weak role for the client while strengthening their own design authority. If professions seek "the right to charge the client for services rendered in accord with the standards established by one's colleagues, even if the client receives no satisfaction or benefit" (Jencks and Reisman 1968:202), then the clients may pay but they are not necessarily happy about it. Eisenman advances that right a step further: the architect should be able to convince a client that the building is separate from but *better* than a solution to the client's self-stated problem. The idealized professional holds the power to decide what is best for the client and to convince the client of the merit of the proposal.

Along with the particular expertise a profession claims for itself must come a degree of standardization and unity through which it can control a market for services, skills, and producers. In architecture the American Institute of Architects works diligently to standardize contracts, the range of services, and ethical behavior while staying on the safe side of antitrust legislation. Other organizations perform similar roles in the domains of registration and education.[16] Efforts to unify members of the profession are counteracted by two factors: first, not all those who practice architecture are registered, and second, not all registered architects belong to a professional organization. Registration and membership are dependent upon years of practice, since one cannot take the registration exam without some practical experience, the exam is offered infrequently (once or twice a year), many individuals must take the exam more than once to pass all portions, and only those who are registered may join a professional organization (excepting associate student members). About three quarters (78 percent) of all architectural practitioners are licensed (Gutman 1988). In a large study of architectural graduates, researchers found that 78 percent of those who have been out of school for ten years are licensed, 56 percent of those out for five years, and 3 percent of those out only one year. Thus, about one third of all individuals graduating within the last ten years are licensed to practice architecture. More than a third of those eligible for membership, however, did not join a professional organization.[17]

Much of the foregoing discussion concerns the knowledge and values that architects possess. Certainly individual architects have distinct personal knowledge and values, but they also hold much in common. This is because they share a loosely structured ethos clearly presented to them in architecture schools.

INTO THE FOLD

For anyone considering a career in architecture, the first formal step taken will be into one of two social domains—a professional practice or, more commonly, a professional school. In 1972, of those taking the registration exam for the first time, 78 percent had professional de-

2.8 This fourth-year drawing room (circa 1900) at the first architecture school in America, MIT, looks much like studios on college campuses today. Note the *beaux-arts* schemes lining the walls and the lone woman student (barely visible at the back of the room).

grees, while the remaining 22 percent were non-degree holders (Hamilton 1973). We can also assume that some of the non-degree holders attended design school but did not recieve a professional degree, either because they did not complete their education or because they were enrolled in a nonaccredited program. While chapter 3 discusses the academic definition of a design problem, and chapter 4 recounts the student phase of an architect's development, I will here consider the school's institutional role in defining the profession.

The primary purveyor of professional knowledge, both tacit and explicit, aesthetic and technical, is the academy. It is in school that would-be professionals are trained, enculturated, regulated, and socialized (cf. Becker et al. 1961). In economic terms, the professional school dominates the production of producers. Since architectural registration does not require a prior academic degree in all states, practitioners may qualify to become licensed solely on the basis of on-the-job training. In 1987, less than half of all states required a professional degree for registration, but there have been dramatic increases in recent years, so that by 1990, 40 states had the requirement.[18] Because academic training has been deemphasized until recently, architecture is less well developed on the educational dimension than other professions (Cullen 1983). Nevertheless, the majority of architectural practitioners hold academic degrees, the academically trained are more likely than those without a degree to become registered, and degree holders are far more likely to head their own firms (AIA 1974). Power and leadership within the profession are thus based on academic training. But unity remains a key to professional autonomy. Still, the presence of non-degree holders indicates that architects, while wanting autonomy, may find unity a distasteful means of gaining it. Architecture's ties to patrons and its pluralistic attitude toward training together reduce its autonomy as a profession.

The ethos of a profession is born in schools. As Larson states, "This basic [academic training] defines the common language and the tacit knowledge that distinguish a profession as a whole from the laity. It is in fact, the main support of a subculture" (1977:45). Tacit knowledge—the unspoken assumptions, interpretations, expectations, and conventions—may be more important to learn than explicit knowledge or skills. Such tacit knowledge is the substance of a professional ethos, affecting both espoused theory and theory-in-use. Studies of professional success corroborate the importance of schools as enculturating institutions, but in an unexpected way. In a review of forty-six studies, Hoyt (1965) concludes that there is virtually no correlation (approaching zero) between success in professional school and success in practice. Success was measured in a variety of manners, including course grades, relative class rank, salary, importance of job position, and peer and employer evaluations. (Unfortunately, architecture was not among the numerous professions examined—they included engineering, business, teaching, and medicine.) Hoyt concludes that "the primary role of the professional school may thus be socialization, not training." My own work indicates that in school, preprofessionals learn the roles, values, vocabulary, assumptions, and set of reasonable expectations appropriate to the subculture. The question remains, however, why some students who are successful in school, and therefore presumably "socialized," do not become successful in the working world. I suggest this stems from the general mismatch between the ethos of professional ideals and values (emphasized in schools) and the circumstances of professional work—a mismatch that rears its head in professional practice.

One way to understand the socialization that occurs in architecture school is to examine the studio, the sine qua non of design education. In the studio, an architect-teacher provides students with guidance on design problems far removed from the untidy, awkward problems that many real clients have. Later, these students may be discouraged or resentful that their real clients do not have problems and resources with greater potential. Students are rarely encouraged to work in groups on design problems explicitly intended to help them learn about the social construction of architecture, about collaboration skills, mutual satisfaction, and the like. Training and evaluation of would-be professionals is thus based almost entirely on the finished products of single individuals. In general, students solve problems with formal design. Technical knowledge plays a secondary role, while drafting ability is ignored except insofar as it corresponds with graphic skill. Drafting is left for more vocationally oriented schools or community colleges; the university deals with art and theory.

In all professions training is relatively difficult and prolonged, and requires students' devotion and undivided attention. In architecture, academic training culminating in a master's degree includes four to five years of undergraduate education and one to three-and-a-half graduate years. The other professional degree is a five-year undergraduate bachelor's in architecture. Although specific requirements vary in different states, to become a registered architect academic training typically must be augmented by several years work under a licensed architect, successful completion of a battery of tests, and sometimes the approval of a team of registered architects who interview the novitiate. Of the 90,000 architectural practitioners in the USA, 70,000 are registered (Gutman 1988) and only for the latter is the title "architect" legitimate in the eyes of the professional body.

Architecture schools' emphasis on design prefigures the importance of practitioners' espoused theory of design as the central element of architecture. Schools highlight the importance of pure design by removing from its study key aspects of professional practice: the client or patron, the coordinated group process of design, and economic and power relations. The principal social relation in school—that between studio instructor and student—is cast as a relation between unique individuals. The primacy of the individual is then carried into practice, promoting the explanation of everyday occurrences as matters of personality, talent, creativity, and convictions. Architects are thus not trained to be alert to significant relations of authority, economics, power, group decision-making processes, management, and so on. In other words, the structural conditions within which individuals must operate in practice are exempted from careful consideration by schools and from inclusion within the belief system. The ideology obscures what Larson calls the "real" social relations. I would argue, however, that ideology and social relations are both part of a composite "reality." The two interact, creating a framework for making sense of architectural practice. The ideology serves functions that are also real, providing inspiration and a model to strive for in addition to maintaining domination (Giddens 1979) or obscuring complex situations that seem beyond individual control.

While individuals learn much about what it means to be an architect in school, that socialization is elaborated and modified in the other significant architectural institution: the office. When Hughes (1958) describes the "gap between anticipation and realization" in professions, he captures the significant differences between education and the work world, between the expectations established by design schools, by the architectural press, and by popular media and the realities encountered in architectural practice. But this characterization obscures the fact that in practice the socialization continues and new expectations develop. Young architects observe their seniors as they more and less effectively integrate ideals and circumstances, as they work with clients, get new commissions, and run an office (see chapter 5). Although there is greater diversity among architectural offices than among schools, the nature of the office enterprise is fundamental.

THE PLACE OF PRACTICE

Every architectural office is a setting where human resources are organized to obtain commissions and deliver services. The way different offices go about these fundamental tasks differs widely, and it is common among young practitioners to sample the range of alternatives. When I ask what distinguishes firms from one another, architects typically characterize offices first by size, for size implies a number of associated features. There are very large (over 50 persons) and large offices (generally over 20 persons) associated with large-scale projects, complex clients such as corporations and government organizations, sophisticated operations, specialization, a wider range of services, higher pay, formalized management, and a hierarchical organization of responsibility and power. At the other extreme, small offices (under 10 persons) are characterized by informal management, less specialization (thereby offering individuals the opportunity to play a number of roles), lower pay, smaller-scale projects, direct contact with clients and consultants, a higher concern for design quality, and few bureaucratic traits. Mid-sized firms are offices between the two extremes and may have the qualities of both large and small practices. Many architects believe that mid-sized offices can have the advantages of both large and small offices while avoiding their disadvantages. On the other hand, some say only small and large firms will survive in the future— those that are truly dedicated and those that are organized to meet demand, respectively. Indeed, there is evidence that mid-sized firms are losing their share of the market through decreases in revenues (AIA 1989).

Besides the size of the office, practices are characterized on a number of other dimensions: extent of recognition of principals or firm as a whole, the building types undertaken, the form of internal organization, and of course the architectural emphasis (for example, stylistics, social mission, or environmental concerns). Although Blau (1984) confirms some commonly held assumptions about these dimensions, she also indicates that stereotypes do not always hold. For example, size *is* related to a firm's ability to win awards, but it is the large firms that are thus advantaged. Large firms do tend to be more bureaucratic or rationalized and to reduce the individual employee's power, but regardless of size, internal office organization varies (team, department, or studio) and with it opportunities for shared voice and participation. In terms of economic health, large firms are more productive, more profitable, and better able to weather a depression than small firms. But the savvy small firm can respond best in a crisis, not simply getting by but pulling ahead.

Because the large firm is advantaged in many ways, particularly under normal economic conditions, it has become a more prevalent player in architectural practice. For at least the last one hundred years, the increasing specialization within the building industry has gone hand in hand with growth among architectural offices. This growth has stabilized in the past decades, with small offices still far outnumbering their larger counterparts. A full 90 percent of all firms have fewer than 20 members.[19] Although only 1.5 percent of the firms employed more than 50 persons, these offices captured 22 percent of all the design service fees paid in 1972. This dominance persists today, since very large firms make up only 2 percent of all firms yet collect 30 percent of all fees (Gutman 1988). According to 1989 data, if we also include large firms (those with at least 20 people), these 7 percent account for 56 percent of all revenues, and this share is growing (AIA 1989). As the corporate client demands an increased range of services and greater economic efficiency from its architects, relatively small offices cannot compete without growing and using their resources as efficiently as possible. For example, a small office needs to match its production staff to the support staff's capacity. The owner of one small firm with a secretary, an accountant, and a business developer, recognizes that these three can easily handle an architectural staff of twelve. To increase the profit margin or offer lower fees, the owner strives to bring in new work in order to add seven new architects to the five who are presently employed.

Large firms employ architectural designers, business developers, marketing directors, project managers, construction managers, accountants, interior designers, public relations personnel, office managers, secretaries, engineers, landscape architects and, so on, turning what was once a studio into a full-scale bureaucracy. Even small firms that offer a range of services, are internallly specialized, and specify formal personnel regulations tend to gain more recognition than the traditional small practice (Blau 1976).

While Blau (1984) finds that the large office tends to win more awards than its smaller counterpart, her data is based on sheer numbers, rather than the percentage of the projects that are award-winning. At present data is not available to resolve this issue, but there is copious professional lore on the subject. As Gutman (1977) states, "[Small offices] are seen as the backbone of the profession, many architects much prefer to work in this kind of setting, and it is widely believed that they are the source of innovation in design." The editor of the professional journal *Progressive Architecture* reported on a well-attended conference where office size and design quality were discussed. "No question: big firms have a harder time maintaining—in some cases, even *attaining*—high quality design. There are lots of mouths to feed, powerful clients to please, and a bottom line that must be taken seriously" (Dixon 1982). At the conference, upper-level management from a number of firms made such recommendations as distributing the decision-making responsibilities and explicitly formulating design objectives in order to guide large and varied staffs toward consistently high-quality buildings. The inherent contradictions in these recommendations should be apparent. The explicit formulation of design objectives—a kind of design policy—tends to bureaucratize an office and centralize (rather than distribute) decisions. Nevertheless, this may be an effective strategy.

The so-called "bottom line" is a serious concern in architectural offices of all sizes, particularly when we look at the economic indica-

2.9 An important service
among firms and a specialization among architects is computer-aided design capability.
Here, a student is shown
working with CADD at USC's
School of Architecture.

tors available. The net profit of architectural offices, based on annual total revenues, is not only small but declining, with the average profit rate being about 6 percent.[20] Why might this be the case? One explanation is the increased supply of architects. The approximately 30,000 students currently enrolled in architecture schools will soon be joining the 70,000 registered architects in America.[21] The number of students is equivalent to almost half the total number of registered architects, and over 4,000 graduates with first professional degrees enter the job market each year, flooding the market for services. While employment is high (98 percent), there is evidence that the abundant supply of architects has led to more competitive fees, so that architects are sometimes working for 4 percent or less of the construction costs, thereby eliminating high salaries and respectable profits (Coxe 1984). An ongoing study by Montgomery, however, points to an increase in the types of services architects perform, and the high employment rate indicates that demand for architectural services is expanding into new terrains.[22]

In a review of the profession's last one hundred years, Boyle emphasizes large offices' transformation of architectural practice. Although the large firm depends upon specialists rather than upon the Renaissance *uomo universale,* the potentially collaborative context has been transformed instead by the division of labor: "As the large office gradually included more and more specialists in an attempt to maintain the generalist character traditional to architecture practice, paradoxically the team of workers progressively lost is original identifying characteristic of collaboration as the coordinating function was taken over by a new level of management" (Boyle 1977:330–1).

WORK AND WORKERS

With specialization comes the "dequalification" of labor, which entails breaking tasks into smaller and smaller components that require less and less expertise (Gutman 1977). In addition, the large supply of architects has served to downgrade work responsibilites (Gutman 1988:28). When asked, two thirds of all architects corroborate these trends, saying they were unhappy with the noncreative assignments they were given early in their careers (Fisher 1987). The jobs of most architectural workers are less meaningful and more alienating; a small but powerful group of architects at the peak of the hierarchical pyramid take for themselves what they consider the most rewarding work. In large offices, the owners or partners of one firm may retain all design responsibility, while owners of another will claim responsibility for business development and client relations. Ironically, executive recruiters occasionally seek exceptionally strong designers for large, established firms offering equally exceptional salaries in the $100,000 range (Coxe 1984). As specialization takes over, the most basic aspect of architecture becomes the most valuable skill. According to Freidson

(1984), a broader transformation is occurring among professionals who are now stratified into three basic groups: the rank and file who perform the productive labor, the administrative elite responsible for supervising the collective performance of the rank and file, and the knowledge elite, the professionals who conduct research in universities. This stratification within professions, visible in architecture, is relatively new, and threatens to unravel the professional community by increasing internal conflicts (see Gorb 1986).

Within an organization of specialists, each of the various specialist groups tends to develop its own priorities, aesthetics, financial interests, and career goals (Becker 1982). Each specialist—for example, the structural engineer, the project architect, and the project manager—employs a unique set of standards. The managerial or administrative function coordinating these specialists becomes crucial to effective professional practice, and has acquired new status among professionals (Larson 1977). In architecture, the project manager or job captain is a prime example of upgraded status without increased design responsibility. (Design responsibility is usually the original motivation for entering the profession, and a disappointed expectation once in practice.) Of 233 project managers surveyed, nearly half responded that they spend less than 10 percent of their time doing architectural design (AIA 1974). Instead of design, the project manager is elevated to an administrative and monitoring function for particular projects, bringing together a crowd of consultants, each with a particular interest and aesthetic.

Gutman (1977) emphasizes a seemingly obvious but often overlooked fact of contemporary practice: the majority of American architects are *employees*, earning wages or salaries not from clients but from fellow practitioners. The replacement of self-employed individuals by architect-employees has important ramifications for the profession's relationship to its clients. With more and more architects working for other architects, what Everett Hughes (1958) points to among lawyers is likewise true of architects: the client and the colleague-employer are equated. Regardless of young professionals' dissatisfaction with a particular project, their jobs are at stake if they choose to take a stand against the person that signs their paychecks. Since the profession requires a certain number of years experience for registration, the employer-as-client phenomenon is to some extent enforced by the profession, prompting an economic, if not psychological, shift in reference group from the lay client to the architect-employer. Young professionals thus have one employer rather than many clients. This distance between architect-employees and lay clients is exacerbated by the fact that firms' owners and chief designers are often the only ones who regularly meet with clients.

In my opening example for this chapter, the draftsperson's comments indicate that architectural employees as a whole feel little allegiance to the "corporation." They tend to be fairly transient within a given locale, moving from office to office if an opportunity arises to better their personal situation in terms of pay, responsibility, or new experiences. In addition, I have observed a mild form of "sabotage" among some architect-employees. This is more common among those at the bottom of the office hierarchy, who are given very little decision-making or design responsibility. These individuals make the seemingly trivial decisions needed to create a model or complete a set of working drawings. Essentially, they must make other individuals' schemes "work." The lowest architect-employees may proceed slowly and somewhat carelessly, to a domineering boss's dismay. In the office, these alienated architect-employees are not burdened by the careful consideration they bring to their own design projects in school or to moonlighting jobs.

The moonlighting phenomenon reveals something about architect-employees' relationship to employers. Young, recently graduated architect-employees search for and accept moonlighting jobs—independent design projects completed outside the office—not only to make extra money but also to be able to make their own decisions. Moonlighting keeps "business" at the office and provides an outlet for design. Sometimes it is a form of economic sabotage, as when architect-employees accept jobs from the same market that their office goes after. They are then in essence competing for work with their own employers. Firms can also be held liable for problems that occur in their employees' outside projects. For these reasons moonlighting is done clandestinely. When aware that many employees are accepting outside commissions, an office may establish a policy that the individual bringing the job into the office will have primary design responsibility. Nevertheless, moonlighting usually continues for two reasons: first, bringing a job through the office will increase the cost to the client or decrease the fee to the architect-employee; second, architect-employees do not believe that the office hierarchy will actually give them the freedom they can have as independents.

According to Aiken and Hage's (1966) study of organizational alienation, the strongest determinant of work satisfaction among professionals in bureaucratic contexts is participation in decision making. By contrast, the strongest predictor of their alienation or dissatisfaction is "formalization" in a heavy-handed bureaucracy where rules are strictly enforced and govern the employees' actions. These rules, like the explicit design objectives mentioned earlier, are another way of removing personal authority. Much of this authority, for architects, stems from design control; they are trained as designers and fully expect to practice this training. The design authority that trained architects would like to invoke concerns important, large-scale decisions. As one office's associate (second only to the owners) confided when asked if it were true that the lower people in the office hierarchy had no design responsibility: "Look *I* don't even get to do any design! The people at the bottom don't realize that, but the 'nuts and bolts' of architecture are emphasized in this office, so we're kind of always doing design and kind of never." Embedded in this comment is the illusion that design is equivalent to broad conceptual decisions (for example, how the site should be addressed). As a result, architect-employees experience Hughes's gap between anticipation and realization. Even for someone who has been in the profession long enough to be an associate, the gap is difficult to bridge.

In a survey of over 250 California professionals conducted by the Organization of Architectural and Engineering Employees (1974), architects were asked about the factors influencing their career choice. The most frequent response (41 percent) was "artistic flair"; next were the far less frequent "parental guidance" (14 percent) and "Frank Lloyd Wright" (11 percent). When the architects were asked whether their employment conditions were better or worse than expected, only 4 percent replied that things were better than expected, while over half (57 percent) found employment conditions worse than they imagined. Many were disappointed with the quality of work produced and with the responsibilities they were given (both at 40 percent). Perhaps these architects were frustrated that their own artistic flair had not been tapped. Blau's more recent study of over 400 architects corroborates these findings: 98 percent of those surveyed said creativity was the distinctive feature of architecture, and 80 percent said they wanted more opportunities to work creatively—that is, more design assignments, especially in the early parts of projects, and more autonomy (Blau 1987).

There is also great agreement about compensation: 95 percent think architects' compensation is too low, and 66 percent are personally dissatisfied with their salaries (Dixon 1986). Architects appear to be the most poorly paid professionals and earn even less than firemen, policemen, carpenters, and truckdrivers (AIA 1974). In the Census of Service Industries (1982), the average annual salary for architects was $22,838, while starting lawyers received about twice that amount. The more recent survey of firms by the AIA (1989, 3,023 firms studied) shows that starting salaries averaged from about $22,000 in small firms (two to four persons) to $24,700 in larger firms (20 or more persons). That same study reveals that only slightly more than a quarter of all architects make over $40,000 per year (reporting on 1988 salaries.)[23]

Although the dequalification of labor continues, it is to the architectural office's advantage to hire architect-employees with a range of skills, so that there is some flexibility in job assignments and missing links are avoided. There is another motivation as well, a more exploitative one that some architect-employers acknowledge. If employees can be hired at a low level—that is, low pay relative to their training, which is not difficult in today's job market—they can be given greater responsibility, the payoff being less frustration and greater job satisfaction rather than the expected salary increase. The office benefits from a low-paid employee ably working beyond his or her job description. Whereas a project architect is paid more than a draftsperson, a draftsperson with a master's degree will accept the greater responsibility of project architect, foregoing the commensurate salary she or he deserves.

**ACROSS THE TABLE:
THE CLIENTS**

The changing architectural office and architect's role are mirrored and magnified by changes in the client population. Historically, the architect's patrons came from the same culture, though generally from a higher social class, yet contemporary architects now find themselves designing in countries and for cultures quite unlike their own. Even as early as 1963, 16 large U.S. architectural firms controlled a total of $118 million in foreign building (*Architectural Forum* 1964). By 1986, 4 percent of AIA members reported some foreign income, but that income accounted for nearly one fourth their operating revenues (AIA Firm Survey 1987). This international work is handled primarily by larger offices, while small offices compete for the local jobs.

At home, it appears that present architectural demand comes not from a tiny elite, but from a broad middle-and upper middle-class support for high culture (Blau 1987). Clients, as mentioned previously, are more and more often corporations, governments, or institutions rather than individuals. In a breakdown of architectural fees by project types, single family dwellings comprise only 4.7 percent of the total fees, far less than commercial buildings (44.5 percent) and public and institutional facilities (26.6 percent) (1982 Census). These client-giants send representatives to client meetings who then report internally to some higher authority, such as a board of directors, vice president, or department head, thereby removing the ultimate approval process from architects' immediate control. Numerous problems incurred by diffuse influence and distance from ultimate authority can be observed in everyday architectural practice and will be discussed in chapter 3. With complex clients, many architects enter the design process expecting the arduous project management will mean a battle to maintain design quality. The art of architecture is pitted against bureaucratic clients. And yet, as Blau and Lieben (1984:242) conclude,

2.10 David Rockefeller (left)
with SOM's Gordon Bunshaft
in 1972, standing before a
model of the Chase Manhattan
Bank and Jean Dubuffet's *Four
Trees*. The Rockefellers are
prime examples of patronage
in a corporate era.

architects realize that their firms' survival is determined by these clients. "Corporate clients are critical in the analysis of [architectural offices's] size change: reliance on them is found either to destroy the firm or to result in substantial growth." They suggest that those architects prosper who have clients who prosper; the corporate clients who go bankrupt bring their architects with them; and those architects who avoid corporate clients are barely surviving.

In this context, the client with whom the architect works and to whom he or she is legally and financially responsible is not the client who will use the building. Historian James Marston Fitch says that instead of direct knowledge of a project's inhabitants, the architect "deals instead with their agents—those corporate or institutional entities who commission the projects. Instead of first-hand observation of real people and their needs and aspirations, the architect is given statistical data with which to work" (1965:236). This takes its toll in terms of whose interests are represented, whose priorities respected, whose problems solved: the owner, the user, the representatives, the persons with final approval, or the architect-employer. Fitch believes, further, that architects' isolation from their "real clients" precipitated a trend toward more formal, abstract, and less humane design.

The growth of architectural offices and clients' increasing complexity have had significant effects on the profession. In 1980, a survey was conducted by *Building Design and Construction* of over 600 "mega-clients" who do at least $1 million of commercial-institutional-industrial construction annually, and whose average expected outlay for the following year was $23.5 million. These clients hired a particular firm for the following reasons (in rank order): ability to complete on budget and ability to make building function (both at 47 percent); ability to complete work on time (36 percent); and ability to work with owner staff (33 percent). Aesthetic quality ranked tenth on their list, along with fee amount (both at 21 percent). Actually, *any* client might have these same priorities, but only a large architectural office can meet the requirements of such mega-clients. And once an office gears up for "big dollar work" it is difficult to take on any other kind. Small projects such as single family dwellings do not make efficient use of resources. The architectural office operation, with its numerous and varied staff, is tailored to provide the services and scheduling for large projects. Generally, a private residence cannot keep more than two draftspersons occupied for very long, let alone compensate the office for the amount of time spent in meetings and design. Some offices may accept single family dwelling projects "just to keep our hands in it"—but these assignments, based on a relatively small construction budget, are notorious for losing money.

Boyle concludes his essay on the last century of architectural practice with the following words: "The ethics of the individual architect were replaced by the ethics of the architectural office, and the more the architectural office resembled businesses in general, the more did its ethics resemble those of the business world" (1977:342).

CONCLUSION

From the early history of architectural occupations to the more recent dynamics of offices and client organizations, the development of professional architecture has hinged upon the link between espoused beliefs and the circumstances found in everyday architectural practice. Since ideology and circumstance are both real forces, I have examined the way that certain beliefs function in the architectural profession. It has been my intention to link certain consequences with their incipient beliefs, not in a causal sense, but as contributing forces. For example, there is a clear connection to be made between the profession's emphasis on design and its distaste for management of office activities, as well as its loss of other marketable skills to other occupations.

I have presented this chapter as a foundation for the rest of the book. The analytic overview of the profession provides a general context for specific issues ahead, such as the nature of design problems, office culture, and design quality. In addition, this chapter demonstrates the critical perspective I adopt throughout the book. It helps establish the shift to a new frame of reference, considering architecture as a social construction created within the culture of practice.

At some level, architecture is understood to be a collective artistic activity, more like filmmaking or theater than novel writing, painting, or sculpture. While scholars argue that all the arts are in fact socially produced (see Becker 1982; Wolfe 1984), architecture presents a special case. Because architecture is inextricably bound up with individuals other than designers, particularly the client or patron, the nature of this bond is hotly disputed, carefully tended, and romanticized. Architects sometimes deny the significance of other actors' roles in design, or suggest that paying attention to these relations is inherently nonarchitectural behavior—that work should be left to businesspersons and managers. From this study it should be apparent that to ignore the social context within which buildings are designed is counterproductive for all parties involved, most assuredly for architects. By devaluing the conditions that frame the creative process, a spectrum of constraints and opportunities are overlooked and removed from the potential control of the architect.

There are twenty-seven people present at the meeting, including the college president (CPres), campus administrators (CAdmin), the chairman of the architecture department (AChair), architects (Arch), campus planning employees (CPlan), a lawyer, and a fundraising officer (FR). The high-powered group convenes every other month to review physical planning and design decisions for the campus. Approximately five projects are reviewed on this day, presented by the architect doing the work or by the client. The first presentation is by Mr. Simmons, an administrator from the medical school, which is located in a valley adjacent to the main campus. He introduces the architect, saying he has asked her to attend in case questions arise. While the project architect listens, Simmons presents a rendering of a parking lot that is being expanded and landscaped, stimulating the following discussion[1]:

CPRES: I'd like to raise a couple general issues.

ACHAIR: I think that's more important than specific design issues.

CPRES: The first is surface water, and the second is the carrying capacity of the valley in relation to the main campus. We need long-range planning that is comprehensive rather than piecemeal, linking the valley with the main campus. [When Simmons responds by talking about recent developments in the medical school's long-range plan, his information is treated as "filler" until the key people begin to speak again.]

ACHAIR: We need an overall view of the valley that includes coordinated materials, a complete landscaping plan, a drainage plan—all these must be dealt with comprehensively. [An administrator continues, explaining the space-planning process and its precincts. As he speaks, it seems that he is establishing the relationship between the medical school and the main campus through environmental issues.]

ACHAIR: We need an overseer for the hydrology issue.

CPLAN1: Really, the problem is the unstable nature of the valley. We must be spending $1 million a year on the problem.

(A few pockets of discussion continue while Mr. Simmons is thanked, and he and the architect leave the room, receiving no comments on their specific proposal. For the next presentation, architect Adolf Reynoso passes out brochures that show the work his office, Hartson/Reynoso, has undertaken for the Southridge athletics department. The office has a two-year contract with the university to design modifications to the physical plant related to athletics. He shows slides of drawings for the same projects, focusing on the current work at the stadium, where his office is adding a physical therapy center, tennis courts, a practice field area, and administrative offices. He shows colored site plans, floor plans, sections, and interior and exterior elevations.)

CADMIN1: Are we doing anything about the seismic issue?

FR: There are no funds for it, and it's not in the fundraising. We estimate it would cost over $3 million.

3.1 Howard Roark arguing un-
successfully with a board of
clients for the uncompromised
modern building that stands in
the window before a backdrop
of neoclassical structures. He
turns down the commission
when the clients insist he alter the facade. Nothing represents society's conservative
architectural tastes better than
a client committee or board.

CADMIN2: What about this astroturf? Why are we doing it when it's going to be so unpopular?

ARCH: You'd have to have another practice facility, since the teams destroy the natural grass before the season even begins. It's administrative requirements in the end, like the scheduling of practices, that necessitate astroturf.

FR: The fundraising is now 80 percent complete. We'll begin with the turfing, then the therapy facilities, the administrative area, and then the tennis courts. [She goes on to explain that they will go ahead with the project without funding for seismic work].

ACHAIR: How much of the construction will have to be undone to make seismic corrections?

ARCH: The plan is salvageable, but a lot will have to be dismantled.

CADMIN1: How can you avoid doing the seismic corrections when all buildings that are remodeled have to be brought up to earthquake codes?

CPLAN1: Since it's a stadium, it was categorized as a "non-building." It's not a good situation, but we're stuck with it. [There ensues some discussion of state-level seismic policy and life-safety regulations.]

CPRES: Even if we had seismic funds, the stadium would be low on the list compared to dining halls and the library. So are we or aren't we going to do this project?

CPLAN2: But this is the only structure built on landfill, and so subject to much more severe problems in an earthquake.

CPRES: Let's find out if we can avoid the most serious hazards and what it would cost to take care of these with the project.

ACHAIR: The detailing of the stadium windows is going to be crucial, and this tennis court raises an overall planning issue again, since it is one of the few building sites left on campus. Stein and Associates are doing a study for us on this now, and on the impact of astroturfing. We should wait for their report.

CPLAN1: Stein has been asked to take the current projects as existing . . .

PRES: We're always in the same boat: in the midst of planning and projects. Plus this whole project is pretty far along the pike. Politically, I don't want the astroturf issue raised again.

(After several minutes of further discussion, Reynoso is thanked, shown the door, and another architect begins his presentation. When we leave the room, I ask Reynoso what he thinks has happened.)

ARCH: I don't know. But nothing was said to slow the wheels of progress, so we have to assume that they've given us the go-ahead. Early on, I had to decide who we were working for—the athletics department or that committee—and I chose the user [athletics department]. But I haven't forgotten that the president has the final word.

The example above is taken from a design session between architects and clients. An architect reading this passage is likely to have two reactions: first, that sinking feeling when client organizations trample architectural issues with bureaucracy (and waste architects'

3.2 This meeting of architects, clients, and consultants in Frank Gehry's office is typical of larger-scale projects, for which such groups might convene once a week to coordinate ongoing activities.

time); second, a forceful denial that this, or anything like it, might be called "design." But design problems in practice, or what it means "to design" in the architect's everyday world, are not part of the expectations we hold about the profession. In the campus planning meeting above, architectural issues catapult client representatives into conversations far broader in scope than the parking lot or stadium rehab on the boards. "The client" is at least two-tiered: the architects work closely with an individual department or school, but they both must answer to the higher authority of this administrative committee. In the vignette, the design projects are characterized by a great deal of ambiguity, a wide set of voices with influence, and consequences that are significant (particularly their implications). These and other characteristics of design problems in practice are the topic of this chapter.

The term design can refer both to a valued quality of architecture (as in good design, formal design) and to the activity of planning environments. The activity of design (as in design process) is commonly thought to be what the designer does, alone, at the drawing board. It is this second sense of the term, referring to the activity, that I would like to reconsider. Temporarily suspend the common definition, and imagine instead that every individual with a voice in the design process is a kind of designer—the client, the engineer, the contractor, the inhabitants, the college president, the fundraiser, and so on. The architect-designer, among those individuals, has the added responsibilities of coordinating all contributions and giving them some spatial expression. Design, then, is taking place whenever any of these actors makes plans about the future environment. While these actors may not sketch their concepts into architectural form, their input will frame design solutions. Moreover, it is from the context of all their interactions that a building emerges. In the opening example, positions on the seismic issue are established, a final approval is handed down on the astroturf, priority is given to fenestration in the stadium's remodeling, and the groundwork for a new building site is laid. None of these is an absolute given, and each will play a significant role in guiding the design solution. This example points out that "design problems in practice" refers to more than design activity in the office; it also means moving a project through the approval process, managing its construction, obtaining the commission in the first place, and so on.

This shift in perspective leads us to view architectural practice in a new light. In the opening case, the architect is relatively passive, observing as the administrators run their own design process. In his last comment, the architect suggests that he is engaged independently in his own design activities with the athletics department but his seemingly simple way of proceeding is in fact risky and limited. It is risky because the committee can decide to stop the whole project at any time, regardless of how well it suits the athletics department. While the architect acknowledges the president's power, he may be overlooking other subgroups (for example, the architecture chairman, the planners, the fundraiser, and their constituents), each of which can be seen as having its own power and set of design problems. It is limited because the architect, by his disinvolvement, turns the planning committee's contributions into constraints. The meeting *is* a waste of time for the architect, but it need not be.

Architectural practice is the setting where ethos and circumstance lock horns, where individual and professional goals combine with budgets, deadlines, skills, organization, power, context and regulations. Architectural practice can be characterized as a series of projects that an office is organized to attract and to accomplish. For each project, the design problem is to create a new environment that somehow improves the existing situation. Traditionally, problem-solving research has studied simple or "tame" problems in contrast to what Horst Rittel, a design methodologist, has called design's "wicked" problems (Rittel and Webber 1976). My own observations corroborate Rittel's characterization of wicked problems, and this chapter describes their key characteristics as I have gleaned them empirically from architectural practice. Based on a content analysis of my field notes from the architectural offices, six principal characteristics of design problems in practice emerge:[2]

1
Design in the Balance. Architecture tries to unite ideologically contradictory forces in the union of art and business, so that at each step, the primary professional value, design, is challenged.
2
Countless Voices. The influence brought to bear on any project is distributed across numerous participants, each having a voice in the matter.
3
Professional Uncertainty. Practice is a dynamic situation in which the responsibilities, procedures, authority, allegiances, and expertise in a project are ambiguous.
4
Perpetual Discovery. Since the information needed to make decisions is never complete and each constraint can be challenged, design is a process of perpetual discovery that could go on endlessly.
5
Surprise Endings. Although a single specific solution is sought, the possibilities are limitless and participants cannot predict the outcome.
6
A Matter of Consequence. Design participants are highly motivated since the stakes are significant and the consequences serious.[3]

While design problems confronted in an architectural practice are distinct from other types of professional problems (for example, a patient's illness, a client's law suit), I will argue that they are also unlike the design problems presented in the architectural academy or the professional society. The unique qualities I refer to concern characteristics of structure and procedures (such as a range of acceptable solutions and design methods) rather than content (such as office buildings versus housing). The design problems of practice will be compared to those presented in studios of North American architectural schools and by the American Institute of Architects. As I have explained, since schools and professional bodies are the chief disseminators of professional ethos in architecture, they serve both intended and unintended functions.

DEFINING DESIGN PROBLEMS IN THE SCHOOLS

In schools, would-be architects learn not only how to solve problems, but also what constitutes a design problem and what constitutes a reasonable solution. The AIA performs a similar function, providing architects with models to present to the public and to the courts. Thus the AIA's documents attempt to formulate the basis for agreement among parties: here's what architects do, this is the contractor's role, here's what the client should expect, sign on the dotted line. The AIA promotes architects and architecture to the public, creating the profession's public persona and official doctrine.

In 1989 there were 114 schools in North America offering professional degrees in architecture (about 90 percent of which were accredited) and another 100 or more schools offering architectural programs lasting two years or less (as at community colleges).[4] I am restricting my discussion here to accredited professional programs, which are typically located in universities and colleges, so that some generalizations can be made.

While there are various ways to categorize schools by approach or by degree program, the one element that all approaches and programs have in common is the design studio.[5] The studio is the heart of architectural education, since one third to one half of the required educational program takes place in the design studio or laboratory (see McCommons et al., 1982), and it is in the studio that we find the purest vision of an architectural problem. While the studio experience has remained the central component of an architect's education, the particular nature of the studio has changed over the years, as evident in the clear models offered by the Ecole des Beaux Arts and the Bauhaus.[6] Each studio varies with the teacher, the school, and the level of student, but the fundamental structure of the studio is relatively constant: the instructor poses a problem (with site and program established) and then works individually with students as they develop their solutions.

3.3 This SCI–ARC studio captures many aspects of studio
life—students working during
off hours, the couch for nap-
ping during charrettes, individual work areas, chairs to pull
around for a pin-up, and general clutter.

Like the architectural office or the atelier on which it was based, the studio represents the social context in which design problems are confronted and resolved. James Polshek, practicing architect and then Dean of the Graduate School of Architecture and Planning at Columbia, offers his description (1981:2–3):

> The design studio becomes home and workplace. Openness to criticism—both from fellow students and from teachers—and the necessity to express private fantasies publicly, further cement the "family." The clannishness is one of the more obvious hallmarks of the "culture of architecture."
>
> Almost seventy percent of an architectural curriculum takes place in or is related to the "studio." This part of the student's education is really a series of design "seminars" meeting for sixteen to twenty hours a week with one faculty member serving twelve to fourteen students. It has been axiomatic that architectural knowledge is transmitted most effectively on a one-to-one basis—the teacher sitting with a single student for fifteen minutes to one hour engaged in an often silent dialogue of pencil lines and fragmentary sketches. This is then reinforced by small group reviews where peer criticism becomes an important ingredient.

Polshek's description captures the ideal sense of the studio, but not the range of extant variations. More common but less fortunate studios may have as many as twenty-five students who meet two to three days a week for four hours a day. Moreover, the *Architecture Education Study,* the most extensive study of the design studio to date, found that students spend only 4 to 8 percent of the time required in studio in direct one-to-one contact with the instructor.[7]

There is a fundamental explanation why studio problems are distinct from practice's problems: they each have a unique and definitive context. First, the intended consequences in each setting are distinct. School must provide the background and foundations to become an architect. Problems are composed for didactic reasons, so complex problems are simplified, variables are isolated for study, and a series of educational experiences is coordinated. The second reason is that the studio can provide direct experience with design as an isolated activity, but not with design-in-practice which students can only learn *about* (see Argyris and Schon 1974; Schon 1983). The third reason is that school problems are self-selected by architect-educators. The teachers, operating under professional values, elect to deal with the issues they consider most significant.[8] This is why a studio problem can be esoteric and conceptual in a way that the problems of practice never are.

The intended consequences of academia are largely brought about. Because school problems are partially the result of an idealized vision, they help to create the ethos of practitioners. As intended, the academic rendition of design problems fosters professional values and unity. Design is emphasized as an art and as a craft. Facility with drawing and conceptual design are highly valued. Since design is also the most mysterious of the architect's knowledge, the learning of it takes place in a somewhat protective setting. The academy serves the intended purpose of providing safe turf for error and innovation.

When we look at the differences, however, between school problems and those of practice, we also can characterize the gap produced by unintended consequences. The school disembodies the primary professional activity of design from its context. This is a paradox, in which design needs to be studied in isolation and yet, by so doing, it is a distinctly different entity than design in situ. To clarify this point, consider the analogous situation in psychology, where purified experimental studies rarely can be applied to the situated human action they try to understand. What is learned in the laboratory (read: studio) is valuable basic knowledge that bears little direct relevance for the way we act in the environment (read: practice). By deemphasizing context, much knowledge and training that would be useful in architectural practice is unattainable.

Since architectural training includes an apprenticeship component, some may argue that students are expected to gain context-loaded experience during their internships. Schools may teach exactly what could not be learned in apprenticeship or practice. But since apprenticeships in architecture (unlike those in medicine) are relatively disorganized, the unintended outcome is that many practitioners are not trained in the social arts of working with clients and consultants, in negotiating a contract, in real estate finance, or in working with regulatory agencies.[9]

THE PROFESSIONAL ORGANIZATION

Founded in 1857, the American Institute of Architects (AIA) remains the primary professional society for architects. From the beginning it has best represented the more established, conservative firms. About 60 percent of those eligible for membership (that is, registered architects) belong to the organization, increasing since 1980 from 40 to 50 percent (Gutman 1988:10). The AIA is perhaps the most abundant source of espoused professional theory, in Schon and Argyris' sense of the term. In spite of the fact that not all, or even a majority, of practicing architects are members, the professional organization sets standards that permeate the entire building industry. AIA contracts are widely used, and the organization issues a range of documents that establish guidelines and expectations about architectural practice.[10]

The espousals of the AIA should not be taken as explicit beliefs of individual architects; rather, the AIA's pronouncements embody the philosophy of the institutions to which all architects are subjected. To gather the AIA's positions, I have relied heavily on *The Architect's*

Handbook of Professional Practice. This collection of documents, regularly revised and published by the AIA, is intended primarily to provide architects with legal and professional information related to architectural practice. The most recent revision (1988) revamps the entire four-volume collection, and comes far closer to a description of practice than its more propagandistic predecessors.[11] The revised *Handbook* also devotes a significant amount of attention to liability issues. Chapters fall into three basic subject areas: a general interest category, including descriptions of professional careers in architecture and the construction industry; a series on practice management, describing the architect's office, project management, marketing and legal concerns; and finally, numerous documents and project forms such as owner-architect contracts and project checklists. The *Handbook* is a reference manual, available in public libraries as well as in the private libraries of good-sized firms.

Both the professional society and the school disseminate their models to practitioners. The discrepancy between both these models and the problems and processes observed in practice, however, are tremendous. The remainder of this chapter focuses on the six characteristics of practice's problems, comparing them to problems as they are construed in school and by the professional organization.

1. DESIGN IN THE BALANCE

In the campus planning meeting that opens this chapter, the quality of the design schemes seems inconsequential in light of the larger planning issues, such as seismic and hydrological conditions. Policy, politics, and funding appear to drive the scheme. Only once is a specific formal design issue raised, when window detailing is mentioned. The architect responds to this multiheaded client by creating a solution that is noncontroversial and by deciding that this project is not going to permit award-winning work. Much later, the same architect commented:

It's fine to say you're going to do award-winning work, but you can't do it without a client. We're trying to do really good work when we get the chance. The trouble is, the only way to do better work is to have better clients, and the only way to get better clients is to do better work. We used to do only development stuff—all our clients were developers. Some of them are good, you know, willing to spend more money and concerned about design rather than trying to maximize use of a property, and get more of everything for less money. . . . Sometimes you just have to admit that a project is going to be a D-O-G. Then instead of pressing hard and putting in a lot of effort for little improvement, you get it out as fast as possible. Everybody designs a few dogs. It's inevitable. On each project, you just have to decide whether it is possible and worth it to do battle for something better.

Rather than try to make allies of key figures on the planning committee, such as the architecture chairman, the architect opts for what he hopes will be the path of least resistance. This strategy specifically places design quality low on the list of priorities.

In practice, design hangs "in the balance," because placing a high priority on design requires tradeoffs in other domains. At the office, design time and design freedom are challenged in at least two ways. The first resistance stems from the common priorities of clients, that the building should be economical and functional. For instance, a small budget places limits on the quality of finishes and materials, which affects the quality of the entire building. A small budget generally goes along with a small fee, limiting the amount of time the architect can spend on the design. Only when the client holds or respects professional values does this challenge to design subside. It is not only clients who question design's preeminence, however, since all participants, such as consultant engineers, design review agencies, and users, come with their own sets of values (Becker 1982). Second, the architectural office's own business practices may work against design quality. To make a profit, even to make payroll, generally means using time efficiently, rather than spending additional time in schematics and design development or making significant changes as the project develops. There is a paradox here: an office without good business practices will not survive, but many of those same business practices can discourage good design.[12] This, as one architect put it, is "no normal business."

While architecture is identified as one of the arts, it is also a profession and a business. Any profession must attend to the business administration of profits and losses. The business aspects of architecture involve, for example, establishing a realistic fee structure, staying on schedule, estimating the amount of work remaining prior to completion, coordinating consultants and in-house staff, maintaining contacts with prospective clients, acquiring new work, managing the number of projects that are in the office at any one point in time, getting agreements in writing, writing legally competent specifications, staying as close as possible to the construction budget, staffing the office in an optimal manner, gaining publicity for work completed, and developing effective office procedures. In fact, every office activity has its implication for the business of architecture.

Within a firm, those at management levels have the greatest responsibility for the business (and, as mentioned earlier, have the least contact with "drawing board design"). In addition, many offices hire someone expressly in charge of business development (marketing, project overseeing, active searching for new work). The design staff tends to view these people as being outside the architectural culture or the real workings of the office. Jokes are made about their stereotypical polyester suits (dress being an identification badge in the architectural world) and about their inability to "organize" architects with all their creative eccentricities. During my early field work, I noticed there was a semi-concealed pleasure taken from minor sabotage of the business developer's goals, reinforcing the notion that a business school graduate cannot begin to understand what goes on in architecture. The underlying intention may have been to protect against economic priorities overtaking design priorities. For instance, an aspect of one young business developer's job was to follow projects and maintan contact with the clients. Often she was unable to get either meeting notes or budget reports from other people in the firm—necessary information for her task. As one member of that office said, "She ought to go work at some insurance company. I don't know why she came to work at an architect's office anyway." But as these jobs grow more prominent in architectural practice, business development will gain acceptance within the office.

In the Bay Area in the early 1980s, business development workers felt so isolated, each alone and ostracized in individual offices, that they formed an organization called Business Developers Anonymous, which met regularly and semi-secretively to discuss business practices, management, and marketing, as well as personal struggles in the design context. The meetings were not public and participants were "anonymous" because, according to my informant, the office hierarchy was concerned that confidential information about commissions could be revealed to competitors—the other offices. The irony of the situation was self-evident: an office admits enough need for a skilled business person to hire one, recognizes her knowledge is valuable enough to try to silence her and then shores up its inviolable self-image by isolating her, making sure to keep both the employee and her function separate from the architect's culture.

On the flip side of business development is a general attitude among architects that I call the "charrette ethos," in which good architecture requires commitment beyond the allotted time, accountant's ledger, and normal hours. It is a widely held notion that the best work comes from offices with a charrette ethos: those willing to charrette and put in overtime (sometimes unpaid) for the sake of the outcome; and that good architecture is rarely possible within the fee. Another aspect of the charrette ethos is that the people involved with a project will care about the building enough to uphold high design standards regardless of the fee. The phenomena of the charrette and working overtime can be seen as reaction to and rejection of the client's control. By working without pay or longer than is reasonable to create a building beyond the client's subsidy, the architect asserts some independence and at the same time justifies decisions that might go against the client's wishes. In a sense, the architect comes to "own" some part of the project.

One office I studied paid little heed to the charrette ethos and is probably typical of many American firms. This office was run according to maxims that might have been learned at weekend business management seminars. Internally, the small office functioned like a full-scale bureaucracy. Commissions were garnered on the basis of "connections" and inside tracks earned on visits to Washington, D.C., or the state capital. Once won, a commission translated itself into profit through a division of labor and finite resource allocation, particularly that of time: two hours for the designer to develop a parti, three hours to study elevations, two hours for the project manager to coordinate plans with the engineer. (This is what Coxe [1986] would call a strong delivery firm.) In this office, the aesthetic dimension of architecture was treated like any other and all aspects were governed by the time clock. This is merely the opposite extreme of the "star" office approach, but both approaches are incapable of merging art and business in architecture.

The separation of architecture as an art from the business of architecture has a long tradition. In the first century BC Vitruvius praised the "gentleman" architect in contradistinction to the suspect architect of wealth: "But for my part, Caesar, I have never been eager to make money by my art, but have gone on the principle that slender means and a good reputation are preferable to wealth and disrepute" (1960:168). More recently, Thomas Creighton, in a foreword to Morris Lapidus *Architecture: A Profession and a Business*, states: "The ability to perform this [business] part of architecture effectively need not detract from the creative act of design; in fact, good business procedures should be an integral part of the total process of producing architecture, that good design is more possible because of them" (1967:vii) Creighton implies that business procedures generally interfere with architecture and creativity. Even the AIA *Handbook* has felt it necessary to state what may not be obvious: "The Client has every right to expect that the Architect will be familiar with and will utilize normal processes of business administration. There is no conflict between the competence in architecture and competence in business matters, and there is no substitute for either"(1976:5:6). Note that this statement reiterates the distinction between the two: business is necessary to but separate from architecture.

On the surface of professionalized problems, good design and good business are not in contradiction. But perhaps this is because the necessary compromise between them has been struck implicitly. There is evidence to support this idea in the AIA's prescribed sequence for solving a design problem. The *Handbook* (1988) enumerates five stages of an architectural project: schematic design, design development, construction documents, bidding or negotiation, and construction. The *Handbook* also used to state the percentage of the total fee for basic services that each phase deserves, before antitrust legislation precluded such standardization (see figure 3.5). From this, we can roughly gauge the amount of time that the AIA recommended architects spend on each activity. What this diagram tells us is that the largest share of a project budget and of office time goes to production—working drawings and specifications writing. Only a small portion goes to conceptualization and the early stages of design, where so many architects want to work (Blau 1979).[13]

The profession as art and as enterprise is not a happy coexistence, as the AIA suggests, nor does good business mean good design, as Creighton wished. Instead, design hangs in the balance in architectural practice—as, for that matter, does good business. One architectural accountant put it this way: "Of course there's a business side to architecture—even though a lot of architects try to keep it low profile. Look, even in our little office, half a million dollars pass through each year. If we weren't good at business, we'd be up a creek!"

The dilemma does not exist in schools, where business concerns go unrecognized. There, design quality is challenged only by the designer's ability. Only occasionally do academic exercises challenge design priorities with pragmatic concerns. A student's scheme may be criticized for the extravagant construction costs it would incur, for not meeting the needs of hypothetical clients, or for its inadequate structural resolution. Many instructors do intimate that the dilemma exists in their private practices, so students are at least exposed to the idea (Beinart 1981). Students do not learn, however, how to achieve design quality within the context of opposing forces. While teaching design is difficult enough by itself, this has not prevented schools from integrating it with other essential design issues such as structure and technology. The pragmatic business component of architecture should be equally difficult to ignore. Nevertheless, in school design continues to win out; according to professional theory, design and business are integrated; in practice, they are in constant battle.

2. COUNTLESS VOICES

I neither am nor will be obliged to tell your lordship or any other person what I intend or ought to do for this work; your office is to procure money, and to take care that thieves do not get the same; the designs for the building you are to leave to my care.

—*Michelangelo (Vasari 1963:v304)*

In replying to cardinals who thought the lighting inadequate at St. Peter's Cathedral, Michelangelo was reasserting the proper roles for

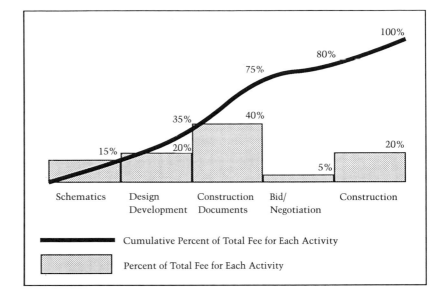

100%

80%

75%

40%

35%

20%

15%

20%

5%

Schematics   Design   Construction   Bid/   Construction
                Development   Documents   Negotiation

━━━━━━━   Cumulative Percent of Total Fee for Each Activity

[▨▨▨▨]   Percent of Total Fee for Each Activity

architect and patron. Historically, however, it appears his ideal was not always upheld. The architects' ideal has traditionally been to control the entire design and building process, though he was not necessarily both designer and builder. Patrons, on the other hand, were expected to subsidize the architect's art as they might the painter's or sculptor's—that is, without having much input. Although our notions of patronage exaggerate the freedom these artists enjoyed, the patron remains a strong model for contemporary architects' clients (see Gutman 1989). The primary patron for architects in the Middle Ages and early Renaissance was the church, which gave the practitioner somewhat greater freedom than the landowner-patrons of later times. Sole ownership gave the latter a more personal interest in the design of their buildings.

Medieval records indicate that responsibility for a building's final form has long been distributed among a number of individuals.[14] Aside from clients, there is a variety of other actors who must participate if the architect's design is to be realized. In *Art Worlds* (1982), the sociologist Howard S. Becker demonstrates that every art relies on a network of collaborators operating under certain conventions. Yet there is a general belief, evident among artists, architects, critics, and even scholars, that the quality of a work of art decreases in proportion to the number of people involved in its creation. This is one reason why the small office remains the ideal of architectural practice. Large or small, any office that produces award-winning work is likely to attribute a particular building to a single designer from the firm. Good offices are typically characterized by their legacy of good designers

(Skidmore, Owings and Merrill being the prime example) rather than their collaborative teams.[15]

One of the few works available on the history of the profession (first published in 1927) strongly emphasizes the importance of individual creation: "We, at any rate, must know that the design and erection of every large and complicated building in the past involved the control of some masterbrain, that no group or committee could have taken its place" (Briggs 1974). By contrast, Spiro Kostof has more recently called for more research into "the social equation that underlies any building of merit" (1977a). He is among the architectural historians who examine buildings not from a formal art-historical perspective, but with an eye to their sociopolitical context.

Even those who support the masterbrain theory of creation acknowledge the important role of clients or patrons in architecture, since it has direct bearing on the balance of authority and, therefore, decision making. As a client assumes a more active and powerful role in the planning process, the architect's role is complementarily transformed. In contemporary America, architecture has been pushed into the public domain, giving voice and decision-making authority to communities, public agencies, regulatory bodies, constituents, planning boards, city councils, neighborhood associations, and the like. Given these groups' influential role in shaping the environment, the architect's decisions are continually subject to "external" determinants.[16] In conjunction with broad social and economic forces, more clients have become less willing to subsidize architecture for architecture's sake. The profession does very little to prepare would-be architects for the crowds of participants who will want a say in their projects. Hence the reactionary oft-repeated calls from schools and architect-heroes for a return to an architecture about architecture.[17]

It can seem frustrating (though indicative of architecture's multifaceted task) that the least significant participants in a project may have a highly significant influence on the building's design. Consider the following examples from my fieldwork:

1
A professional renderer who depicted the architect's preferred scheme from a "bird's-eye view" is blamed for the clients' selection of a less preferable alternative. The clients were so overwhelmed by the odd conglomeration of solar equipment on the roof, that they selected a scheme rendered at eye level.

2
A contractor reviewed an architect's construction drawings for a residential remodeling that entailed reorienting the entry, expanding the kitchen, and adding a dining room. He informed the clients of what he considered several poorly resolved design problems, and with their approval, made such changes as moving a wall, changing the dimensions of the kitchen, and rearranging circulation in the foyer.

3

A bank loan officer, reviewing plans for a house built on speculation, insisted that every new home within a certain price range had to have skylights, at least one and a half baths, and a jacuzzi. All of these had to be incorporated into the scheme, to the architect's dismay, before the necessary financing could be obtained.

The coordination of all these contributors is no easy task, and architects struggle to maintain control. Even though a single participant may be involved with a project for only a short duration, that individual has a voice in the process; the combined impact of all such participants can overwhelm an architect's best intentions. The architect's office must act as a control point, as one practitioner put it, providing continuity and leadership over the life of the project.

The ultimate test of authority or influence in the design process is the capability to call an end to the entire project. Both architect and client hold this power. The situation in architecture is thus one of "conditional viability," as defined by decision theorist Kenneth Boulding (1962), since each party has the ability to eliminate the other. The architect-client negotiations are somewhat "secure," in Boulding's terms, since it does not pay either party to eliminate the other. In Boulding's model of conflict theory, dominance is typically assigned to one of the parties involved. Between architects and clients, however, dominance is unclear. Architects are most likely to dominate negotiations by observational criteria, whereas clients may ultimately dominate since they can stop specific negotiations, take their business elsewhere, and continue the project there. In the current highly regulated climate, there are others who can terminate a project. The writers of an environmental impact report, the city planning commission, or a design review board can easily upset the design process.

The influence of the client naturally varies with client, architect, and project. Any client, however, wants her or his input to be significant; at the same time the architect is expected to know best and to be able to foresee consequences. This strikes the unusual balance of power characteristic of architecture. It has confused both players; one client commented: "When I made a suggestion, say to change the pitch of the roof, and Ben accepted it, it made me really nervous. I mean, why should he listen to me? How am I supposed to know if it would look okay—fit in? He's the one who's supposed to know about that; that's why I hired him. Otherwise I would have done it myself." Inherent to the architect-client relation is the simple fact that clients hire architects to help them. At the same time, as this client reveals, there's a sense that clients can perform some aspects of the desired services themselves. It is this sense that gives some clients the confidence to contribute in more ways than the architect might wish.

DESIGN PROBLEMS IN PRACTICE

Some architects assume that the more participatory the process, the more time-consuming and the less profitable. An office may try to protect its design authority by rendering collaboration less frequent and less meaningful. One instance, arising between architects and consulting engineers during my fieldwork, exposes the negative consequences of this strategy: Each of two offices confronted a similar rehabilitation problem. In the first, the structural engineer said the the turn-of-the-century building needed diagonal steel bracing either on the exterior or just inside the shell. The architects chose the second alternative and planned office spaces to work around that structure. They felt this was functionally awkward, and discordant with the building's character, but preferable to exterior bracing. In the second office, a structural engineer confronted a similar problem and suggested the same diagonal steel bracing. When the architects explained why this alternative was unsatisfactory, the engineer developed a means to use reinforced concrete abutting and tying into the shell. The final result was similar to what the first office had been trying to achieve but was unable to work out with their engineer.

Examples like this point out why offices try to find consultants with whom they can establish a long-term relationship, working as a team with full knowledge of one another's abilities and methods. From my observations, it appears that with heavily involved clients the time spent in these meetings pays off; approvals are easier to obtain and changes relatively easy to resolve.

Architects' responses to diffuse influence vary, but one of the most common attitudes is to treat others' contributions as constraints. As evident with the first engineer above, this position tends to rule out negotiating such constraints and thus means a reduction in the architect's freedom. The architect who accepts alternatives with no further exploration *converts* the consultant's or client's contribution into a constraint. The second engineer demonstrates that the first alternatives are not the only ones. In fact, each actor makes *willful choices* about solutions, and each of these choices has implications for the building's design.

Even if an architect maintains design authority, only the smallest jobs can be completed by a single individual, since nearly all projects involve a collection of in-house architects and draftspersons. Of course, the diffuse influence within the architects' own office is more manageable than that distributed among independent outsiders like consultants and clients. Many offices maintain a steep hierarchy, in which partners and project architects make nearly all decisions. Rarer is a team approach to projects and participation in design by all strata of the organization. Blau's study of firms indicates that the more participatory the office, the more effective it is in terms of both business and design quality (1984:143).

Although design problems in practice involve numerous voices, both from within and outside the architect's office, both the professinal organization and the schools continue to emphasize the importance of the individual architect. The AIA takes a highly optimistic, if not unrealistic, view of the situation. A look at the following lists of participants indicates the extent to which influence is dispersed in design decision making. The first list (Table 3.1, top), published by the AIA, shows a range of consultants whose services may be needed in a building project. Compared to the second list (Table 3.1 bottom), compiled from my own observations of individuals who participated in actual design projects, the AIA's list looks almost manageable.

The roles and responsibilities of various project participants is indicated in a relatively hazy manner; the actors are loosely tied to activities in different phases of the design process. For example, the *Handbook* states: "Beyond the first conceptual steps, however, the process becomes more complex. In all but the smallest and simplest projects, the steps that follow the concept involve a team of people. While it is true that most significant works of architecture are usually developed under the guidance of a single strong design leader, it is important to realize that few projects have fewer than 10 people involved in the decision making (architects, engineers, interior designers, specialist consultants, construction managers, public agencies, and, of course, clients). Thus, design excellence results in part from the effective management of a complex team, all of whose members contribute to the quality of the final result" (*Handbook* 1988:2.5:9). The AIA's basic strategy for confronting the outside voices of participants is to establish both confidence in and control for the profession. The AIA accomplishes this by claiming a powerful role for the "single strong" architect at the hub of all activity and a more peripheral role for other participants. Consultants are to provide factual and technical data in a timely manner; they are presented almost as tools for the architect. A romantic version of the relationship is portrayed by architect Morris Lapidus (1967:48): "A team of experts like these [consultants] is a vital and wonderfully knowledgeable group. We need them all. They and their services form the complete package when we offer our services to a client. He expects, and should receive, the benefits of such a talented crew of consultants, with you, the architect, at the helm." Similarly, in the professionalized problem, the client is expected to provide a site, create a program (usually limited to a list of functional areas and approximate square footages), review and approve documents as they are produced, and pay bills: "The Architect functions as creator,

Table 3.1
TWO VIEWS OF THE PARTICIPANTS IN AN ARCHITECTURAL PROJECT

FROM THE AIA HANDBOOK OF PROFESSIONAL PRACTICE (1975, 5:5)

PRIMARY CONSULTANTS	ADDITIONAL CONSULTANTS	
Civil engineering	Survey and soils engineering	Audio-visual
Structural engineering	(provided by owner)	Communications
Electrical engineering	Foundation engineers	Space planning
Landscape architecture	Value analysis engineer	Environmental impact
Interior design	Construction cost estimator	Energy conservation
Construction management	Zoning and building department	Legal
	Special building types,	Financial
	e.g., hospital, school, library	Surety
	Illumination	Insurance
	Food service facilities	Graphic designer
	Elevator and escalator	Photographer
	Materials handling	Model maker
	Irrigation	Renderer
	Traffic and parking	Computer service
	Acoustical engineering	

LONG-TERM PARTICIPANTS	PAID CONSULTANTS	REGULATORY AND APPROVAL BODIES	INTERESTED PARTIES	INFORMAL CONSULTANTS	INCIDENTAL INFLUENCE
Client	Landscape architect	Client	Community groups	Client's friends	Renderer
Architect	Structural engineer	Client "body" (corporate representatives, board of directors, etc.)	Tenants, users	Previous clients	Photographer
In-house architectural staff	Mechanical engineer		Financial backers	Constituents	Model builder
Interior designer	Electrical engineer	Building inspector	Architects from other firms	Product representatives	Workmen, carpenters
Architects from other firms	Interior designer	Fire marshal	City manager	Financial backers	Proposal writer
Tenants, users	Lighting expert	Building department	City architect	Architects from other firms	Typist
Community groups	Energy consultant	Plan checker	Neighbors to the site		Lumber company
Landscape architect	Fire safety expert	Tenants, users			Product representatives
Structural engineer	Soils consultant	Voting public			Constituents
Project architect employed by client	Geologist	Planning director			Environmental impact report writers
	Biologist	Planning commission			
	Lawyer	City council			
	Historian	Board of supervisors			
	Programmer	Design review board			
	Proposal writer	City architect			
	Cost consultant	Bank loan officer			
	Business developer				
	Contractor				
	Construction foreman				

3.6 Herbert Johnson, Frank Lloyd Wright, and Wesley Peters (from right to left) watch the testing of a column at the Johnson Wax Building. This trio represents the essential network of collaborations that architecture demands, between architects and clients, engineers, and other architects. Wright had an ideal assistant in Peters, who arrived as one of his first apprentices from an engineering background at MIT. Wright relied on Peters for decades as his chief technical assistant on many projects.

coordinator, and author of the building design and drawings and specifications with which it will be constructed. . . . Even those [Clients] who are continuously engaged in building are the customers of the various branches of the building industry rather than the active components" (*Handbook* 1969:2:3). In a subtle way, the AIA suggests the importance of the client while protecting the primacy of the architect in statements like these: "Architecture is a responsive art. Without a client, there is no architecture. A successful client-architect relationship constitutes the cornerstone of fine architecture" (*Handbook* 1975:5:2). Like an artist, the architect can respond to the subject without much interaction, perhaps more as an artist responds to a life model than the way a therapist responds to a client. At another point in the *Handbook*, the AIA suggests that the architect's basic services include "providing design" to the client. From one point of view, this notion is as odd as a psychotherapist providing mental health to the client, who by definition must take part in the curative process. This way of dealing with clients may originate in architectural education, where students respond to programs from nonexistent clients.

The school upholds the primacy of the autonomous designer by focusing all its attention on the student's experience as an individual. The relationship shared with the instructor is an exception, yet is played out with virtually no explicit pedagogical comment. Likewise, group projects occasionally provide the opportunity for students to experience design as a collaborative process. Generally, however, the groups' negotiations occur without preparation or reflection, and even when a group is involved in the early stages of a project the final outcome is generally divided into the individual solutions.

The academic client is usually described or fabricated by the instructor. If in practice outside participants seem an unruly crowd, in school "implied others" are created as opportunities. Fabricated clients, for example, are frequently created in the architect's own image. In the rare circumstances when live clients participate in the studios, they do not wield much power. The instructor, in fact, replaces the client as the most consistent and significant influence on the student-designer. Since the instructor is the sole evaluator of the solution, students must consider the instructor's tastes and preferences in their work. Thus an architect is trained to respond to challenges from another professional, and not to those of a layperson. J. M. Fitch's comment—that the architect's distance from the client has led to less humane design—is again pertinent.

The simplicity of the academic model—the diad of influence (student-as-designer, instructor-as-client)—dissolves in architectural practice. Both schools and the professional societies represent the architect as dominant and competent, the situation as manageable, and the

3.7 The primary relationship in architectural education: studio instructor and student.

3.8 Some studio problems require collaboration among students, like this solar housing project for Ralph Knowles (kneeling) at USC.

roles of participants as clear and complementary. Comparing this ideal with observations in practice, it is easy to see the discrepancies. As Argyris and Schon predict, however, beliefs about other participants become self-fulfilling prophecies. The architect *gives up* control if consultants or clients are kept in pigeon holes, as when, for example, the architect accepts the client's program without challenge. The architect who strives for client approval achieves a similar result.

3. PROFESSIONAL UNCERTAINTY

In the Southridge College example, Reynoso's project exhibits a high degree of uncertainty: the purpose of the meeting and its outcome are unclear; there are at least two different clients; the seismic issue is unresolved. Ostensibly, the meeting is about ongoing architectural projects, but the conversation centers on long-range planning issues. The loose and unfocused qualities evident here are typical.

The fundamental source of such professional uncertainty is the constant change that every problem and organization undergoes over time. That dynamic state contributes to uncertainty in four primary areas: expertise or knowledge, authority and responsibilty, allegiances, and procedures. There is a standard reply when an architect is asked such questions as "How does a typical project move through your office?" "Who usually works out the schematic design?" "How do you decide when it's time to move on to design development?" The answer is, typically, "It all depends." The architect's constant litany—that every probelm is unique—is an appropriate response to an ambiguous situation. Knowing that problems and outcomes cannot be predicted, the architect emphasizes "experience." As with the seasoned lawyer or the country doctor, direct experience with a range of problems is considered the best foundation for professional practice. Thus, although design problems may be unique and complicated, professional knowledge generalizes from one problem to the next.

EXPERTISE

Let him be educated, skilful with the pencil, instructed in geometry, know much history, have followed the philosophers with attention, understand music, have some knowledge of medicine, know the opinions of the jurists, and be acquainted with astronomy and the theory of the heavens.

Ever since the first century BC, when Vitruvius (1960:5–6) spelled out the tremendous range of knowledge an architect needs, the burden of such an unwieldly bundle of expertise has weighed upon the profession. In order to coordinate the input of the many collaborators, an architect is expected to be knowledgeable in all the fields brought to bear up on a design project. Even consultants brought in for their expertise, such as engineers, other designers, or specialists (kitchen, fire, lighting, and so on), will not be the sole proprietors of their domains. The overlap of expertise supports the adoption of more integrative design solutions, but with this integration comes ambiguity about each member's responsibility. In planning a museum facility, for instance, the architect will consult with the interior designer about rooms appropriate for exhibit display; the interior designer will in turn work with the lighting expert to create the desired ambiance; the lighting expert also works with the landscape architect to illuminate the exterior spaces pleasantly and safely; and the landscape architect may work on issues of siting with the architect.

Areas of expertise themselves are ambiguous: the engineer's facts are contestable, acoustics is an imperfect science, the landscape architect may not know much about specific plant materials. The ambiguity of expertise is particularly evident for the architect. Although the architect's education is primarily focused on design, in practice the architect is variably a designer, businessperson, market analyst, psychologist, contractor, politician, and arbitrator. In meetings, I have heard architects make statements like "The social grouping in a dorm should not exceed 20 people," "Its hard to sell a condominium with more than two bedrooms," and "The city planning commission will never approve that." The foundations for such statements are uncertain, but architects can assume or be assigned responsibility for such expertise.

AUTHORITY

Since it is not always clear who has the authority to delegate responsibilities, even assigning responsibility can be difficult in architectural practice. Many of the liability issues now seriously threatening the profession are based upon the uncertainty within a building team over who is in charge of what. In one four-hour project meeting I attended, some 18 participants (mainly consultants) focused solely on issues of responsibility and coordination. Because there was little overall coordination of the project, major components had been overlooked, including storm drains and computer power lines. The participants realized they were operating on different bases of information, since not all had received updated drawing sets. As one disgusted engineer commented, "The right hand doesn't know what the left hand is doing." The meeting ended with two people, the client's in-house architect and an engineer, assuming responsibility for central communications.

The reluctance to assign responsibility stems partially from uncertainty over who has authority to do so. The client, as initiator and owner of the project, is the ultimate authority. But because of the architect's expertise and role as coodinator, the client may bestow—or the architect may assume—that authority. Inside the architect's office workers are assigned certain responsibilities for a given project, yet they can be overruled at any time by persons with higher authority in the firm. Since clients are generally the least experienced participants in design processes, they are the most uncertain about their role: when their opinion is expected, whether they can challenge the material presented, when they have overstepped their bounds, whether they can thwart some undesirable development, what the impact of any given debate will be on the whole project. Since the design process is a recurrent setting for architects, they know the range of possible roles they can assume. The architect can often assume a strong posture, thus shaping the roles of other participants.

It is likely that ambiguous authority definition is the reason why meetings often fail to lead to definitive action. As the campus planning example shows, participants discuss ideas and alternatives without making any explicit choices. They express opinions and preferences and on that basis the architect develops the design. Especially in the early stages of a project, the client's uncertainty can be advantageous if it permits wide-ranging negotiation about a solution. The decisive rejection or approval of an alternative (approval being far more specific than rejection) is a limitation when new ideas and information inevitably arise.

ALLEGIANCE

When authority lines are uncertain, participants with strong interests may assume and hold tenaciously roles of power. Inevitably, too, each participant's role undergoes alterations that in turn reinforce the ambiguity of authority. There is a strong tendency, therefore, to form temporary alliances or coalitions in order to safeguard one's interests. Note how the architect in the opening example defends the college president on the astroturf question against doubts from within the client's ranks. He forms a slender alliance that may serve him later on. The allegiance of consultants and clients is important to the success of any architectural project. Particularly when the architect must work with client representatives, a coalition ensures that the representative will act as a lobbyist (rather than as a more neutral middleman) when reporting back to staff and superiors. All these allegiances are, however, relatively fragile, since two participants rarely agree on all issues. The motives for and short duration of most alliances contributes to their ambiguity as does the basis for their formation.

The fragility of allegiances can sometimes be detected in the pronominalization of a participant's speech. Consider the following example, in which a fire-safety consultant talks with architects:

I thought *you* guys were different [from other architects]—that *you* were really trying to make this place work.

[After a bit of massaging by one of the architects, the consultant joins them.] If *we're* going to be safe, can *we* move this building a few feet this way?

[But only a little while later, after making a concession, he returns to the other side of the fence and remembers his professional identity.] Now, how am *I* supposed to justify pulling burning bodies out of the building when *you* don't even have access roads?

[The architects assure him that they really need his help, and the fire consultant is the first to agree. Eventually he gives them advice about what can be slipped past the review panel, what can be pushed through, and what will never wash.]

Transferring allegiances is in fact part of the standard agreement between client and architect. Prior to the selection of a contractor, the architect is the owner's agent; after that point, however, the architect is expected to become a neutral arbitrator between client and contractor, upholding faithful realization of the contract documents (see *Handbook* 1988:2.8). This arrangement contributes to the ambiguity of allegiances.

PROCEDURES

As if the above ambiguities were not enough, the procedures for a project's evolution are often also unclear. By procedures I mean the methods of action exhibited during the course of a project, including the sequence of events adopted, the means of developing ideas, and the ways of going about reaching agreements. In the campus planning meeting, it was unclear whether the council would vote to approve a project or whether one powerful negative voice could stop everything. Were the architect's plans approved, or did the questions about seismic problems need to be addressed before proceeding?

If procedures are often left unclear, then the impact of each phase on subsequent phases is hard to predict. Such confusions are most apparent when someone tries to establish and then manage the architectural fee for a project. In order to justify a particular fee and then allocate resources adequately, an office tries to predict what a particular project will entail. Since it's useful to maintain some consistency in the way projects are handled, the office will use past experience as a basis for planning ahead. Each project manager guides projects idiosyncratically, however, with many procedural inconsistencies that are as much the result of differences among projects as personal style. For this reason, some offices develop a standard procedures manual to define consistent routines for projects; these have little day-to-day application, however. As one skeptical architect commented, "Even when a plan is explicitly developed for a proposal or to establish the fees, it's always forgotten or ignored once the work begins." Another said, "This is a manic office, not a methodical one."

Ways of holding meetings are also uncertain. Methods of discussing issues, reaching agreement, and conserving time are all unstructured, so that even when an agenda exists, conversation will skip from tangent to tangent:

CLIENT 1: How many people are we planning on in the cafeterias?

CLIENT 2: Well, how many people are in each of the complexes?

CLIENT 1: People in smaller apartment suites should not be expected to share kitchen facilities.

ARCHITECT: Do we really want the smaller suites?

CLIENT 2: If we have suites, we still have to have separate bathrooms for men and women.

There is no clear procedures at the macrolevel for the overall development of a project, nor at the microlevel of the meeting or decision-making process.

The radical uncertainty that pervades architectural practice is generally not recognized by the professional society. Although the AIA acknowledges the complexity of the process, the *Handbook* maintains its manageability: "The Architect must be knowledgeable in many fields—creative design, construction, engineering, business administration, and he must be familiar with construction law. Being at the center of the design/build process, the Architect's skill, training, and conceptual ability equip him to coordinate these components throughout the course of the project" (Doc B551, *Handbook* 1972:4). As discussed above, the architect's is a position of control, one that can be unambiguously defined according to the AIA. The AIA also limits the role of the client to the most unambiguous role conceivable: the client pays for the architects' services, provides a program, and periodically approves the development of the solution. The client is also directly responsible for hiring the contractor. The AIA works to clarify the procedural ambiguity by dividing an architect's work into phases, and then dividing those phases into a series of activities. These appear on the "Project Checklist" (Doc D200; see figure 3.9), published to help architects clarify the activities of "basic services" and keep records. This thirty-two page document is the professional organization's attempt to cope with ambiguity, and while I never saw anyone use this list exactly as it was intended, many of the suggestions are followed informally.

The AIA does acknowledge the complexity of the architect's task: the collaborations are numerous, many with overlapping expertise, and each phase of a project comprises a number of distinct activities. "Since areas of authority are frequently difficult to delineate with respect to liability, situations can arise in which the Architect and Engineer or Consultant are jointly liable for the same error or omission, even if one is more at fault than the other." (*Handbook* 1975, 10:5).

Part A—Ongoing or periodic tasks accomplished throughout this phase.

	Dates	Initials	Item	Remarks
25.			Review periodically internal office budgets and production schedules and check against actual progress. (AIA Doc. F721, F723 and F800 Series)	
26			Initiate and update project record book.	
27.			Maintain expense accounting records.	
28.			Submit monthly or periodic statements to Owner for payment. (AIA Doc. F5002)	
29.			Submit monthly or periodic reimbursable expense statements to Owner for payment. (AIA Doc. F5002)	

Part B—Tasks prior to starting schematic design.

30.			Determine from Owner the name of Owner's authorized representative.	
31.			Confirm Owner's space needs and other program requirements for the project.	
32.			Establish project filing system.	
33.			Initiate project directory. (AIA Doc. G807)	
34.			Initiate project data form. (AIA Doc. G809)	
35.			Assign personnel to the project.	
36.			Assemble and review all necessary legal requirements such as codes, ordinances and OSHA standards.	
37.			Establish schedule including completion dates for each phase of the project. Advise staff, owner and all consultants.	
38.			Verify requirements for environmental impact study, if any.	

AIA DOCUMENT D200 • PROJECT CHECKLIST • AUGUST 1982 EDITION • AIA® • ©1982 • THE
AMERICAN INSTITUTE OF ARCHITECTS, 1735 NEW YORK AVE., N.W., WASHINGTON, D.C. 20006

9

3.9 Project checklist, American Institute of Architects.

Likewise, a means of working with clients is outlined, based on vague foundations of cooperation, understanding, trust, and confidence: "During the Owner-Architect Agreement negotiations, a solid base of cooperation and understanding must be established between the Architect and the Owner. The success of the Project depends in a large part upon this relationship of trust and confidence" (*Handbook* 1969, 11:2).

The revised *Handbook* describes an "experienced" client who appears quite businesslike. "Experienced owners understand the importance of constant communication, the need for clear and unambiguous decisions, the dangers of excessively revising decisions already made, the importance of writing things down, and the value of strong financial management and predictable cash flow for all concerned" (*Handbook* 1988, 1.1:7). This description gives concrete procedures that can clarify the design process for participants. But by neatly listing the procedures and stressing the importance of strong financial management and of documentation, the *Handbook* implies that though the professionalized problem is complex, the architect alone can tame it. Ambiguity is manageable; the procedures for coming to clear and unambiguous decisions are known. In each of the problematic areas of practice, the AIA defends its members and tries to create for them a position of strength.

The extreme uncertainty and contingency of architectural practice is intentionally avoided in the architectural academies. Focusing on the first two characteristics of design problems, the academic exercise is typically simple and unambiguous, since design is rarely threatened by pragmatic considerations and since the individual is held in high esteem relative to the collective. Studio problems narrow the full range of issues that any architectural project entails, either by selective focus or by schematic treatment. Few studios ever deal with certain issues of practice: changes in the middle of the project, budget cuts (or any type of budget issue for that matter), new information learned during the process, conflicts among parties and interests, ambiguous roles, working with consultants, and so on. By nature practice involves an ambiguous, complex situation that undergoes constant change. While the professional may be well aware of the realities of this situation, the student knows nothing of the sort.

Not only are many aspects of practice difficult to simulate, it can be pedagogically undesirable to do so. When novices learn any complex field, it is common to break the task into simpler components. Academic problems are ideal ones. the problem has potential, an appropriate site has been selected, a reasonable program has been created, there are no clients, consultants, or planning commissioners to demand revisions, and the budget is irrelevant. There is little uncertainty about the problem or the process. The latter is relatively clean as well: only one problem at a time must be solved, the designer works alone with feedback from a more experienced designer, an a priori schedule is determined establishing the degree of completion or detail expected in the solution. It is not surprising that young professionals are frustrated by the circumstances surrounding architectural commissions and by the high degree of uncertainty they find in practice.

4. PERPETUAL DISCOVERY

Curb the impulse to spend endless time on design.
(Lapidus 1967:xv)

When outcomes are uncertain there are no rational means to determine the work a project will entail or the time required to complete it. The objective is to develop a solution of unspecified content so that the process is not inherently timebound. Of course, schedules and deadlines are established, but these typically conform to external pressures (a building's advertised opening dates, balance of fee remaining, planning commission meetings) overshadowing the internal time demands (complexity of the project, familiarity with the building type, changes in the program).

Time management is one of the most common ailments of architectural practice. Like the AIA, most architects break design activity into three phases: schematics, design development, and work drawings. Although each of these phases has a different purpose and focus, it is not at all clear when one ends and the next begins, particularly during the first two phases. Architects say that the end of a phase depends in large measure upon client approval. The decision to seek client approval, however, while influenced by the established schedule, is somewhat arbitrary. The approval, then, and not the conclusive development of the work itself, determines the end of a phase. The work is not intrinsically complete; architect and client agree to call it complete.

With even the smallest and simplest projects, years can pass between the moment a client first steps in the door and the time when construction is completed. Perhaps because the scheduling is rarely fixed, few projects are actually habitable on the projected move-in date. This problem is related to architects' claims that they "lose money" on projects since they work more days than their fee will cover. There are several reasons that schedules resist participants' best intentions and projects take longer than either clients or architects anticipate. First, in the architect's office, seemingly straightforward activities can be extremely time-consuming: these include, for example, selecting fixtures, building a model, and coordinating the set of working drawings. Second, there are unforeseen delays cause by participants outside the architects' office: a consultant can't get to the job for another week, the first set of soils reports are insufficient, the contractor goes bankrupt, or it takes six months to obtain city approvals. Third, no issue or constraint is nonnegotiable, nor is the information needed to make decisions ever complete. In the design process participants can admit any issue for debate, can consider an issue at any level, and can turn any constraint into a design variable. Finally, there is the overarching phenomenon of perpetual discovery to which all the above characteristics are subjected. That is, any change in the scheme has repercussions for every other part of the design. The architect is continuously tempted to go back and redesign what has already been decided.

Deadlines can be useful in drawing a limit to the perpetual discovery phenomenon. Often they are set specifically to prod architect and client. Architects admit to depending on deadlines as a way of curtailing design deliberations. "Without them, nothing would get done around here. When time gets short, you have to make decisions. And with the current rate of inflation and interest rates, clients want things to move fast. Architects get squeezed—there's not enough time for serious design, so we end up charretting more." Although deadlines are often extended they nonetheless establish a frame of reference for a project, apparent in statements such as "We're six weeks behind schedule on this building." A schedule thus plays a significant role in a bulding's design; establishing a good schedule, however, is not easy. The architect of an enormous and complex museum facility was ecstatic at the completion of working drawings. To her own surprise she had accurately estimated time, fees, and consultant services for the project, so that the office would actually make money on it. She was genuinely amazed that a project so unwieldy had "worked out." In large part, this was the result of her good management: once deadlines are created, someone must synchronize the work effort to adhere to them.

Given the large numbers of influential actors, a project schedule can easily slip through the architect's fingers. Architects try to avoid delays by working with trusted consultants, by establishing a critical path chart, and by carefully coordinating activities. Since even a small project can take years, many internal changes occur between inception and completion. An institutional client undergoes departmental reorganization, the community group's constituency grows more conservative, a federal housing project is postponed by a new presidential administration. In the catalog for an exhibition called *Processes in Architecture* (MIT 1979), architect Donlyn Lyndon explains the numerous changes that occurred during the eight-year planning life of the

Pembroke Dorms at Brown University. Attitudes changed about security and coeducational living, functions were added and others eliminated, and the budget fluctuated—all of which influenced the outcome. When a project's information and issues do not remain constant, the potential for endless deliberation is increased.

Determining which issues are negotiable and which are constraints is usually within the architect's ken, providing another degree of control over the outcome. As experts, architects can open and close lines of inquiry with their authority and knowledge of the process. In such matters they can dominate clients who are not familiar enough with the design process to recognize its potential flexibility. Generally, architects accept two basic constraints. First, architecture is assumed to be an appropriate response to the client's situation. When a corporation wants a new image and a building to convey it, the architect will rarely suggest an advertising campaign instead. The second assumed constraint is the site. When a client already owns a site, only occasionally will an architect deem it unsuitable. Beyond these limits, however, architects vary in terms of what they consider constraints; for example, some feel it is their responsibility to evaluate and reconsider the client's program, others will accept the program at face value.

Besides the potential negotiability of all issues, the overwhelming number of relevant issues leaves design open to perpetual discovery. There is simultaneously too much and too little information. Clients can never explain all their needs and desires, and those who attempt to do so will encumber their architects with excessive detail. One architect felt certain his client was more interested in the planning process than in the house being planned. This client sent page after page of prescriptive minutiae such as "I need storage space for my roughly 25,000 slides from Africa" and "Storage is needed for food, dishes, pans, appliances (though I have none now); my present cupboard space . . . might be adequate if I did not presently use a good deal of it for books, photographic supplies, sleeping bags, [and] magazine storage."

According to Churchman (1981), in any specific problem one can discover a network leading to all other potential problems –for instance, by moving to different levels of the problem or by revealing a new problem brought about by the first solution. As new aspects of the problem are resolved, old decisions must be reconsidered—the temptation of perpetual discovery. In conversation, the tangents taken by each speaker display a personal view of the problems' interconnections. The following case in point features an architect describing to a colleague a competition project—a museum and gatehouse for a women's college: "The site is a real problem since you can't see the school from down at the bottom of the hill. And this big open space really should be preserved. So, anyway, we need something that recalls the classic arrival,—we have to consider the notion of entry. But it's important that the exhibit designer doesn't do some Eamesian thing. We want it to be clear, straightforward. You know, you could just about bury the whole building underground!" (See figure 3.10.)

Why burying the building underground results from this protocol is unclear, but it seems to be the beginning of a solution. An invisible set of interconnected problems reveals itself to the speaker, leading to a concept for the solution. Selecting some central concept or issue provides a direction that will limit consideration of other issues.

A design process is a perpetual discovery, potentially endless, for reasons such as the negotiability of all issues, the relatedness of problems, the difficulties of coordination, and the disproportionate time taken by relatively insignificant tasks. Even when construction is complete, the design project is not finished. The building is continuously inhabited, personalized, weathered, landscaped, ventilated, viewed, and visited. The building solution is the answer to one set of problems, yet will inevitably bring other problems into view. The life of the building in its environment, both social and physical, will bear the approvals, satisfaction, dissatisfaction, and redesign long after architect and client stop meeting. This was shown quite clearly by Boudon (1969), who visited Le Corbusier's Pessac some forty years after its construction to inquire about the substantial alterations made by its inhabitants. The burden of perpetual discovery of problems and their design resolution shifts from architect to inhabitant. Boudon introduces his well-known study thus: "It remains nonetheless true that

3.10 Relationship of ideas for museum project.

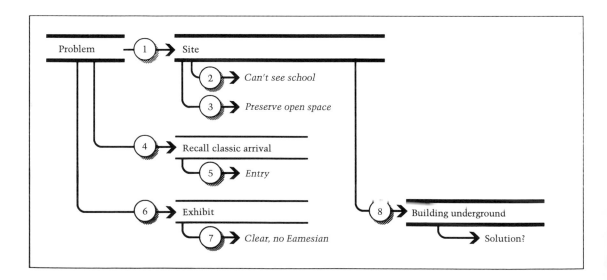

both the way in which we live and the homes we live in are products of the human mind and as such are subject to constant modification" (1969:2).

The theory that there are problems within problems, so that each decision holds implications for earlier as well as subsequent decisions, creates an image of a nested or circular process. Based on what I have culled from the AIA's literature, that organization can be seen to promote a linear process. The sequence of phases and activities does not admit, for example, that once in design development a given process might return to schematics-type activities. For the AIA, the architect has specified responsibilities in each phase of a project—phases that are broken down further into subactivities, creating a seemingly endless description of the necessary elements of architectural services. The AIA's project checklist (see Figure 3.9), with its implied linearity, disguises what is actually a much more fluid process. The checklist also masks any indication of what these tasks migh entail. For example, Item no. 32 states that the architect should "establish project filing system," while no. 31 seems far more complicated: "Confirm Owner's space needs" (Doc D200, *Handbook* 1988). Each of these tasks has a completely different nature, level of complexity, and time length. By implication, however, each task is given equal weight in the project checklist. Again, the professional society paints the process as complex, but knowable and predictable. Design as a problem of perpetual discovery is tamed into one of time management.

In school, however, the designer-student is specifically challenged to rethink solutions. While academic problems are simplifed by their emphasis on design and on the individual, the process of solving even simple design exercises can go on endlessly, or at least until the due date for an assignment. Thus, of all the characteristics of practice, perpetual discovery is the best represented in the schools. Although the motivations for reconsidering previous decisions are different in school—as are the rationales for constraints—the similarities exist. Academic design processes also are open-ended, with arbitrary deadlines that are established and enforced. Many problems given over a two-week period could easily extend to fifteen weeks. It is commonly understood among students and instructors that the time allotted to academic design problems will never be sufficient. This reinforces prevalence of "all-nighters" or charrettes in design schools. On the other hand, although deadlines help students learn to manage time, the focus is on their own time and not on group deliberations or contributions from consultants.

5. SURPRISE ENDINGS

Unlike a buyer and seller negotiating, say, the price of an existing house, an architect and client do not know the object of their negotiations: architects do not know what they are selling until after it is sold; clients do not know what they are buying until after they have bought it. *This is because the object of the negotiations, the building, is created within the negotiations.* In the course of discussions about the impending project, decisions do not *derive* from an overall vision of what ought to be; instead, those decisions help to construct an overall vision. In fact, professional services are bought and sold, not buildings.

The entire design process, as conceived by the AIA, practitioners, and academics, is intended to reduce ambiguity about the outcome. In practice, architect, client, and consultant work together to create a building that will have the desired consequences and will avoid unforeseen negative consequences—at least, they try to limit the range of surprises.[18] But the finished building always does hold surprises that participants were unable to predict from simulations. Several aspects of design problems make it difficult to predict design outcomes. First, there is no one point in time in the life of a building when participants can evaluate it definitively, saying, as it were, "Ah yes, this is what I expected." Buildings take on their character over time, through use, and can be continuously reevaluated. The dynamic nature of the outcome complicates our ability to predict it and its consequences—a particularly disquieting notion for developer-clients who seek a marketable "product." Second, people and institutions seeks architects when they experience a shift in their own expectations. They seek environmental changes to reflect and catalyze less tangible changes in their lives and organizations, so that design becomes not just the expression of a new attitude but the formation of it (see, for example, Wittman 1984; Ellis et al. 1985). In this sense, architecture is very much like psychotherapy. A third characteristic of the design process leads to unexpected outcomes: the principal planning media (drawings, models, and conversation) are *simulations* of the outcome. It is actually words and images that are negotiated under the belief that they determine the final form of the building. Of course, these media are effective; architects do create buildings without first making full-scale mock-ups. The gap between planning media and the object being planned is exacerbated by clients who may be graphically illiterate. Consider the following example:

An architect was planning a hair-cutting salon for a client who took all drawings and revisions home to show his girlfriend, getting her advice and keeping her informed of the progress. The architect, near the end of design development, presented the client with a model that represented in three dimensions all that they had previously discussed. When the architect suggested that he show the model to his girlfriend, the client thought for a moment, then declined: "I'd rather keep it a surprise." The architect was stunned, for the comment meant that the client himself was surprised by the model and had not fully understood the three-dimensional implications of the drawings. The architect, having gone through months of meetings, had been certain that the client understood every detail of the project.

The example illustrates that a client may understand the drawings as an internally consistent two-dimensional world without making a spatial connection between the drawings and the three-dimensional building they define.

Conversations between architects and clients revolve around the consequences of certain hypothetical actions—as if conducting an imaginary experiment by constructing a word-and-sketch building. In the following example, the conversation is about the traffic flow in a cafeteria line. The place seems to come alive as they draw-talk, creating a three- or even four-dimensional mental image of the future environment.

"We could have two serving lines on both sides of a food island, but then food has to cross through the lines [sketch 1]. Diners can cross diners, but food and diners shouldn't cross one another."

"Maybe we could feed the second line in halfway down the food counter like this [sketch 2]."

"Plus the checker could help direct traffic. But what about replenishing the salad bar? It's important that the servers can get to the salad bar easily. We need to have a pass through for them. [This seems to have outweighed, at least temporarily, the diner and food crossing issue.] Maybe by defining the two separate serving lines we could also leave some space for that [sketch 3]."

On the other hand, participants prophesy certain contingencies that must be considered in the design: "By 1995, all students will have personal computers in their rooms"; "We're going to have a lot more public contact in the future." Predictions are made about occupants and then factored into plans to accommodate their behavior—plans based on hypotheses. Because these hypotheses are also "designed" by project participants, the building will encourage and discourage uses according to such negotiated hypotheses. Hence the notion that "form follows fiction." The outcome—the building and its use—is impossible to predict from the start.

The ability to form expectations is complicated by the fact that no problem brought to the architect automatically dictates an environmental design solution. Each issue raised in architect-client meetings can be taken outside the realm of the architect. For example, after testing a number of alternatives, the participants quoted above found circulation in the cafeteria remained awkward. Finally, the architect said, "You'll just have to have another ticket-taker at this door." The building thus creates a job, the architect moves the responsibility to

3.11 Sketching possible
solutions.

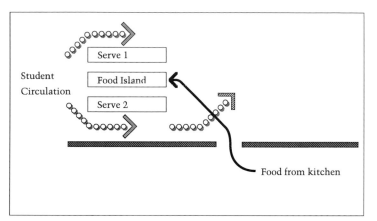

Cafeteria Diagram Sketch 1

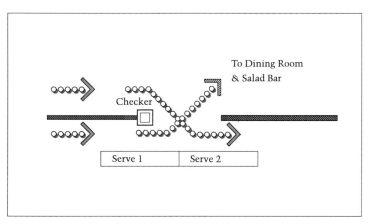

Cafetieria Diagram Sketch 2

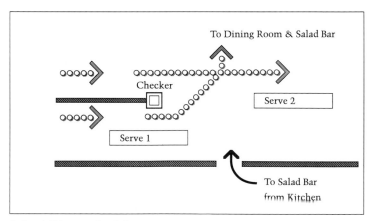

Cafeteria Diagram Sketch 3

the client, and the problem becomes managerial rather than environmental. As such, even the *realm* of the solution's outcome can be surprising.

Although there are innumerable possible outcomes that could evolve from the design process, both architect and client persevere toward a single, specific solution. When similar situations arise in different projects, the architect or client will often rely on precedent: "We used this kind of sheathing at the San Marcos Mall. You must go take a look at it." Even if a solution "works" in one situation, however, there is no assurance of its appropriateness in another context. Office landscaping satisfies the twelfth-floor sales counselors but makes the tenth-floor analysts miserable. The air conditioner can be placed in a roofwell in San Francisco but not in the San Fernando Valley, where it overheats and shuts down completely. Nonetheless, it is understandable why "comparables" are commonly used, since clients need guidelines for predicting an outcome even when they are potentially unreliable.

Architects look for extant buildings similar to ones they are planning as a means of seeing into the future. For example, it is common to locate a building of the desired level of quality in order to estimate the current price per square foot of a planned project, or vice versa: the known cost per square foot of several buildings is used to predict the quality that can be achieved for a specific price. Clients then are shown the comparables: "If you want an office that looks like this, it's going to cost about $150 per square foot." Although the term "comparable" generally refers to a cost-quality determination, architects and clients often want to find buildings that are comparable in other ways: building type, program, scale, exterior materials. For a new retail project, one troop of six architects and clients traveled around the United States exploring well-known shopping centers. This experience became a shared basis for much of the subsequent decision making. The collective review of comparables is common practice for significant institutional projects.

While architects in practice spend much of their time worrying about the building and the suprises it may hold, the AIA documents appear to sidestep the entire issue of surprise endings. The typical agreement between architect and client does not center on a finished building; instead, it is the contractor who is responsible for the physical result: "While one or more building contractors assume responsibility for the construction work, it is important for most projects that the architect remain involved to observe the construction work. . . . Some owners tend to undervalue or even eliminate the architect's role in administering construction contracts. Owners, however, are advised not to skimp on these services; a successful project may well depend on the architect's involvement during construction. Moreover, architects are exposed to professional liability claims arising from the construction of the project even if they are not on the project team during the construction phase" (*Handbook* 1988, 2.8:1).

It is the architect who is responsible for making plans, but while some architects make sure the contractor follows the drawings to the letter, others lose interest once the final fees are paid. Architects, contractors, and clients make design improvements as they see the building take its actual form. The range of attitudes toward the construction phase is further evidence that outcomes cannot be fully anticipated.

Architects learn in the course of professional socialization that it is the process of doing the work that matters rather than the product, and this view so overwhelms the profession that concepts of mistake and failure become lay terms (Stelling and Bucher 1973). Instead of products, architects and other professionals are required by contract to deliver certain services. These services are intended to create a building, which is always implied but rarely given specific mention. An even more tacit issue is the quality of the building toward which those services are directed. Even though the quality of service is discussed, the link between service and built product are not: "This type of owner, who sees you as a provider of a product and not as a provider of professional services, will likely be disappointed and dissatisfied if your "product" is not perfect" (*Handbook* 1988, 2.2:4). "The Architect's primary function is to act as the Owner's professional adviser. He develops *his best solution* for the project from the Owner's criteria, prepares statements of probable costs, advises on the selection of materials, systems, and equipment to be used, advises on the selection of contractors, and acts as the Owner's agent in dealings with others associated with the project" (*Handbook* 1970, 9:3 [emphasis mine]).

The architect is objectively developing "his best solution" (an idea for a building, not an actual building) and the owner must "inform the Architect about all functional and occupancy requirements to be considered in the design of a project" (Doc B551, *Handbook* 1972:8). The architect will provide professional services, working with the material given. Shortcomings or unforeseen consequences can be blamed on insufficient information. Logic indicates that the nature of architect-client interactions precludes clear, exhaustive formulation of needs and requirements, since these develop or become understood through the design process itself. My observations of design practice corroborate this reasoning. Because needs are not fully known there will always be insufficient information, in the AIA's sense, for the provision of satisfactory services and hence for the design of a satisfactory building.

A principal topic of the revised *Handbook* and of recent AIA conventions is the liability issue. Litigation is evidence of surprise endings in the negative sense. Indeed, the professional society may avoid written discussion of surprise endings because it is such a volatile subject. The society tries to protect, not expose, its members by removing them from responsibility for the surprises that arise in practice. The AIA is promoting something it calls a "standard of reasonable care," which is designed to establish the legal basis for determining professional negligence, that is, the reasonable expectations society may hold for the architect's performance (see *Handbook* 1988:1.6; Franklin, n.d.). Guidelines like these are themselves tricky, since antitrust laws forbid the profession from setting exact standards, pricing, and so on.

The professionalized problem is conceived as having predictable outcomes so long as all the proper procedures are followed. This stands in contrast to practice's problems as well as those posed in the academic setting. Although fine distinctions can be made between problems in practice and in academia with regard to the unexpectedness of the outcome, in this area, their problems are quite similar. Earlier it was noted that even though academic problems are simplified and less ambiguous than those of practice, the design process remains one of perpetual discovery. Stemming from this open-ended process is a wide range of solutions—academic endings are often surprising, as any studio instructor can attest. The final form a student's project will take remains uncertain even a few days before it is due. But since academic exercises cover a limited range of issues, the surprise factor is likewise limited. The instructor sets the program which frames and guides the students' design activity, and although variations are dramatic, solutions display consistent characteristics and exclusions. Nevertheless, there is often an "anything goes" attitude in studio, since academic solutions are relatively free from constraints. In terms of content, therefore, studio problems embody greater unpredictability of outcome than practice's problems. With regard to the unexpectedness of the outcome, the problems in practice and in academia differ in kind, but both result in surprise endings.

6. A MATTER OF CONSEQUENCE

Architects, because they can do harm, must learn to be open-minded.
Denise Scott Brown, 1981

To conclude an outline of the nature of architectural practice, this final section acknowledges that architectural deliberations involve significant stakes. Buildings are a matter of consequence. They have a significant impact on the lives of the people who plan them and those who use them. If they did not, the architectural profession itself might not exist.

Since the outcomes are uncertain and important, design decisions are calculated risks. Participants thus have significant stakes in the design negotiations (see Rittel and Webber 1973). The result of the negotiations is imposing: a building is big, expensive, immovable, and public; it cannot be stored away after one tires of it, nor can it be easily replaced. Even if a dissatisfied client sells the building, a new group of individuals must cope with it. Only when little is at stake, in the rare instance when the building does not really matter, are participants nonchalant about the negotiations.

The work of architecture is a matter of consequence to at least the following parties: architect, client, funding agent (including investors and lenders), consultants, neighbors, and inhabitants. The interests of these various parties are not always congruent, however. Here, an architect speaks to a client who represents a funding agency for public housing: "We'd like to do something nice for the people who are going to live here, but there are so many essentials, so many requirements, we have to work just to get it built [within the budget]. It's better to take [our proposed housing development] as it is, even with its problems, than not to have it at all." Not all negative consequences can be avoided; not all participants have an equal voice (in this example, the future residents appear to have no voice). Relations of economics and power, as evident in this example, can determine whose consequences will matter most.

Because a building functions at many levels, those with a voice in the process are concerned about wide-ranging consequences. They have a great deal at stake, from potential law suits to public presentations of self. A building can ease a financial situation or cause bankruptcy; it can accommodate its inhabitants or make their lives miserable; it can instill in its creators pride or embarrassment. A building's consequences are serious and so, therefore, are design deliberations. Participants take the design process seriously, knowing that their decisions will matter in the long run.

The design process is lengthy (and tends to extend itself) partially because the stakes are significant and the consequences serious. The answers to planning questions such as "How many students should form a basic social grouping?" will matter to generations of dormitory residents, the architects and clients may decide upon residential suites for eight or double-loaded corridors for eighty. In the campus planning meeting cited at the beginning of the chapter, the safety of tens of thousands of people slips past as a semantic problem: the stadium structure is termed a "non-building" and is therefore free from seismic regulations. The planning committee here takes a tremendous risk.

Since there are no true or false answers in such situations, the actors rely upon informed judgment and an assessment of immediate needs to make decisions—decisions that are risky and lead to unpredictable outcomes (Rittel and Webber 1973). The campus planning committee takes the risk that a big quake will not strike during game time.

The different and common interests of parties involved are the necessary bases of negotiation (Zartman 1973; Strauss 1978). There must be some overlap in objectives for negotiation to be a feasible strategy, and some conflict to feed the process. Clients, architects, and consultants all hold both common and conflicting interests.

The clients' initial motivation to invest time and money in architectural design is the anticipation that, with careful planning, a building will be designed to accommodate their future activities, needs and desires. If the clients' respective needs are not met, the consequences can be disastrous, and so their stakes in the design negotiations are high. In my studies, clients looking to architects for answers had fears about possibilities ranging from terrorist threats on a research institute, to children falling out of a second-story window, to unrentable office space. Clients generally prefer to hire architects who have experience with their particular building type, since this may reduce the risk of negative consequences.

Along these same lines, as subsidizers of the architectural enterprise, clients have their financial resources at stake. Since it is not easy to start over (they are expected to pay the fee regardless), clients want to be sure that the architect will satisfy their requirements, that they can afford the building being designed, and in many cases, that the building will give a good return on their investment. On large projects, clients sometimes hire cost estimators who monitor the process to insure conscientious budgeting. Whether the clients are corporate, private, governmental, or community, few are financially prepared to pay for a building that goes significantly over budget. Architects have a reputation for exceeding the preestablished budget. As one practitioner put it, in the unabashed language of an earlier day, "Clients—and I like clients—have a mean and nagging way of never forgetting how much more their buildings cost than their architects told them would be the case" (Murchison 1930:225).

In addition, the building makes a statement about its inhabitants (Cooper-Marcus 1974), even though clients may not be able to articulate the statement they wish to make. A husband and wife, upon seeing the first perspective sketch of their house, said, "It looks, well, funereal . . . like a mausoleum"—obviously not a desirable association. The architect had consciously attempted to design an appropriate statement for the couple, offering a building he thought "solid, stable, and monumental." The clients, who viewed the house differently, held to their own interpretation and were not convinced by the architect.

Because of the high stakes, clients are highly motivated participants in the design process. They see the importance of their own input to a solution that will have favorable consequences. Unlike a patient, who typically will not challenge the doctor's diagnosis or prescribed cure (Illich 1976), the architectural client, with a more ambiguous role, exerts greater influence on the outcome. Other social science researchers have noted this difference between professions' clients. Gutman (1977:56) suggests that doctors and lawyers assume the authority to prescribe on the basis of scientific and objective knowledge. Architectural clients, on the other hand, have "needs [that] are acknowledged to be subjective. They can be met equally well by several different prescriptions and the client or user is allowed to have a voice in choosing which one might be best for him."

From the perspective of architects and consultants, all projects are linked to a network of other commissions and thus have consequences for their careers. Every project helps form the basis for subsequent projects and for the economically stable office. Young architects find it difficult to get commissions until they can present a sizable body of built work, since one project breeds another. Architects want to have a portfolio of various building types, constructed projects, and satisfied clients, so that prospective clients can speak with previous clients and examime past projects.

A problematic project can foster a bad reputation, law suits, and long-term headaches. Many offices pay very large liability or malpractice insurance premiums (in the tens of thousands of dollars annually), since one freak accident can wipe out a firm.[19] I observed one case in which an architect was accused of designing a faulty mechanical system for a library. The client, on the manufacturer's advice, had relocated part of the system in a functional but unsightly manner and was suing for damages. Client and architect, both dissatisfed, became embroiled in a lengthy lawsuit. Another firm was asked by a developer to design high-density housing on a sensitive site that was the focus of much community attention. The office turned down the commission because there was "no way we could come out unscathed." Even though the firm felt it could do a better job than another office that would inevitably accept the commission, the architects did not want to jeopardize their reputation with a controversial project.

A successful project, on the other hand, helps bring work into the office. Satisfied clients will return to the architect with more work when they have it. Word of mouth through friends of friends, and neighbors of past clients are modes of informal marketing on which architectural offices typically rely. According to a survey of 600 AIA members, a full 98 percent held that referrals by current and former clients were very important to developing new clients (AIA Marketing Survey 1988).[20] These informal means, combined with formal referrals or clients with continuous building programs, lead many architects to attribute their success to their particular "track record." "We don't go out searching for work—it just walks in the door." Another office claims that three-fourths of its work comes through referrals and return clients—the satisfied customer. Yet another holds that it attracts clients because its buildings always come within 5 percent of the preestablished budget. Each office exaggerates these contentions as a way to promote their success. During a six-month period when I studied the office that claimed "work just walks in the door," it submitted several unsolicited proposals for public projects, no new jobs began, and a sizable portion of the staff was laid off. Self-promoting statements indicate, then, the important consequences that any project has on the future life of the office.

Professional recognition is another kind of success. A publication in a prestigious professional journal or an award from a professional society is personally satisfying, and while it may not ensure future commissions, it can help to convince prospective clients. (If it did not, offices would not so consistently frame and hang their awards and publications where clients can see them; see Figure 4.1.) Published projects expose not only prospective clients to an office's work, but also other architects, who for a variety of reasons refer clients to their colleagues. Some offices prize quality design and peer recognition above all other stakes. The professional model is the innovative young firm, with numerous outstanding projects and awards but no capital, pursuing aesthetic goals that outweigh business interests.

There are certainly economic interests in every project; the office's solvency as a business is at stake. Architects must "negotiate a fee" (the phrase used by the profession) that allows them to pay themselves and employees, provides seed money to follow up on prospective jobs, and pays office expenses, without pushing clients to take their business elsewhere. Architects will also test the limits of the project's budget. A relatively large budget for a particular project type is associated with a better outcome, in part because it normally means higher quality materials and more design time. Architects will often risk going over budget if they think clients can be persuaded to dig deeper into their bank account. This is often, but not always, a successful tactic.

In any office, commissions also have consequences for staffing and thus for a firm's ability to do good work. Good, qualified draftspersons and architects, of the kind every office needs, want to work on interesting projects and receive a reasonable salary. If a firm's services are in demand it can charge a higher rate, as well as select the commissions that will be most rewarding in terms of design and financial opportunities. Such offices will be better able to attract and maintain appropriate personnel to do the work. And while recent architectural graduates may sense that they are competing for a small number of jobs, those who do the hiring complain of a shortage of talent, particularly outside major metropolitan centers.

The important consequences of professional action enhance architecture's professional status. The AIA would like to impress upon the general public the intrinsic importance of architecture, and, as mouthpiece, become an essential institution itself, as have its medical and legal counterparts. Its statements again reflect the ideals of the architectural profession: "No longer is the Architect committed solely to the interests of the client; he is as much concerned with the best interests of the community, the people and the land" (AIA *Handbook* 1972, 4:3). Part of the AIA's mandate is to convince the public that architecture's value is greater than has heretofore been realized, deserving more respect, compensation, and opportunity. The organization's past theme of "value architecture" stemmed from such promotional thinking, as well as from a need to go on the offensive with regard to litigation.

In the schools, on the other hand, the stakes are less high. Outcomes matter only to their makers: the students. Compared to actual buildings, the academic design solution is relatively inconsequential. Still, the stakes are significant to the student, whose self-esteem, academic standing, and portfolio are all improved by good work. An architects' training may include winning competitions or forming friendships that will later become partnerships, though these are fortuitous and peripheral to education's main focus. The academic setting is intended to provide, as far as possible, a risk-free environment for students to learn and experiment. Yet the very opportunity that school offers is exactly the reason why students have little at stake—nothing at risk. Hence it is easy to see why design values can easily dominate in a context where design ability is the only element at stake.

In practice, income, profit, reputation, liability, not to mention environmental accommodation and fit, are all implicated by design. Each project, once completed, will live on to help or haunt its makers. As Frank Lloyd Wright counseled young architects: "Go as far away as possible from home to build your first buildings. The physician can bury his mistakes, but the architect can only advise the client to plant vines" (1953:236)

Table 3.2
COMPARATIVE DESIGN PROBLEMS

DIMENSION	ARCHITECTURAL OFFICE	ACADEMY	PROFESSIONAL SOCIETY
DESIGN	in the balance	master value	balanced practice
PARTICIPANTS	countless voices	solo and duet	architect at the helm
DYNAMICS	uncertainty	clarity	manageable complexity
PRODUCT	predictable building	unpredictable design	predictable services
PROCESS	open-ended, circular	open-ended, circular	linear sequence
STAKES	significant to many	significant to one	significant to many

CONCLUSION

To summarize, the problems confronted in architectural practice differ substantially from those presented by either the professional society or the academy. Practice's problems are generally more uncertain, involving internal contradictions and many participants with something at stake. The professionalized problem is presented as a complex task that competent architects can manage, resulting in benefits to clients and society. The academic problem is a complex task that requires design ability on the part of the individual student, whose performance is subjected to professional evaluation. Table 3.2 compares the six characteristics of design problems in practice with those of academic and professionalized problems. Appendix D elaborates this comparison.

School, the professional society, and practice do operate at one level as a single system, a mark of the profession's early attempts to promote a degree of standardization and unity. University-based training is regulated through vehicles such as the ACSA and the NAAB. The American Institute of Architects regulates entry into the profession, represents architects' interests in the public domain, and distinguishes quacks from bonafide practitioners for the public. These institutions currently function to promote certain professional goals. For example, at present the closest similarities between school and practice concern perpetual discovery and surprise endings. The emphasis in school is on design, and those highly valued qualities of discovery and invention are carried into practice. The relationship between school and practice, then, is bidirectional. While practice's problems (as they are theorized) help to shape academic training, the reverse influence also holds true: approaches to academic problems help to shape those in practice. The emphasis on the individual designer, the downplaying of budget considerations, the charrette ethos—all are internalized by the student and carried into professional life.

Indeed, while in their presentation of problems the schools represent the designer's ideals, the professional society represents the designer's dream for a *public* ideal. The AIA, in other words, attempts to articulate the architect's ideal role in society. Thus neither the academy nor the professional society describes practice in a way that matches observed reality, even though they may intend to do so. Instead, these institutions act as agents of change, albeit in a less-than-radical fashion. Viewed as instigators of change, it is possible to see how they acknowledge the dilemmas of practice. Beneath the surface structure of competence, design, risk management, and predictability lie the uncertainty and contradictions that the professional institutions work to overcome. For those characteristics intrinsic to design practice, however, such propaganda will have no effect.

According to my analysis, the schools and the professional organization, which tacitly operate as agents of change, are incurring unintended consequences that work to defeat their own goals. The emphasis on design, competence, leadership, management, and the individual tends to distance the architect from the laity, both the clients and the public at large. What is missing, and could point the way for the profession's next evolutionary phase, is attention from the institutions to the social art of design. I suggest that education can extend beyond context-free design, to include the social aspect of architecture, and that the professional organization can lead design process participants into more meaningful roles that would be beneficial to the profession. In the next chapter, I describe existing roles for architects as they develop from layperson to student to practitioner.

PAUL'S INITIATION

In 1986, when Paul finished graduate school in architecture, he moved to Massachusetts and found a job in one of Boston's most innovative firms. The salary at the three-person firm was low ($1,000 per month), but he took the job because he wanted to learn about practicing the kind of architecture that interested him most, figuring he would also have the time to study for his licensing exams and to learn more about regional architecture outside the office. Within weeks, however, Paul found himself spending long hours at the office, usually twelve hours a day including Saturdays and sometimes Sundays. The other three, all partners, often worked even longer and drew no salaries. Still, the office was not making much money, partly for reasons that Paul admired—yet he recognized this to be the reason why so much of his (and the others') time was spent at work. Their commission on any project was always small, even though they designed not only the building but the lighting and sometimes the furniture. At every major juncture in a building's design, all four brainstormed possibilities in group meetings. One alternative might be pursued for several days, until George, the charismatic founder of the firm, would come up with an ingenious new idea. Then the process began again.

At one point, with George's consent, Paul took a long weekend to visit his family. When he returned, the newest partner of the three told him coldly that he should not plan to go away again. Paul began to wonder who had authority in the office, and about the formal and informal relations between his three coworkers. He was also unsure of his former ideas about weekends and five-day work weeks. Though he wanted to become a responsible member of the office, he also wanted some time for his own personal and professional pursuits. Could he suggest curtailed but more efficient methods when he saw them? Though it seemed clear that the office needed to hire another person, he suspected they could not afford it. He wondered if he could talk to them about money matters, and how they might go about collecting larger fees so that they could pay another employee. Did he have a voice in officer matters? He wanted to help organize the office to run more profitably, but it was not clear that anyone else was interested or that his ideas were reasonable. He was, after all, fresh out of school.

Paul didn't think he had a right to shorter hours when the others put in at least as much time. He wasn't even sure what constituted a legitimate reason for going home. He wanted them to know that he would work as long as necessary in exceptional cases when the office was under deadline pressure, but that he needed to be able to distinguish the exceptions from the everyday. Finally, and perhaps most importantly, he wanted to know whether they were pleased with his work and commitment thus far—was he doing a good job, a mediocre one, or was he being exploited?

This portrait catches Paul at the transition between school and practice. He arrives unprepared, even though he has worked in other offices before graduation. School has not readied him to be a cultural interpreter, so that he might quickly make sense of his situation. Paul stepped into an ongoing cultural scene and became an active participant without knowing some important, tacit rules about how to interpret both his own and his coworkers' actions. Landing in the midst of an unfamiliar architectural arena, he adopted the most universally acceptable approach he knew: charretting (that is, working as long as need be to complete a project). For Paul, however, charretting always preceded a specific deadline; it was not an everyday modus operandi. The answers to some of Paul's questions were as yet unformulated, being shaped and emerging only as the four people established a manner of working together. By the same token, on the day Paul started work, a panoply of patterns already existed of which he was unaware. There was no one already working in the office in a similar capacity who could initiate him or give him the insider's story. To George and the other partners who had moved beyond the early throes of their careers, their own way of working had become invisible—they were unable to articulate their patterns. Even if they could have done so, those patterns would change as the impact of Paul's presence was absorbed into the worklife of the office.

In architectural offices, the meanings of actions, utterances, and intentions are fluid, to some extent formulated anew in each office and to some extent governed by the broader patterns of the architectural profession at large. If one does not know the meaning or significance of one's acts, an ambiguity arises between appropriate and inappropriate behavior. A novice in the office can never be sure about what others seem to be saying, or if his or her own points are being understood. This was the crux of Paul's problem: he had not yet adapted to the architectural office's culture. This culture is a complex social arena patterned around people, projects, and modes of behavior. Paul's example depicts aspects of the system through which meaningful, coordinated action transpires in an architectural office. With time, Paul not only learned that system, but his participation contributed to the evolution and reconstitution of that system.

The purpose of this chapter is to examine architectural practice as a well-developed social phenomenon, indeed as a culture. By so doing, we gain a better understanding of the uniqueness of the architectural profession and what it means to be an architect. In previous chapters I discussed the sociological underpinnings of the profession and the nature of design problems. These considerations outline the structural context of practice, which "is that 'within which' the negotiations take place, in the largest sense" according to Strauss (1978:98). Aside from the larger social order that frames each architectural office and project (for example, the economic climate, the strength of the architectural profession, the hierarchical relations among actors), structural conditions consist of what is currently being accomplished and the actors' theories of how to get things done (Strauss 1978: 5, 102). The structural conditions constitute the backdrop before which people in their everyday worlds work together in specific ways on particular projects.

The one characteristic of architectural practice that is consistently and unmistakably present at all levels of analysis is change. To describe practice without reference to time is to miss its central feature. This is one reason that design practice has defied explanation, since each level of analysis confronts a moving target, from the individual architect to the office make-up to the building industry as a whole.

In this chapter, I explore how an individual becomes an architect. Just as Margaret Mead saw Samoan culture encapsulated in what it means there to come of age, the metamorphosis from layperson to architect tells us much about how the architectural profession sees itself. As a group teaches its prospective members how to belong, the observer grasps the important traits of the culture. The evolution from student to draftsperson to full-fledged architect entails first gaining knowledge, then gaining experience, after which comes increasing responsibilities, and finally assuming leadership.

THE OFFICE CULTURE   If we asked an architect to describe what was going on in Paul's case, it is unlikely that the term culture would be mentioned. It might be suggested that either Paul was too inexperienced to know what was happening, or else that the office was highly disorganized. To distinguish among architectural practices, few architects would speak of their "cultural" differences. Instead, we would hear of the differences among the works they design, the types of services they deliver, their leaders, or perhaps the differences in their management styles (see Coxe 1986). The AIA *Handbook* mentions the "culture" of architectural firms but notes that architects are more comfortable referring to the "environment" of the office (1988:1.10:2). Social scientists, for their part, analyze professions in terms of socialization processes that establish standards of truth, realism, and right and wrong (Stelling and Bucher 1973). But these socialization processes are typically disembodied from the situated cultural contexts within which that socialization occurs. These two distinct ways of describing an architectural firm have dominated previous discussion, deflecting attention from the complex but systematic social organization that I call the culture of architectural practice.

In light of past studies of work communities or work cultures, it might be argued that the term culture is misapplied to a context as limited as a workplace. I contend that many workplaces are by no means limited and that the professional office is just such a workplace—an encompassing setting that is, by definition, primary to its members. Moreover, the benefits of a cultural analysis of architectural firms are great. In fact, services, design talent, leadership, and management style are all part of what I am calling the culture of practice, but these terms do not by themselves tell the whole story. The notion of an office's management style, for instance, includes the norms and values appropriate to the office, the patterns that projects and teams follow, and the rewards and incentives for workers (see Burke 1982:221). Cultural analysis broadens the scope of investigation, involving an exploration of the office's dialect, mores, activity patterns, power structure, and roles. Such an analysis first requires examining the important facets of a firm's culture: its origins, evolution, and implications for the profession.

Serious analysis of occupational settings as cultural systems has been too often supplanted by more popularized considerations. The concept of organizational or corporate culture grew fashionable in the early 1980s with Deal and Kennedy's *Corporate Cultures* (1982). They argued that a corporation's success is partly dependent upon its so-called culture—the values, beliefs, and rituals that its members share. *Business Week* (Byrne 1986:52) called it a fad that management could latch onto for a quick fix, citing one particularly enthusiastic executive: "This corporate culture stuff is great. I want a culture by Monday." In spite of this simplistic reductionism, the concept of culture carries appropriate implications for the present analysis, offering a map on which the geography of our particular setting and its actors—the firm and the architects—can be explored.

Besides Kennedy, there have been a number of managerial researchers who have examined and refined the concept of culture applied to organizations (see Bate 1984; Vrakking 1985). Fewer studies have been made of professional cultures. Bledstein, in his book *The Culture of Professionalism* (1976), describes a general theory of professions with power over certain worldly experiences within their jurisdiction. They in turn provide society with explanations, turning morals into science. This leads to a cultivated elitism, to a separation from the public that the profession serves, and to a culture of professionalism that thrives among America's middle class. The foundations of this analysis are similar to more specific cultural studies of professions such as the study of medical education (Becker et al. 1961) or the world of high-energy physics (Traweek 1988).

A DEFINITION OF CULTURE

Some anthropologists argue that culture is the knowledge needed to act appropriately, while some say it is the complexes of behavior patterns (such as customs and traditions) in a society; still others suggest that culture is the manifestation of basic and essential human characteristics. Clifford Geertz contends that culture is "a set of control mechanisms—plans, recipes, rules, instructions (what computer engineers call 'programs')—for the governing of behavior" (1973:44). The programs are organized systems of significant symbols, giving sense and meaning to experience. Culture thus becomes the accumulated totality of these programs, an essential condition of human existence. According to Geertz, to inquire about culture is to ask about the import of our actions, to expose both the normalcy and the particularity of those acts. The more we examine the architect's world the more logical it seems, the better we become at guessing what an architect might do in certain circumstances, and concurrently, the more architecture appears to distinguish itself from any other profession or art. This is what it means to gain an understanding of the culture of architectural practice. The culture operating in each firm permits its many members to work toward a common goal and to understand the significance of their actions.

We can learn about culture because its "webs of significance" are shared and public, even though they do not exist in any single individual's head (Geertz 1973). Every architectural office has a unique web within which a portrait of its culture can be discerned. That web is apparent when scores of otherwise unremarkable features are examined together. Consider the following clues, which can be found in any architectural firm and which begin to sketch its particular profile: the framed messages on the wall (past work, credentials, favored kind of paintings), the reception area and its circumstances (a guard for the inner sanctum, a greeter, direct entry into the everyday workings of the office), the quality of materials and their disposition (polished marble and Mies chairs, a drafting room cluttered with old drawing boards) the differences between work areas for principals, associates, and draftspeople, the ambiance of the lounge and conference areas, the artifacts individuals keep on their drafting tables, the prevalent office costume, the sayings that go around the office, and the permissable relations between staff and management. It is important to note that such aspects of an office both express its culture and promote it.

When we observe a newcomer or an outsider in the office, the otherwise half-hidden culture grows more visible. The "inside" can be defined by the newcomer's display of inappropriate actions, postures, and values. When I first began my research within architectural offices, I was treated to an accelerated and articulated enculturation process. Office members spent a great deal of time explaining to me what the inside looked like to them, and, especially at the beginning of my

4.1 The reception area of
Frank O. Gehry and Associates
introduces the visitor to the
firm with chairs that Gehry
designed, magazine covers
featuring the office's work,
framed awards, and models of
past projects. The office is
finished with the basic,
unadorned materials that characterize many of Gehry's
buildings.

work, what they wanted me to believe about the firm. The following comments came from various senior members of one firm:

FOUNDING PARTNER: One of our principal goals here is to keep everyone in the office happy.

PARTNER 2: We discourage moonlighting, because it drains people from the office work.

ASSOCIATE: We never take calls during meetings with clients.

PARTNER 2: When someone [a potential employee] comes in to interview, we'd rather see loose sketches in their portfolios than hard-lined, agonized sheets [of drawings]. Loose drawings, soft pencil drawings, have so much more personality and communicate so quickly with people. If I had my way, I'd take away all the 2H pencils—I wouldn't even let them have pen and ink.

Whether or not these statements reflect the facts, acculturated members of the office know what they should say as well as what they can do. Each of these statements suggests that there is an office culture of acceptable and appropriate activities, reliable expectations, beliefs, and values that members of the office are expected to share, implied by the frequent reference to "we." The tacit agreement among those who share these values, or at least know them, permits a number of architects and draftspeople to work together without stopping to argue at each step about how to proceed. They can rely on relatively accurate expectations about their coworkers. A new architect who wants to work and advance within the office will need to learn the culture's basic morphology. Assimilated members of an office interpret behavior in relatively consistent ways; they know what it means when a partner invites the office out to lunch, who to seek out for help with a design problem, whether the project architect has the final word, who must be obeyed and who can be ignored.

I want to make clear, however, that this so-called office culture is by no means monolithic, with only one way to act and to interpret actions. Within any firm there are subgroups that share perspectives, such as project teams, constituted to handle project-related activities inside and outside the office. Internally, the group must coordinate to produce architectural services; externally, it must gather information, services, and approval. There are also distinctive subgroups organized according to status within the office—these hold different beliefs and ideals (see Blau 1984). It is misrepresentative to talk about *the* office culture, just as it is to speak of any culture as homogeneous when it is made up of diverse sets of individuals in complex relations. The subcultures, the factions, the newcomers, and the oldtimers work together as a dynamic system that constitutes the everyday life of an architectural office.

It is my contention that the social context of a work of architecture is at least as influential as the properties of building materials or the building site. Within the office, the roles, relations, and tacit individual theories are a significant part of the conditions that frame architectural problems. Since any architectural problem is addressed through some form of concerted social action, people must be able to work together with some shared sense of purpose, meaning, and method to produce a building. The culture embodies conventions that allow group members to concentrate on the projects at hand (Becker 1982). It defines a world with an inside and an outside, offering membership, exclusivity, identity, boundaries for growth, and both the criteria and the judges of achievement.

FROM LAYPERSON TO EXPERT

What does it mean to become an architect? What are the programs, behaviors, rituals, and knowledge that architects must learn? What is the metamorphic transformation of a layperson into an architect? By studying the process of becoming-an-architect, we discover what it *means* to be an architect, thereby gaining further insight into the culture of architecture. "Architect" is a legal term, but it is not the legal sense that interests me here. Rather, I am concerned with the more tacit, more intricate evolution of an individual through a sequence of distinct periods: as an architectural student, an entry-level architect, a project architect or associate, and finally as a principal. Only in the last two stages can one be said to be a full-fledged architect. Normally, these developmental phases are not described explicitly, even to the novice, but reveal themselves only during the process of becoming. If we envision a black box, into which we place the raw materials of a layperson, and out of which comes the well-informed architect, then the contents of that box, and in particular the way the mysterious production line operates, need to be explored.

The following analysis was inspired by Sharon Traweek's excellent study of particle physicists and their culture (1988). Traweek's subject, the world of physicists, organized around linear accelerators, appears more conventionalized and rule-governed than that of designers. The patterns existing in the workings of the architecture world are certainly discernible, but there are also many variations on those patterns. Like Traweek's, my own investigation uncovered a sequence of characteristic developmental phases, as well as the evolution of professional attitudes about status, appropriate gender roles, and so on. My study diverges from Traweek's, however, for she gives relatively singular interpretations to stages of the physicists' development, their socially produced emotional states, and even the information they are to assimilate during their socialization. This is possible because of the coherence of the physicists' realm; for example, major universities use the same physics textbook in any given year.[1] Such consistency does not exist in architecture, even though there is a core of knowledge on which the profession founds its expertise and a cohesive international publications network in which architectural heroes and award-winning work appear. While the press and the professional organizations establish some continuity among members, they do not promulgate basic knowledge as do physics textbooks. Given architecture's less-than-homogeneous culture, in the discussion that follows I will focus on the most common path to becoming a full-fledged architect; but it should be remembered that there is tremendous variation within the actual population.

At the very outset, we must ask how one decides to begin the journey of becoming an architect. There are always those few individuals who seem to have known from an early age that they were meant to be architects, as if by providence. A more common motivation, as far as I have been able to tell from my interviews with freshman architecture students, might be termed society's prudence. Counselors, parents, and teachers steer toward architecture those young men and women, but especially men, who exhibit the telltale signs commonly associated with a budding architect: doing well in both math and art; being good in art, but needing to earn a living; excelling in mechanical drawing. Reflecting the increasing trend toward professionalization in our society, students themselves often choose an architectural career by process of elimination: "I didn't want to be a lawyer or a doctor." They are likely to have read *The Fountainhead* and to have heard of Frank Lloyd Wright (but probably have not seen any of his buildings). Thus all the individuals who are part of the decision, from high school counselors to the students themselves, hold strong social stereotypes of architects—stereotypes that are relatively ill-informed and go unexamined. In his essay "On Becoming an Architect," Mark Howland (1985:4) characterizes the novitiate when he describes his own experience: "Few of my freshman classmates at Rice [University] had a clear idea of how architects worked. We had taken mechanical drawing in high school, had poured [sic] over house plans in popular magazines and perhaps had even been shown around an architect's office. But in general we had not read professional journals, worked summers or grown up with architects. From our high school counselors we learned that an architect is part artist and part engineer, while from our parents we heard that professionals live responsibly, joined the Rotary and voted Republican." I do not mean to imply that the decision to become an architect is a random one; it is systematic insofar as society's stereotypes are systematic. These stereotypes are in many ways inappropriate, however, and many of those who begin the journey do not complete it: they change majors, take a nonprofessional degree, or work in related but nontraditional careers. Along the path there are numerous means of escape, and various branches to follow, but there are only two ways to begin: education or a form of apprenticeship. Most novices enter the field through an architectural education, and this tendency will increase as more and more states mandate education over the apprenticeship route. Once set forth on this path, the individual undergoes what social scientists call professional socialization, defined succinctly as the "decline of idiosyncracy" (Stelling and Bucher 1973).

THE ARCHITECTURAL STUDENT

Amid the diveristy of design-related educational programs, there are two basic options for completing a professional architecture degree, offered by about one hundred accredited institutions in North America. The five-year undergraduate degree has been the staple of design education, leading to the bachelor of architecture. More recently, the master's degree can be added to an undergraduate architecture degree in one to two years, or in no less than three years with a bachelor's degree from another field. Either route involves the intense indoctrination characteristic of an initiation rite: a high degree of commitment, a certain amount of isolation from nongroup members, cohesion within the group, sacrifices, and rituals marking passage at various stages. Architectural programs share certain elements that have symbolic as well as functional value. These are the studio, the crit, and the charrette.

For graduates and undergrads alike, first impressions of the architectural scene can be overwhelming, just as are first impressions of a new foreign culture. The architecture students are a distinct bunch on campus, their behavior as clear an identification badge as that of the football team. "Arkies" (the name coined at one university) stay up late, are never home, spend all their time in studio, and belong to a clique of other architecture students. Again, Howland's reminiscences are apt (1985:5): "The long hours of work in a common studio space forged us into a close knit group of men and women who were marked by our dedication, endurance and talent. We shared the excitement of learning to see the world in a new way, of learning to distinguish between well and poorly designed glasses while our friends were drinking coffee unaware from styrofoam cups. We were the imaginative professionals with certified taste." Cohesion among students is developed early, building the strong reference group that is characteristic of all professions. Here, in this earliest phase of becoming an architect, we see kernels of architects' later values, such as the principle of peer review and a developing segregation from the general public. In school, the student is immediately exposed to key concepts, and perhaps more importantly, to architecture's heroes. To Wright and Howard Roark are

4.2 Students gather around a
studio instructor to learn the
requirements of their next
project. This is the modern
equivalent of the atelier (see
figure 2.4).

4.3 Typical studio scene,
showing students making
models for a midterm critique.

added such twentieth-century greats as Le Corbusier, Kahn, Aalto, and Mies van der Rohe, along with historic figures like Palladio, Brunelleschi, and Ledoux. While historical greatness is to some degree revised by evolving contemporary biases (and has only begun to include non-Western architects and women), at any point in time the list of heroes, in contrast to concepts, is relatively well-established and shared.[2] Unlike physics, architecture admits a multiplicity of theories and while there may be a fair number of hard facts to learn in the more technical areas (for example, materials, building codes, structures), convictions occupy a significant position in relation to factual knowledge.

An architecture major, like other professional degrees, is characterized by a high number of required courses that dominate all but a small part of the students' entire educational experience. Requirements fall into several basic categories: art, architectural history and theory, structures, professional practice, social sciences, and environmental controls, with relative emphasis varying from school to school.[3] Regardless of which institution students attend, however, they learn that the most important part of their education and the core of the architectural curriculum will be the studio. All courses are secondary to the studio assignment, both in terms of the number of units and hours devoted by students in this atelier-like setting. Each term, students evaluate their studio by the problem or problems given and by professor. The studio problems are important first because they must hold the students' undivided attention for a term, and second because students include these design solutions in the portfolios they later present to prospective employers. Likewise, the studio instructor will be their semester-long guide into the mysteries of design. The typical studio instructor is a practicing architect who provides a living example of what it means to be a designer. In studio, students gather the individual instructor's method and Weltanshauung, and with each new studio another possible approach to architecture is layered upon the last, from which students will determine their own professional course. A studio instructor acts as master to apprentices modeling appropriate behavior, values, design strategies, and thought processes (Schon 1983). The role models are predominantly male, for among studio masters (as they are sometimes called) there are even fewer women than women teaching in architectural schools as a whole, and far fewer proportionately than female architecture students.[4]

The relation between instructor and student in studio can be the richest source of learning, and thus the most envied student is generally the one with whom the professor spends a great deal of time. From Princeton University come tales of Michael Graves announcing at the beginning of the semester that he will only be interested in working with a few of his students, those being the most talented.

The others (who have also paid their costly tuition) are expected to get along with minimal supervision. Whether or not this story is true, it reflects the perception of the instructor-student relation as a limited, valued resource, and it reifies the belief that the talented (both Graves and his chosen students) can claim special privileges in architecture. This talent is not taught; it is believed to be a natural gift bestowed upon the best designers.

Talent aside, good students exhibit certain behavior: they produce more drawings, sketches, models, and studies of alternatives than anyone else, setting the pace for the entire studio. Such fluidity of thought, with prolific graphic expression, when added to a degree of natural talent, are the traits of the best students. In addition, within the student population, there are usually one or two creative rebels who do not follow the above patterns, yet are widely regarded as being among the best students. Creative rebels are sometimes defined as those who "break the rules for the right reasons"—that is, by breaking with convention or going against the instructor's program they achieve great results. These rebels do not follow the normal course of becoming an architect, often skipping development phases.

If the studio is the core of architectural education, literally and symbolically, then it is important to examine the primary form of interaction between studio teachers and students, the "crit." Short for critique, crits are discussions about design solutions that teachers "give" and students "get." There are desk crits, given to individual students at their drawing boards in studio, during which the instructor reviews the progress of the student's project and the student looks for assistance with specific problems and future directions. At a desk crit, the student is likely to receive graphic and verbal advice about how to proceed. In addition, there are group crits, pin-ups, and juries, when a number of students display their drawings for review. These occur in the middle of the project and always at its end, the latter being the final review or jury. At the final review, a critique of the students' completed work becomes a formal ritual in which several respected jurors are invited to evaluate students' projects. Some critics are drawn from the pool of in-house studio instructors, some from the local community, and some schools fly famous architects to the campus to participate in the juries. Most guest critics are not only architects but architect-teachers; rarely are clients, users, engineers, planners, or neighbors invited, even though their evaluation of architectural projects is important in actual practice. Again, the socialization process appears to sacrifice public responsiveness for intraprofessional strength. It should be remembered, however, that the jury is not intended to provide a lesson in professional practice.

4.4 Student presenting model
of final project at year-end
jury (visiting critics Eugene
Kupper and Sarah Graham in
foreground).

4.5 Pictured here is a pin-up, a
mid-semester review of the
progress a student is making
on his project. Two faculty
members are present (Mark
Cigolle and Roger Sherwood,
USC) to give advice in a relatively informal manner.

4.6 Compared to the pin-up, the final jury presents a highly formal, rather intimidating ritualized context in which each student's work is evaluated publicly by a group of experienced practitioners and teachers. Reviews such as this one at SCI–ARC (in Santa Monica, California) attract large audiences of students and local architects.

THE MAKING OF AN ARCHITECT

Dinham (1986) attributes three purposes to juries: to criticize individual students' designs, to provide general instruction, and to initiate scholarly, seminar-like exchange, all of which are intended to further the student's growth. From the students' perspective the crit is probably the most grueling and potentially humiliating experience of their education, akin to hazing. A student publicly presents his or her project by describing the drawings and models on view, then remains before the group to accept criticism. The best critics find avenues for constructive instruction that focuses on the crux of the problem and the student's present solution, but this is a difficult art. Criticism is sometimes leveled without much apparent regard for the student's growth, as educators and renowned practitioners parade their own talents verbally. In other circumstances students are frustrated by critics who, rather than address the work displayed, discuss (in seminar fashion) the broader issues and theories that the projects raise. Critics, for their part, argue that such discussion is an important part of the students' education, and that the quality of the work on the walls determines the specificity of the criticism.

Juries, depending upon the jurors, provide contexts for listening to heroes and assimilating values as well as for learning to design. Nevertheless, many students complain that they never "got a good crit" during their education, generally meaning a crit that was positive, specific, and perhaps showed a way to improve the scheme. As the terminology indicates, crits are not two-way discussions: for the most part, students are the passive recipients of jurors' opinions. As a ritual, the crit teaches students that their work should be able to stand the test of harsh professional criticism, doled out by those with greater experience. It offers a model of professional behavior, implying that full-fledged architects hold positions that can be challenged only by other full-fledged architects (other jurors) and not by the public, other professionals, or clients. It sets students in relation to their seniors, who publicly judge the strengths and weaknesses of their early works.[5]

These lessons remind the would-be architect that much hard work lies ahead before he or she can become a bonafide architect and enter the realm of practitioners. Students put a tremendous amount of time into their studios; their commitment to the design task is best demonstrated by the charrettes that precede each group crit. The charrette is the last of the key features of educational enculturation, along with studios and crits. The final push before a project deadline, it begins with the student dedicating all available waking hours to the production of project drawings and ends with the addition of sleeping hours as well. The test is to see how many consecutive nights one can work without sleep. It is not uncommon to be "on charrette" (the American bastardization of "en charrette") for a week, culminating in two or

4.7 For final reviews, schools
invite nationally respected
critics to evaluate student
work over a period of several
days. Here, giving summary
remarks, are Lars Lerup, Tod
Williams, and Robert Mangur-
ian (from right to left), among
others.

even three all-nighters. This is a competitive arena, for not only is everyone racing against the clock, but students compete with each other: for the most complete set of drawings, the most precise model, the most elegant presentation. The first student who begins to ink or apply color sets the rest of the group into rank ordering thereafter. But the charrette, along with its competitiveness, is a setting in which those who struggle together become even more closely bonded. In a studio, members often get and give advice from one another rather than wait for a desk crit from the instructor. Those who are available help out fellow students on charrette by assisting with the most laborious and time-consuming tasks. And the charrette paces the rhythm of energy devoted to studio—after the crest comes a much-needed valley in which attention can be paid to other business.

A common story with many versions illustrates the dedication, sacrifices, and difficulties of the architecture student. I myself have retold it since it was told to me during my first semester in architectural graduate school, as having happened to the ubiquitous friend of a friend.

It was midnight, there were only twelve more hours before the project was due, and the studio was packed. It was the end of the first semester of architectural grad school. After a solid week of charretting this friend of my friend was nearly burnt out on beer, then coffee, and too many cigarettes. He had almost finished inking his drawings, which were really beautiful, when his wife walked in. He hadn't been home for days, and he was so bleary-eyed that he hardly recognized her. But she looked mad, and before he could say a word, she took his coffee cup and poured its remains over his drawing, and then she dumped the ashtray in the same place and ground the cigarette butts into the paper with her fist. All she said was, "I want a divorce."

The charrette is frequently presented as a "macho" scenario of all-night endurance tests, hard work, and dedication, with students drinking lots of coffee, playing loud music, sleeping on available couches, and temporarily sacrificing everything for the sake of their projects. Of course, women also work late in studio along with the men, participating just as fervently in the rituals. Still, as with the profession, the schools are male-dominated cultures where female students are treated differently (see Anonymous 1980). Female students are faced with implicit assumptions about their lack of physical stamina and commitment when the charrette, and architectural school in general, is likened to a kind of designer boot camp.[6]

As the charrette legend implies, the school as a physical setting plays an important part in the profession's socialization process, for working at home is discouraged, especially during charrettes. The institution's stated rationale is that working in studio is best for the student, who will benefit from other students' criticisms and from spontaneous visits by the instructor. Professors drop in on studio after hours, evenings and weekends, expecting to find a full house. But working in studio also serves another purpose: the process of becoming an architect is far more easily guided when the novitiates are conveniently gathered together under one roof in the enculturating institution.

The significant task of architectural schools, that of initiating the formal development of future architects, does not lend itself to simple summations. In school, students gauge the enormity of the knowledge an architect needs and begin to cultivate some of that knowledge as well as some of the necessary skills. In order to command even a portion of these skills, a student must be dedicated, with a commitment to the task at hand above all else. In school, students also learn that only skills and knowledge can be acquired; certain qualities essential to the architect—talent, passion, good aesthetic judgment—must come naturally. Those students who exhibit these qualities along with commitment are expected to become good architects. The principal message of the next phase of development, that experience is everything, does not hit home until the student leaves school to look for work.

ENTRY-LEVEL ARCHITECTS: GATHERING EXPERIENCE

After graduation, if the architect has chosen a career path that begins in college, the second development phase ensues. Naming this period in the young architect's development is difficult, since, in contrast to medicine, no single label exists for it in practice. The response one young architect gave to my question about office hierarchy is typical: "There are principals, associates, project architects, and then everyone else." The category "everyone else" consists typically of individuals en route from school to a responsible position within an office. These employees can be termed entry-level architects, intern architects, production people, apprentices, technical staff, junior architects, or more commonly, interns and draftspersons. Draftsperson is the title given to most young architects in their first jobs, and as the name implies, drafting and production will be their most common activity. This is, however, a specific job title that can be kept for an entire career as well as a transitional phase that most architects move through. Interns, on the other hand, are technically those architectural employees who prepare for registration by performing a range of tasks under the supervision of a licensed architect. Were it not for medieval crafts guild connotations, apprenticeship would be the proper term, for what characterizes this phase of an architect's evolution is the gathering of practical experience under the contemporary master, the architect-employer. Instead, I use the somewhat cumbersome but apt phrase "entry-level architect" to describe the recent architectural graduate who may or may not have passed the registration exams, but has yet to assume a position of broad responsibility within the office (such as project manager or project architect). Although the length of this stage is indeterminate, it might last three to five years after graduation.

When applying for a job, an entry-level architect is expected to have some skills that will quickly develop further—skills such as drafting, producing working drawings, model building, and lettering. These expectations stand in sharp contrast to academia's high regard for talent, knowledge, and commitment. The dramatic shift in focus from academia to practice was earlier characterized as the contrast between theory and practice, or mystical and technical expertise (chapter 2). Regardless, the transition from school to office work is rarely graceful, as even the most advanced student can be entirely lacking in that trait most valued by architect-employers: experience. There are, within the entry-level phase, several significant activities or programs: landing a job, doing bathroom details, and learning the humility of practice. There are, too, rebels who break from this model, though these represent exceptions that prove the rule.

LANDING A JOB

Whether it is after school or during the summers before graduation, landing the first job presents that old conundrum: one can't get a job without some experience and one cannot gain experience without a job. As a result, some first jobs consist of running prints and errands while others come through personal connections or from a willingness to work for little or no pay. During the summer months, for example the better architectural students will be invited to work in the small firms of their professors, for relatively low wages and sometimes for free. There are even examples of architects who actually charge students and recent graduates to work for them, offering the opportunity to collect a range of office and construction experience. It is surprising that the practice is not more common, given the current vast supply of architectural graduates. Because demand for architectural services has been rising along with the supply of architects, unemployment among architects is very low (2 percent according to Gutman 1988:24). There are two reasons why draftspersons are willing to work for low wages or none at all, and in some cases even pay to work: first, the vast supply of candidates for low-ranking jobs (a condition further exacerbated in offices of high professional esteem), and second, the need to gain direct office experience.[7]

For the architectural student and recent graduate, the architectural labor market most resembles the market for unskilled labor. The supply of inexperienced draftsperons is greater than the demand, producing the twin effects of low wages and high turnover. While inexperienced architectural labor is not in high demand, the demand for

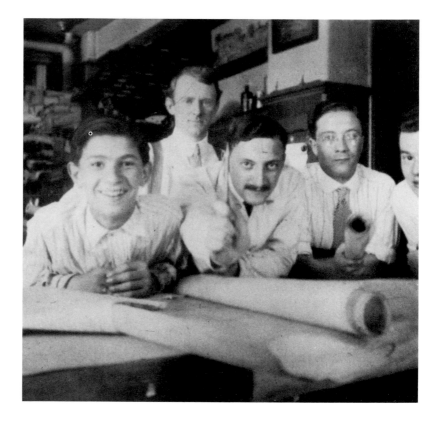

4.8 Rudolph Schindler (center), at the Ottenheimer, Stern
and Reichert office where he
worked as a young draftsman
in Chicago in 1914. Schindler
gained experience at this firm
and others before starting his
own practice. The very young
office boy at left is probably
just beginning his own architectural career by running errands and helping out with
odd jobs.

cheap architectural labor is great, given the relatively small revenues most offices generate. The high demand for cheap labor meets the low demand for unskilled labor to create low-paying jobs for novices. It also creates a turbulent labor market. Job security is nonexistent; draftspersons are hired and laid off by the project. Reciprocally, after gaining more experience, entry-level architects move to take jobs that offer higher pay or more responsibility. Because of these persistent fluctuations, principals of even small firms cannot state how many people work in the office at any point in time.

A group of senior-level architects discussed the reasons they "let people go." Their comments shed light on the dynamics of the entry-level architects' labor market.

ARCHITECT 1: A few years ago, I had a big job that fell through, so I borrowed money to make payroll when I should have let people go. Now I know you've got to be ruthless and make these tough decisions. I'd lay them all off if it happened again. You can't get too people-oriented or you'll lose your firm.

ARCHITECT 2: I think you have to identify who you're willing to carry and who's expendable.

ARCHITECT 3: But that will leave you with a top-heavy organization [because lower-level staff is most expendable], which is exactly wrong in a financial crisis.

ARCHITECT 4: There's a big investment in every employee in terms of training them, so it's bad to lose them.

ARCHITECT 2: But the cost of training differs, and draftsmen are very cheap.

ARCHITECT 1: You've got to have a survival instinct.

ARCHITECT 5: I did the same as [Architect 1]. Even though my staff knew I was borrowing money, when I finally had to let them go, they still didn't understand. I'd be tougher next time.

The partners are committed to their firms' survival; employees are viewed as potential liabilities in financial crises, evaluated by weighing the cost of keeping them against the cost of their training. While entry-level architects are not paid much, they are inexpensive to replace. The senior level architects above reveal the tremendous uncertainty that their organizations face: big jobs can be lost, the size of the loan needed to stay afloat is impossible to estimate, and it is difficult to know who to retain and who to fire. Architect 1 mentions a "survival instinct," an apt phrase, since instinct is all there is to go on when one is unable to make rational, informed judgments. This real uncertainty of practice is not well understood by entry level architects except insofar as it affects job stability.

Even though the overall supply of entry-level architects is great, architect-employers insist that the supply of "good" entry-level architects is slim. Definitions of "good" vary according to the firm's orientation, but generally it means competent, skilled, quick, and perhaps talented. To demonstrate their qualifications, young architects, like other professionals, submit a resume for review by a potential employer, but they also submit a portfolio. The portfolio communicates many of its creator's qualities, including skill level, experience, biography, design ability, school of thought, and stylistic predilection. It typically includes reproductions of drawings and models explaining the architect's design projects from school and office work, if any. All architects maintain and add to their portfolios from the early years in school until the ends of their careers; thus the portfolio, at any given stage, is the visual expression of an individual: "This is what I can do. This is what I think is good." Over time, school projects and early work tend to be replaced by documentation of actual buildings as the architect's career develops, since the portfolio's viewers are more often prospective clients than architect-employers.

Potential employers of entry-level architects look for the experience and ability they need in their office. These are most often working drawings skills, since up to about 40 percent of the total fee for any project is dedicated to production, or construction documents.[8] Another prized skill is the ability to "letter well." Lettering is a rather small part of architectural work, yet skill in lettering is disproportionately significant for architects. In the technical sense, good, clear, consistent lettering on working drawings is important to avoid ambiguity during bidding and construction. It is also one of the skills needed in practice that *can* be developed in school. But good lettering is also symbolic. Just as spear throwing might be the measure of a young man among hunters, so lettering is taken as an art that novices should work to develop and from which elders can make deductions about a candidate. The design of a letter, the care taken in its creation, and its consistency allow for predictions about the way an individual will perform in the architectural office. This belief merges with the larger conviction that the dictates of design sensibility carry through all aspects of life, from the way one letters, dresses, and cooks, to the way one designs buildings.

TITLE BLOCKS AND BATHROOM DETAILS

The everyday life of most entry-level architects, particularly in their first jobs, resembles that of a laborer more than that of a professional. There are regular hours with little flexibility, repetitive tasks, piecemeal undertakings that give little sense of accomplishment or overview, and scant control over one's own activities. The opportunities for design, as practiced in school, exist only on a very small scale, since fundamental design decisions are made by higher ranking architects. Novices are expected to complete what seem to be trivial undertakings, such as working out the title block for all the drawings of a particular project. The task that best explains entry-level architects' dislike for their tedious work and its lack of status is doing bathroom details. In actuality, few people have ever had to do bathroom details as their primary work; the task stands for other menial assignments.

Young interns rarely get much responsibility, design or otherwise; at this stage they are treated more like architectural tools than architects. If they prove to be good tools, with speed, accuracy, and endurance, eventually they may be given responsibility. Interns are given small tests—doing a model, working out a detail, developing an elevation—and as they prove themselves able, gradually they receive more responsibility. The profession's intention, institutionalized in the Intern-Architect Development Program, is for offices to provide apprentice-like education to young practitioners by exposing them to the full range of office activities, from office management to client contact to site analysis.[9] While young architects inevitably learn a great deal in their early jobs, few actually receive systematic exposure to the full range of office activities. Economic rationales generally outweigh the professional duty to shape interns' training: offices give interns exposure to a narrow domain to keep training costs to a minimum; the intern works at those tasks that he or she is already best prepared to undertake; interns are given tasks for which errors are not costly and which require minimum supervision. These criteria in part explain why entry-level architects are relegated to model making and lettering rather than client relations, specifications writing, or construction management.

To gain new responsibilities more quickly, novices leave to work for other offices where different boundaries will be drawn around their appropriate domain. Young draftspersons are highly mobile, moving from office to office, creating a steady flow of new faces in firms. Seniors keep an eye out for promising young architects who work quickly, learn quickly, act assertively and congenially, make few mistakes, and have some design sense. If experience is the primary condition for gaining employment, error-free speed is a key condition for keeping it. Working quickly—something hardly mentioned in school—becomes central in practice, where hourly or salaried employees in large part are judged by their productivity. Working quickly and accurately once again raises the importance of experience; the more familiar a task, the more quickly it can be completed without oversights. If the ideal architect-employee is quick, careful, and talented, these are likely the results of extensive experience.

THE HUMILITY OF PRACTICE

Gathering experience is the task of entry-level architects, and the firms that employ them have conflicting interests about providing it, since they want experienced workers without having to train them or pay commensurately higher wages. Thus it is quite often difficult for young architects to get the range and kind of experience they seek. The ideals of the well-rounded generalist architect remain embedded in schools and formal intern development programs, yet office operation depends upon the coordination of specialists and technicians. The entry-level architect is caught in a schism between ideals and contemporary architectural practice, expecting to become an architect-designer yet humbled by his or her status as a laborer who has yet to learn the trade.

As with other initiation rites, becoming an architect has phases that state and restate in symbolic terms the relations of the individual initiate to the larger society being joined. In the phase where young architects gather experience, they relearn the academic lessons of humility before their elders; they also learn that academic theory means nothing without practical technique. As young practitioners gain experience in actual rather than academic design and building processes, they also learn how to work for masters—partners, associates, or project architects—who are in control. Although students also learn to take advice (from instructors), their work remains their own. By contrast, entry-level architects rarely receive credit for their efforts in the office, their identity being indistinguishable from that of the many others who could have filled their positions. The whole question of authorship, an important part of the architecture culture, does not arise again after school until the mid-level phase of project architects.

A word about the mavericks and rebels who defy these norms. These individuals tend to aim straight for acceptance as full-fledged architects, skipping over the entry-level or project architect phases of development to begin their own practices or alternative careers as early as possible. Dispensing with the interim phases where humility, obedience, and technique are engrained, mavericks may more easily retain an idealism about architecture than their more conventional colleagues.

The recent graduate who rebels must have, in addition to motivation, a means of avoiding the necessity of wage labor as an architect-employee. A single client, a teaching appointment, family money, an established partner—these are the common conditions allowing a maverick to start a practice rather than join one. The rebel confronts a unique set of problems, however, most of which stem from lack of experience and of models for getting, keeping, and performing architectural work. Very few architects entirely escape working for others, which is so contrary to the professional culture's fundamental values as to be law: eligibility for the registration exam requires several years' experience under a licensed architect.

4.9 While few architects fully
escape working for or with
others, creative isolation is a
kind of ideal. Shown here is a
student who has found that
late-night hours are one way
to achieve privacy.

But even though few individuals successfully rebel against the conventional evolution of an architect's career, the guiding vision for many architects from the time they are students onward is to work for themselves. Working independently means freedom, along with responsibility for the entire architectural practice, which is diametrically opposed to the entry-level architect's experience. In the phase after entry-level, additional responsibilities are assumed, providing the context to develop individual strengths and to gain more independence. This mollifies the rebel in many architects, who come to realize they are well suited for a specialized task, that the small private practice has limitations, or that there are opportunities within existing firms to achieve their goals.

THE MIDDLE YEARS: JOB CAPTAIN, PROJECT ARCHITECT, ASSOCIATE

While the entry-level beginning is clearly marked by the first job, its end is virtually imperceptible. There is no predetermined duration for entry-level status in architecture, as there is, for example, for the internship portion of residency in medicine. Depending on the office and the individual, one might remain a draftsperson for as little as a year or as long as a lifetime. But for most novices who intend to become full-fledged architects, progress begins almost immediately toward the next developmental phase, the architect's middle years. A variety of signs may indicate that an architect is moving forward, such as an invitation to client meetings, a shift from hourly wages to a salary, assuming responsibility for designing more significant elements of a project, a direct working relationship with principals, less supervision, or the hiring of a new cadre of entry-level architects. Any one of these changes can signal that the metamorphosis has begun; an intern becomes a job captain, a drafter becomes a project architect. But in fact no drafter becomes a project architect, just as no accountant becomes chairman of the board, without a myriad of intervening steps. The metamorphosis is slow and sometimes uneven, and the formal mid-level job title is likely to follow rather than initiate the transformation. In Blau's studies of architects, she uses just three categories to encompass all practitioners: managers, staff designers, and staff architects (Blau 1979). While these categories are relatively clear-cut, they do not reflect the tremendous uncertainty that accompanies any architect's development, an uncertainty that is most apparent in the middle years.

Because the onset of the middle years is so difficult to identify, this phase is especially interesting as a cultural phenomenon. The middle years can be characterized most simply as the period of greatest ambiguity for the architect—an ambiguity that is eventually replaced by the significant choices that end the middle years. By resting between the two clearer periods in the architects' identity, novice and full-fledged professional, the middle years take the individual from a generic beginning to a very specific end. That is, the similarities that all entry-level architects share are outweighed, over the course of the middle years, by the idiosyncratic characteristics that shape an individual's career. Specialists emerge, along with upstarts, administrators, loyalists, and so on, and the rate and direction of professional development are established.

The early middle years are often awkward, analogous in terms of human development to the early teens, when we are no longer children and not yet adults. The ambiguity of the middle years in architectural practice is sensed by novices who frequently complain that they want to do "more interesting work" but cannot find the means to realize this goal. There are few if any established routes to more interesting work and the greater responsibility that it implies. The mysteries of advancement are inherent to architectural practice and serve certain functions in the enculturation process. Not only are the means of advancement mysterious, but so is the status an individual achieves in the middle years. Even the American Institute of Architects cannot clearly describe this transitional phase, as indicated by their categories of employment status defined in Table 4.1.[10] The groups labeled "Technical III" and "Principal" clearly correspond to what I have called entry-level and full-fledged architects, respectively. The remaining categories are more problematic and warrant further discussion.

The first mention of job titles with professional status—such as job captain, senior designer, and construction administrator—appear in the Technical I group. The lowest category (Technical III) has junior versions of those same positions, that is, junior designers and drafters, technical II contains intermediate versions. This categorization, a taxonomy in its own right, indicates that all positions prior to those with full professional status (at Technical I) lead up to that end. In other words, jobs at entry level and in the early middle years are viewed as lesser forms of true professionalism, which is identified with the highest *technical* positions.

At Technical II, where one is "usually not licensed," I suggest that the individual has entered the fuzzy domain of the early middle years. Here, the individual's personal situation is the most ambiguous, for although a useful degree of experience has been gathered, the greater responsibility that should accompany it has yet to materialize. There are no formal tutors or policies to instruct the architect about crossing this next bridge—there are only visions of the other side, in the form of architects who have successfully made the crossing. Young architects, for example, may start to ask how project architects get to do what they are doing, or discover how much the job captain makes and compare it to their own earnings.

Table 4.1
JOB CATEGORIES

AUTHOR'S CATEGORIES	AIA DEFINITIONS[1]	
FULL-FLEDGED	PRINCIPAL:	owner, partner, corporate officer, participating associate.
LATE MIDDLE	SUPERVISORY:	general manager, department head, project manager, project architect, project engineer.
MIDDLE AND LATE MIDDLE	TECHNICAL I:	senior professional staff, frequently licensed, highly skilled specialist, job captain; senior designer; senior draftsperson; senior specifier; senior construction administrator.
LATE ENTRY AND EARLY MIDDLE	TECHNICAL II:	intermediate technical staff, usually not licensed; includes intermediate levels of positions listed in technical I; manager of clerical staff.
ENTRY	TECHNICAL III:	junior technical staff, not licensed; includes junior levels of positions listed in technical I; secretarial or clerical staff; office assistant.

1. Source: The American Institute of Architects, *The 1983 Firm Survey*, (Washington, D.C.: AIA, 1984), 16.

If the surface structure of mid-level status is comprised of new circumstances such as invitations to client meetings, a new cohort of entry-level staff members, and less supervision, the underlying significance of these circumstances is greater self-determination and responsibility. Part of what it means to do more interesting work is to have more control over larger pieces of the architectural project. The metamorphosis from entry- to mid-level architect, then, is a transformation from gathering experience, to displaying competence, to gathering responsibility and autonomy.

The archetypal realization of greater self-determination and responsibility in architecture is to become the lead designer and credited author of a project. Within firms, some project architects are permitted the pride of authorship, that is, public recognition of responsibility for a project. In such cases, a building is attributed to an individual as well as to his or her office, as are, for example, the SOM buildings designed by architects Gordon Bunshaft or David Childs. This coveted role is, however, rarely assumed in a pure form, because such positions make up a very small proportion of the total professional staff, many offices do not give public credit to project designers, and most project architects and designers have a variety of privileges and responsibilities besides design. For the project architect in particular, these include meeting with clients and consultants, overseeing the work of others, keeping the work effort and fee in check, and monitoring the project's overall progress.

Rising to the level of project architect or lead designer is only one conclusion to the middle years. Architects can achieve greater self-determination and responsibility not only by gaining control over their own designing, but by gaining control over the work of others or by taking charge of a more particularized part of the building project. The first architect becomes a manager or supervisor, while the second becomes a specialist. Either of these career choices represents a break from the more linear development outlined in the AIA's three-step technical ladder. Such a career choice, then, is the clarifying result of the middle years' initial ambiguity. After the entry-level architect has gathered a respectable level of general experience, and has been given some responsibility, he or she is able to make particular choices among the opportunities available in the late middle years. Some architects become project managers, others become lighting specialists or historic preservationists. It is also common for architects at this late middle stage to change offices or start their own offices, since their opportunities can be expanded dramatically with such a move.

Not only are opportunities to advance expanded by moving out of an office, but those opportunities are also made more explicit. Within an office, the mysteries of advancement are difficult to unravel. Even offices that have personnel manuals keep some of their criteria for advancement obscure. For example, one founding partner of a two-hundred-person firm described office policy on advancement: "In our firm, if you want to be a partner, you have to bring in work and you've got to be a track-layer." The fist criteria is explicit; the second is quite vague, effectively leaving the ultimate decision about who should become a partner to the current partners.

In one of my case study firms, four individuals were considered for promotion to the associate level during a six-month period. The senior members' evaluation of these mid-level architects highlights the mysteries of advancement. The first architect, the youngest and most recently hired of the four, was viewed as a potential associate because he was talented. As one partner explained, "James needs experience, but you can see he really has architecture in his blood. Maybe that's because his father was an architect." A second man with no academic architectural training had worked in the office for over fifteen years. His dedication was rewarded when he was made an associate. A third man, a close personal friend of one of the partners, was brought into the firm after his own small office failed. He became an associate in record time—after just one year. The final architect, another man, nearly as young and inexperienced as the first, was being considered for promotion because he was the favored assistant of the office's chief designer, and the office wished to woo him from his plans to quit and start his own practice. In each situation, a slightly different set of circumstances led to the individual's promotion. If these four cases are representative, we could conclude that advancement depends upon experience, talent, dedication, and personal connections. There is no formula, no job description to match. It has more to do with having the "right stuff." A principal explained it to me this way: "To become an associate has nothing to do with a time element or length of stay in the firm—it's really a performance thing. It's hard to define exactly. It has to do with your personal philosophy, what you draw, how you work, whether all that fits with the firm. It's someone who does the right thing at the right time. You can hardly train anyone to be an associate, but you know it when you see it." While the move from draftsperson status into the middle years of project architects, designers, managers, or associates is generally ambiguous, larger and more bureaucratic firms are more likely to state some advancement criteria. Likewise, the developmental process is warped by the smaller office, where there may be no such thing as a mid-level; there is only the founder and the draftspersons. One reason young architects move out of such offices, especially to larger firms, is to have the chance of gaining more responsibility.

In a mysterious socialization process such as job advancement, it is common to call attention to certain points in the process by rites of passage. A rite of passage marks the bridge that an individual crosses at a culturally significant transition. These are usually grueling experiences that test the individual's mettle and worthiness to proceed (see Van Gennep 1960). In the middle years, the two most intense rites of passage are the licensing exam and starting an office.

The profession's institutional means of conferring status is to administer, and the official means of becoming an architect is to pass, the registration exam. While registration is a kind of institution, by all accounts it is also a rite of passage. The exam, given across the country for four days each year, includes approximately ten tests, two of which are design problems that entail drafting for hours on end in a room filled with other applicants.[11] The applicant can take and pass any number of individual tests, so that only those portions failed must be retaken. Most applicants do not pass all portions on the first try, thus extending an already arduous rite of passage. The exam is not

4.10 The design portions of
the Architectural Registration
Exam are graded by at least
two jurors drawn from registered practitioners all over the
country. Here a group of "master jurors" establish grading
criteria to ensure that all solutions are judged consistently.
They then oversee jurors who
will grade individual exams.
(The exam itself is highly secretive, and no photographs
are allowed to be taken while
it is in progress.)

about design ability, talent, or any of the other more mysterious architectural qualities; it is about competence. A brilliant designer will not pass without technical knowledge of construction conventions, graphic standards, and building codes about fire safety, accessibility, and energy. Because the less technical and more mysterious architectural abilities are not testable, the exam was first instituted amid much controversy (Jenkins 1961) and still has limited validity within the profession. If a surgeon practiced without professional credentials it would be scandalous; this is not the case among architects.

Even though registration is legally required for designation as an architect, it is only tenuously related to what practitioners consider criteria for membership in the profession. While registration is viewed positively in offices, and is commonly expected in the late middle years, it does not guarantee advancement. Just because an entry-level architect passes the registration exam does not necessarily mean she or he will be paid more or given more responsibility. Shluntz and Gebert's study of architectural graduates shows that just over half of those who have been out of school for five years are licensed (1980). By the time architects have been out of school for ten years, over three-fourths are registered, which corresponds roughly to the time when one becomes a full-fledged architect. Thus, registration is likely to occur during the middle years of one's career. Licensure literally attests to the architect's competence in the range of knowledge necessary to professional practice, but if we are interested in what registration *means* to professionals, then its significance lies in the independence it confers. The registered architect can act alone; an unlicensed counterpart cannot. Since independence is a highly valued professional attribute, the unregistered practitioner will occasionally be found in the undignified position of needing someone else to sign off on the drawings.

The other principal rite of passage that occurs in the late middle years is starting one's own office, or "going out on your own." This rite is not institutionalized, as is registration, but it does have regular patterns. It usually entails an extremely difficult financial period, and the rate of failure is high.[12] When architects go out on their own, they may have only one or two small commissions, no staff, and a garage for an office. The test is whether the architect can "stick it out" until he or she becomes better established, that is, with more work, the ability to hire a draftsperson, and the money to pay rent on a bonafide office. The entire test ultimately rests on getting enough work. These conditions lead to two stereotypical characterizations of architects starting their own practices: the starving artist and the young entrepreneur. The former, in a typical scenario, lives on the small salary received for part-time teaching at the local university while working

4.11 Julia Morgan's office,
opened when she returned
from Paris and her studies at
the Ecole in 1902. As with
young architects today who
want to work on their own,
Morgan's practice had modest
origins in a converted part of
her family home in Oakland,
California.

in a converted garage on competitions and small residential remodels. By contrast, the young entrepreneur sends out a mailing to all his or her contacts announcing the firm's opening, rents a commercial space for an office, hires an answering service, and goes after government jobs. Among those offices that survive, these first years will be regarded in retrospect as an acid test that marked the transition to later success. These years are a rite of passage between dependence and autonomy, taking orders and taking responsibility, mid-level and full-fledged status. Using the categories of Van Gennep (1960), an anthropologist who studied the forms of rites of passage, both starting a firm and registration are rites of transition that come between the rites of separation (which students and entry-level architects experience) and rites of incorporation (which are restricted to full-fledged architects).

A NOTE ON GENDER

The middle years, because they are transitional, uncertain ones in which the vast pool of entry-level architects becomes professionally differentiated, are particularly problematic for women architects. The mysteries of advancement by definition partially conceal access to power, permitting discriminatory biases against minorities as well as women. In the 1983 survey of AIA members, more than three-fourths of the women reported that they had encountered discrimination in their work, and about two-thirds specifically mentioned discrimination with regard to advancement (AIA Survey 1985). In fact, when the number of years' experience is held constant for men and women, men are nearly twice as likely as their female counterparts to reach senior-level status (57 percent of men and 33 percent of women with 10 to 14 years' experience were partners). In terms of compensation, for every dollar that a male architect is paid, women earn 68 cents, and women are three times as likely to earn less than $20,000 per year than their male counterparts (in 1983 dollars). This is true even though proportionately more women in practice hold graduate degrees in architecture than men (33 percent to 20 percent). All these figures indicate that women are discriminated against in terms of compensation from entry level onward, and will be further disadvantaged in the middle years in terms of advancement.

Indeed advancement for women architects is less mysterious because it is so evident that it is gender-biased. Women report that because of the discrimination they experienced as architectural employees, they decided to become independent practitioners sooner (of the women who altered their professional plans as a result of discrimination, 25 percent decided to become independent). The enculturation process indirectly teaches that full-fledged architects are supposed to be men, and so the later stages of an architect's development are less accessible to women. Without question, advancement within an office is more difficult for women architects, who instead choose to start their own firms, following the general rule that independence and rebelliousness from conventions are more possible outside the established office context.

If school is about learning what it takes to be an architect, and internship is about gaining experience, then the middle years are about acquiring self-determination and responsibility. Most importantly, the architect enters the middle years fundamentally undifferentiated from peers with an equivalent amount of experience, and leaves the middle years with a particular set of responsibilities that reflect his or her unique career path. To be judged capable of handling responsibility, one must meet the vague criteria of one's superiors. This fosters a system in which the tacit decisions of senior architects go relatively unchallenged by the rank and file. As individuals move up the ladder, they hoard their new responsibilities—those very responsibilities jealously kept from them by their predecessors. Thus the system perpetuates itself.

THE FULL-FLEDGED ARCHITECT: AUTHORITY AND BUILDINGS

ARCHITECT 1: Regardless of our clients, I'm not sure I could build a canonical work right now. I'm still putting it all together for myself, coming to terms with what our ideas are.

ARCHITECT 2: Canonical work comes from a talented architect and from [the situations you find yourself in]. We are having trouble moving out of the first stage of our careers—what can you do with the single-family house, after all? Our strategy is to move away from residential work.

ARCHITECT 3: This comes with time, as you move from small-scale work to bigger projects.

ARCHITECT 4: Canonical works are done by middle-aged men and old men.

ARCHITECT 5: You have to get to the point where you can turn down work. Regardless of scheduling and staffing, you have to have faith that the phone will ring again. And if you take a [bread and butter] job now, you may be giving up a later, better project.

All the young architects speaking above have started their own offices, and are moving from their late middle years toward full-fledged status in the profession. That movement is consciously acknowledged in their conversation, even though the means to accomplish it are unclear. For this group of practitioners, what it means to become a legitimate, full-fledged architect is tied to the buildings produced: creating a significant work, doing nonresidential work, and landing large-scale projects. In larger offices, the onset of full-fledged status is also bound to the buildings an individual works on; here the middle years come to a close when an architect has authority over an

4.12 Frank Lloyd Wright as an
old man, seated at his desk at
Taliesin surrounded by objects
and furnishings he designed.
This portrait embodies the
authority of the full-fledged
architect. According to Brendan
Gill, the visitors' chairs are
intentionally lower than
Wright's own, to keep them
in proper perspective.

actual building project. Partners, principals, founders of the firm, and senior associates—these are architecture's full-fledged members. To become a full-fledged architect, the practitioner must have the experience and responsibility that derived from entry-level and middle-year jobs. The amount of each needed for full-fledged status is not absolute; the true architect is not born once some experience-and-responsibility threshold is crossed. Rather, at the stage when architects capably see through a significant building project, they enjoy full-fledged professional status. This is what the young architects above are trying to achieve.

Whether an employee or independent practitioner, the full-fledged architect has responsibility for and receives credit for an actual building. But the means of achieving full-fledged status is quite different for the architect-employee than for the independent practitioner. An architect who works in another architect's office has entered the middle years by the time he or she first receives primary but not entire responsibility for a project, as is the case for first-time job captains, project architects, project designers, project managers, and associates. The first assignment with such responsibility marks the peak of the middle years, after which full-fledged status sets in. The rate of progress from the middle years into full-fledged status then depends upon the structure of opportunities within the office as well as the abilities of the individual. If, for example, the senior partners protect the major design decisions and credit for projects, then their employees will find it necessary to leave the firm to become full-fledged architects in their own right. On the other hand, architects with independent practices such as those in the above example are considered full-fledged when they have projects of a certain scale or merit in the office. One architect who recently founded her own firm had a teaching position, two competition prizes, and a house designed but as yet unbuilt. She felt she had crossed the invisible professional boundaries when she got the commission to do a small private school. Large projects, new construction, and nonresidential work typically go hand in hand with a more stable, financially secure practice, thereby affirming established professional status. Authority for a project, in the full sense, implies not only responsibility for the actual services rendered but responsibility also for the costs incurred. Thus the established architect typically has some fiscal responsibility for the work (as owner, partner, or participating associate). The full-fledged practitioner is one who can lose income when a project costs more than the fee, who will benefit when the work is done efficiently, and who may need to take out a loan to make payroll. The established professionals are most concerned about exposure and liability, not only because they pay the insurance premiums, but because their practice is at stake in a law suit. It is also the full-fledged architect whose reputation is at stake in a project, whose standing will help or hinder the acquisition of new clients. And it is the full-fledged architect who interviews with the client to get the next job. As such, in this last stage of the architect's development the balance of activities shifts away from actually doing the work to getting the work and keeping it. Ironically, although the established practitioner has less responsibility for doing the work than in earlier stages of professional development, he or she is generally the one to receive credit for a building. Indeed, the right to authorship is an important element of full-fledged status.

Those practitioners who have chosen to become managers or specialists within an office exist on the margins of full-fledged status. That this is true within the professional community is evident in statements like this one by a senior business partner: "The AIA as an institution only recognizes design—the only awards programs are for design, and mainly for the building's exterior at that. There's no recognition for good business in architecture. I think it's about time we gave management a better rap. Let's give out awards for good managers, and publish the project manager's name next to the project architect's in the glossies [the professional magazines]." The clearest focus of identity for the full-fledged architect is the Renaissance architect who was required to be competent in the full range of activies that constitute the architectural task, from art to structures to geometry. Today, the Renaissance equivalent of the full-fledged architect is one who has breadth and some contact with design. Other activities, from project management to special architectural consulting, are considered important by other professionals, but they are not core pursuits of full-fledged architects.

It is important to recognize that being a full-fledged architect is not a static condition, nor a status that, once achieved, ends the overall developmental process. I now turn to the final goals toward which full-fledged architects strive—goals that define an ideal held within the professional community. The full-fledged architect's career evolves into the search for a market for services, significant commissions, public recognition, and a widening sphere of influence.

As established architects seek greater professional accomplishment, they try to establish a stable market for their services, in order to produce a steady flow of building opportunities and to provide financial security for both the office and themselves. This is what the last young architect in the example meant when she remarked, "You have to have faith that the phone will ring again." A stable market for services can take forms ranging from private clients with a solid network of referrals to corporate clients with continuous building programs. Because full-fledged architects supposedly have a ready clientele, architects tend to make statements like "We never go out looking for work; it comes to us." This litany is more often based on hope than fact, as pointed out earlier, but it indicates the ideal state of affairs. A stable market for services is related to the desired condition of having a large backlog, that is, services contracted but not yet performed or projects waiting to begin. A ready clientele and a large backlog are insurance against economic misfortune. Beyond the desire for economic stability, architects try to achieve greater profitability.

In addition to a steady flow of commissions, the quality of commissions is important to becoming an established architect, as the young architects above are well aware. Every full-fledged architect attempts to gain prestigious commissions, generally projects with either public presence or large budgets. A well respected and much published architect said, for example, "Somehow we [at my firm] have to get out of houses for Mr. and Mrs. John Q. Public and break into the big time." Similarly, the head of a large, established firm hired a renowned designer to help him get into the award-winning design arena and out of the developer market. There are many means of getting better projects: entering competitions in order to break into the market for a new building type, hiring talented designers to attract prestigious clients and win awards, restructuring office policy to give greater emphasis to the interests of certain clients, and so on. These strategies, while they may lead to higher quality commissions, do not necessarily bring higher profits. Indeed, many architects would argue the two are inversely related.[13]

With more prestigious projects comes the full-fledged architect's desire for greater recognition both from fellow professionals and from the public. Public recognition is a part of marketing, since architects who are better known and respected by the general population will have the advantage in gaining commissions over their lesser known competitors. Professional recognition, on the other hand, is widely rumored to be of little practical value in gaining commissions.[14] Certainly, however, the architect's status is heightened by the respect of fellow professionals. Among architects, such respect is the highest form of recognition, since professionals learn that they themselves are the best arbiters of the quality of their works (see chapter 2). Counter to professional beliefs, the respect of fellow professionals often does translate into greater professional and financial success. One young architect, for example, gets all his work from a former boss who has enough projects to regularly turn work away and to refer his clients elsewhere. Architects will recommend that a client call a colleague when their own offices are unable or unwilling to do the work, for reasons such as scheduling, the scale of the project, relevant expertise,

Table 4.2
SUMMARY OF THE ARCHITECT'S STAGES OF DEVELOPMENT

LEVEL	JOB TITLES	PERSONAL PROGRAMS	OFFICE PROGRAMS
STUDENT	None	Gather knowledge Gather preliminary skills	None
ENTRY	Intern Draftsperson Junior designer	Gather experience Display experience	Doing work
MIDDLE YEARS	Junior designer Job captain Senior designer Project architect Associate	Demonstrate competence Gather responsibility Gain autonomy, management tasks	Doing work Keeping work
FULL-FLEDGED	Associate Partner Principal Owner	Gain fiscal responsibility Oversee widening sphere of influence	Keeping work Getting work

and so on. In addition, other forms of subsidy and marketing, such as awards, teaching appointments, public lectures, and competitions, are all decided by teams of architects.

Finally, in addition to a market for services, prestigious commissions, and recognition, full-fledged architects seek a widening sphere of influence for their works and ideas. Power in professional communities is linked to influence among followers, clients, and colleagues. By achieving a sphere of influence, a professional goes one step beyond the original goal of autonomy and exerts superordinate authority over others. Charismatic, inspirational leaders within the profession—the heroes whose works are studied as models—have achieved a sphere of influence. At different periods in these architects' careers, they may have a following of students (Michael Graves at Princeton in the 1980s, or Walter Gropius at IIT in the 1950s), of powerful clients who act as patrons (as did Hearst for Julia Morgan, or the French government for Ricardo Bofill), or of young architects who derive principles for their own work from a contemporary master (such as Frank Gehry or Peter Eisenman). The architect's office can also spawn new offices, as did Eero Saarinen's, thereby casting off satellites of architectural work that reflect their origins. Each of these means of extending the boundaries of influence is also a means of achieving some fame, living beyond one's years. The presumed means to achieve notoriety is through the material record—through the buildings an architect designs over a lifetime, but since architecture is so wholly bound to the

THE MAKING OF AN ARCHITECT

4.13 Richard J. Neutra standing behind Frank Lloyd Wright
at Taliesin in 1924. Neutra,
like Schindler, immigrated
from Austria to work with
Wright. Taliesin, perhaps more
than any other architectural
studio or office, has always operated as a distinct cultural
context with rules and values
set by Wright.

social network that produces and consumes its services, that is, to other architects, architect-employees, and clients, fame rarely comes without such extended spheres of influence. Even those architects known to have been rebuked in their own time and later hailed as true heroes had a sphere of influence. Le Corbusier, for example, while rejected by the French government, has his M. Frugès at Pessac and the Cistercian monks at La Tourette; Louis Kahn died in debt, but managed in his lifetime to gain commissions from powerful institutions like the University of Pennsylvania and powerful individuals like Jonas Salk and Mrs. Kimbell.

Full-fledged professionals gain their status as they acquire authority for actual buildings, for getting projects and keeping them, for finances and liability. When all this has been achieved, as it is for partners and principals of an office, there follows a search that continues until the end of an architect's career. That search is rooted in truly fundamental goals—the desire for stability, challenging prospects, prestige, power, and notoriety.

CONCLUSION

From this description of the making of an architect, three rites of passage are discernible (van Gennep 1960). First are rites of separation for the student and entry-level architect, who learn they are distinct from the laity. Second are rites of transition that occur in the ambiguous middle years, when architects take their registration exam and perhaps start their own offices. Last are rites of incorporation, when full-fledged architects undergo rituals that document their membership in the culture: winning awards, attending the national AIA meetings, getting published. Nevertheless, entering the established ranks of architects is not a clear-cut process. Unless we believe that certain individuals are "born architects," there must be some process of *becoming* an architect that precedes *being* one. It is this process of enculturation that I have tried to illuminate here, a process that transforms layperson into architect through the knowledge, experience, and authority gained over the course of a career.

There are two qualities that neither employers nor educators can instill and without which, it is assumed, one cannot become a "good" architect: dedication and talent. In addition, architects must have opportunities to demonstrate their talent, dedication, experience, and responsibility, which means that the architect must have commissions. For those who try to go out on their own, this is the primary hurdle to overcome. For this reason, it is sometimes assumed that successful architects were born with the necessary connections and conditions for success. Hence the advantage of architects born wealthy; they are provided with independent means that remove them from dependence upon commissions or with a ready supply of potential clients.

In Traweek's study of particle physicists, she examines how science breeds conformity. As she notes from Kuhn, scientific training is "rigorous training in convergent thinking" (1988). Architectural training presumably intends the exact opposite. Architecture, like other arts, is expected to breed innovation. But this represents a conflict when professional schools and offices have as a primary goal the achievement of unity among otherwise independent practitioners. Becoming an architect is about becoming an artist, but a peculiar kind of artist who stays within certain boundaries. It is not surprising that some of architecture's greatest heroes did not long subject themselves to school or offices and to the boundaries respected there.

Becoming an architect can be seen, therefore, as the broader culture's way of assimilating certain individuals with creative impulses. The process of becoming an architect is one of learning socially appropriate avenues for creativity. On the other hand, as Traweek considers gender (notions of masculine and feminine) to be socially produced, I consider creativity, too, to be socially produced. That is, individuals are socialized to understand what constitutes a creative act, when creativity is appropriate, what the types of creativity are, the degrees thereof, who should have it, and what can be done with it. In architecture, creativity and individuals deemed creative have been associated traditionally with the building design. My research, however, indicates that the profession needs to expand its creative domain. In recent years, recognition of other creative aspects of an architectural project has increased within the professional community. While still considered most present in the designer, creativity is attributed more readily now to project managers, computer-aided design specialists, and facilities planners. New specialized university programs and offices that utilize services of top consultants are promoting this trend. Inevitably the making of an architect will acquire new components and new concepts of creative work.

The architectural firm locates the individual practitioner's actions in a coherent system of meaning, so that those actions become intelligible in the social world. The firm is, in this sense, a culture. Each practitioner undergoes the metamorphosis from layperson to architect within a frame created by the surrounding social milieu of practice. Key creative opportunities for the practitioner transpire both in the office and with the client; each warrants closer attention. From my field work and interviews I have found regular patterns of interaction recurring within very different firms, and it is these similarities I discuss here rather than the particular differences.

As noted in chapter 2, most architects do not practice in corporate-sized organizations: of the 25,000 firms in the U.S., about half are one-person operations, and among the 12,000 firms that have one or more employees, half have fewer than five employees; fewer than 10 percent of the firms in America have 20 or more employees. Remarkably, there are only 250 firms in the United States with over 50 persons.[1] Since so many architects choose to practice alone, it is reasonable to ask why the architectural firm exists at all. The pragmatic response is revealed by statistics: the largest 2 percent of architectural firms take in 30 percent of all the architectural fees; firms under 20 persons, which make up 90 percent of all firms, bring in just 50 percent of all fees. Like other successful businesses, size correlates with revenue, and like other professions, the majority of practices in architecture operate on a fairly small scale. Moreover, the data indicate that the large architectural firm captures a disproportionate amount of fees, and their proportion is growing. The economic reasons for collective practice are linked to specific characteristics of the building industry. Since over 40 percent of the nation's nonresidential building stock encloses less than 5,000 square feet (Ventre 1987), such commissions can be handled by most firms, including small ones. However, the most coveted jobs (both for design opportunity and for profit) are generally institutional buildings, high-rises, corporate and public work, and these typically belong to the small proportion of commissions that are large-scale. Competition for these jobs is keen, restricted to firms large enough themselves to handle large projects, so architects must be part of an office to gain these commissions.[2] Another reason to practice in groups is for purposes of specialization and

CHAPTER 5

5.1 These three men—from
left to right, Louis Skidmore,
Sr., John Merrill, Sr., and Na-
thaniel Owings—founded one
of the best known practices in
America. Merrill, an engineer,
joined the two architects in order to offer appropriate expertise for the completion of large
projects. They are shown here
with a model of Fort Dearborn
in 1953. Now, with offices in
five U.S. cities and an office in
London, SOM employs nearly
1,600 people.

diversity: a larger office can handle more commissions with more variety, and the large office is comprised of enough positions that individuals within the firm can specialize in design, marketing, construction
administration, and so on.

There is another, more complex and subtle reason for collective
practice that is the subject of my analysis: architects work together in
order to establish meaningful worlds for themselves and their actions.
This is a chief element of culture, without which the individual is
"incomplete" according to anthropological theory (Geertz 1974). A
professional community such as architecture is a cultural microcosm,
giving practitioners their bearing in the world.

In practice, the individual architect is provided a milieu to forge
and express a coherent professional identity. This milieu is not a
static, predetermined social scene; rather, the architects in a firm together create the setting for their actions. The setting is dynamic,
shifting slightly as the firm grows, adds and loses members, gains new
clients, and as the broader context evolves with subtle changes in the
economy, the building industry, or the available technology. Firm
membership fluctuates dramatically among low-level (and low-paid)
employees; finding a coherent practice within such confusion can
prove difficult. In order to produce a body of work with integrity, individual architects must construct avenues leading out of the disorder
toward collective work and coordinated practice. The milieu of each
firm is unique and in flux, but underlying their uniqueness, firms
share certain structural characteristics. The first is an office's heritage,
which involves the origins and founders of a firm, often recollected in
legends analogous to creation myths. Other characteristics include office members' use of language, their power structure, and their prevailing practices and values.

OFFICE HERITAGE

Each office has one or more founders who shaped the practice, and if
the firm has been relatively successful under their leadership, the
founders have become role models. If the founders have either char-
isma or widespread professional recognition, or both, their influence
increases. The example below comes from a conversation with a firm's
partner, part of which was reported at the beginning of chapter 2 to
introduce the discussion of beliefs and actions. Here we see how beliefs and actions are transferred from one generation to the next:

Robert is the senior mentor figure in the office. He has strong, dedicated, passionate interests. He taught us how to lose money [laugh-
ing]—I mean to work on a project until it's right. When I started to
work with Robert almost 30 years ago, we had a little garage for an
office. Robert gathered people around him who liked to work with
him. Lots of people left, but Frank and I were willing to stay under

5.2 Wright and apprentices in the Taliesin drafting room. Wright, as founder, hero, and leader, shaped a practice that still lives on at Taliesin, though its vitality has suffered since the death of the master in 1959.

Robert's hand and principles and design command, to carry out his wishes. Maybe others felt this was too constraining and left to start their own practices.

When the office was small, we all shared Robert's vision. He's always been able to go straight to the core of things and turn out a simple, straightforward solution,—he's established that here. Building buildings is really his art. He can always cut through the bullshit. But now we have trouble keeping our standards with all these new people. It's good that Robert showed slides of the office's work last week because the new people need to see how our work has developed.

In this example there are vestiges of a creation myth, recounted by Henry, the first of two partners to be handpicked by Robert. There were humble beginnings in a garage, attracting those who had enough vision and dedication to stay with Robert. Robert's talents are magnified: he can cut through bullshit, go to the core, knows what is right, and embodies the art of building buildings. He is a legendary figure with a legacy that lives on in the everyday activities of the office. Founders like Robert, who play a strong role in their firms, gain much of their charismatic authority from their own creative ability—they are designers with a following (see Blau 1979).

A firm's founders serve as role models through their own actions, but also through the memories and actions of "old-timers" who play a critical part in passing down office heritage to throngs of newcomers, the "rookies." Most offices have their Henrys, who are dedicated members of the firm by virtue of their tenure. In the office, old-timers tell about their early days with the founders in stories that embed an office ideology. For example, from Henry we learn it is more important to do a project the right way than to make money; solutions should be simple and straightforward. Newcomers are expected to internalize that ideology, so that all members of the office practice on common ground. Those that have internalized the office ethos, typically the old-timers, adopt appropriate behavior. Sometimes this behavior parrots that of the founders, so that they practice not only with the same architectural style but also the same working style. For instance, Henry complains that Robert's only fault was an inability or unwillingness to communicate, yet just a few minutes later he talks about his own problems working with underlings:

Robert would ask me to draw something up again and again until it was right, without telling me what that was. I used to waste a lot of time and get pretty frustrated, because Robert's own mental picture seemed extraordinarily clear.

[Later] Now we bring in lots of young people and we have to give them a sense of the way we work. It's really a ritual of making buildings—that's what our process is. But when people haven't worked with us for long, they don't understand. Now I have to say, "We don't do things like that" and they don't know what I'm talking about. I can't spend the time to lead each person through the office philosophy.

I have to take command. I'm not ashamed to say that's how the office runs now. We can have academic discussions and question the program, the design, and all that. But at some point, I'm going to say, "We'll do it this way," and then the argument should end and we should draw it up.

Henry is not entirely unaware that he treats young practitioners the way he was treated when he was young. When he explains the delegation of design authority, he says he was not invited to client meetings for fifteen years, and does not intend to give rookies the advantage that took so long for him to earn. Such inherited behaviors promote a set of values, which in this case includes the importance of seniority, the difficulty of explaining design, and the necessity that chief designers dictate the actions of those who work for them. The firm's central values, by nature, appear to believers as objective, basic truths. Those values and the actions that express them are, in and of themselves, right, not requiring—sometimes even precluding—explanation. Thus a way of designing was passed down from Robert to Henry, who learned it the hard way: without explanation but through example. Now this is the only way he knows to pass the truths along.

The values held in any firm are shaped by various forces, the most significant of which are the principal's own values. The formative period, particularly during one's time as an architectural student, when professional values are first encountered, live on in practice, establishing a baseline for a firm's development. Each of the various architecture schools has a reputation for promoting certain values, be they formal, social, technical, or pragmatic, and the alma mater survives in the offices of its graduates. The other significant inspiration is the architect-mentor under whom the apprentice works in the first years out of school. Young architects working for a senior figure they respect collect values they carry with them into their own practice. One office's partners worked for Kahn, another's for Saarinen, another's for Wright—and the legacy of those heroes lives on in the new practices. The architect whose mentor was a New York postmodernist, a Southwest regionalist, or a developer will emerge in each case with different values and likewise a unique practice.

Office culture can be passed along through individuals, their words, their actions, and their legacies, but also through the portfolio of buildings designed by the office. These artifacts are the most permanent and objectifiable legacy of an office's culture. In the buildings, office members learn the prevailing values and how they are expressed in form. To become a responsible participant in Robert's firm, architect-employees need to learn not only that simple, straightforward solutions are the right ones, but just what those look like. An office's family of buildings expresses the developing ideology of the firm. From

the series of buildings the office produces, newcomers begin to grasp what Henry means by the art of building buildings, going straight to the core, or knowing when a project is right.

Because the office's artifacts—its buildings—do not automatically express their own meaning, and because their meaning is multifaceted, some shared interpretation of them is fundamental to office cohesion. The important task of interpreting these artifacts rests with senior members, who reveal their meaning to the waves of new employees passing through the firm. Most of the time, the appropriate reading of the buildings is imparted in informal conversation, but occasionally formal ceremonies take place like initiation rites, as in Robert's slide show of the office's work.

FIRM GROWTH AND CHANGE

The type of office described above is relatively common, with one or more founding fathers or mothers who act as spiritual leaders, role models, or mentors to younger firm members. Some of these younger members will eventually assume positions of leadership in the firm, and become role models themselves, thus changing the office profile. The office starts small, grows at least a little over the years, and changes its profile over time. Both growth and change are part of the model office evolution, but it is worthwhile pointing out that there are many exceptions to this pattern. There is the office that grows but does not change much. These offices typically cling to one leader or set of leaders, whose retirement brings about the death of the firm. This category includes firms made up of young contemporaries who start out on their own and grow old together, and firms that have a single charismatic founder who never takes on any partners; in the current lingo of organizational management specialists, there is no "transitioning." Then there are the firms that neither grow nor change significantly, as in a state of continual emergence or subsidized stasis. The ever-emerging practice is one in which an architect's promise remains unrealized, typically because he or she cannot break out of small-scale work, and even that work is irregular. Other architects practice in offices that remain static because the practitioners are subsidized outside the firm, as with university teaching positions. None of these forms, it should be pointed out, preclude doing good work. Finally, there are practices in decline, that shrink or go out of business gradually, an alarmingly common phenomenon in periods of economic crisis.[3]

In Blau's (1984) study of growth, decline, and survival among New York firms, she found that no single model of practice could be upheld as the model of success; success depended on economic circumstances, size of the office, orientation, and many other factors. She also found that no one strategy that offices employed to survive an

5.4, 5 The photograph above was taken in 1949, in the early days of the firm now known as CRS–Sirrene, based in Houston. From left to right are Caudill, Scott, Rowlett, and Peña. Below, the same four partners in 1970. Their firm grew from a small operation over a grocery store to become the largest firm in America, measured by dollar volume in design commissions.

economic crisis seemed particularly effective—that too depended upon circumstances. What Blau did uncover was an ever-present state of flux brought about by the dilemmas that confront every firm. My own observations suggest that the level of flux varies from firm to firm, with some offices moving very slowly and others undergoing cataclysmic restructuring. These firms manage to survive, each with a commensurately distinct culture for practice.

The office described by Henry has a respected, charismatic founding partner. Other offices, however, are organized around a set of objectives (for example, to make more money, revitalize historic districts, or dominate the market for hospital construction). Architect-employees stay in firms not only to work with a mentor but because it's a good job (for example, they have responsibilities they want, they are paid well, it's where they want to live), or they may be rebels or entrepreneurs, hoping to secure more powerful positions to establish their own values in the office. Another point that should not be overlooked is that Henry is rather unique: most architects have worked in a number of offices, and many principals begin several firms as a result of economic crises, relocation, new partnerships, the creation of branch offices, and so on. The evolutionary path of any current architectural office culture is generally the result of internal upheaval and external pressure. The particular responses to these dilemmas shape the office culture and prepare it for the upcoming problems.

It should not be forgotten that material conditions also significantly affect the office heritage, including the type of projects gained, the budgets that come with these projects, the recognition received from established professional channels (awards, competitions, the professional press), the level of craftsmanship in the local building industry, the availability of low-cost talent to staff the office, and the availability of new technology. For example, when the U.S. experienced an energy crisis in the 1970s, the building industry, and architects in particular, responded with the development of a series of energy-efficient building strategies, solar technologies, and analytic tools like computer software to evaluate problems and the efficiency of various solutions. This specialized focus developed by many offices at the time has now become a part of the standard services those architects deliver.

The economy, the labor pool, current fashion, the sociopolitical climate—all guide an office's entry into the professional mainstream. Each firm has a way of making sense of itself, beginning with a kind of creation myth with founders for role models, and with shared interpretive readings of its artifacts, the buildings. The office develops systems for passing its culture on to new generations, and the resultant coherence helps the firm run smoothly.

While culture implies multifaceted relationships among individuals and the material world, the cultural scene of an architectural office can be more specifically delineated. The members of the office come together for economic, practical, and personal reasons in order to get work done. Robert's office, described above, also reflects a professional ideal of creative practice and a competitive building economy.

To understand an office's culture, we must know the kinds of programs—rules and plans for behavior—that pertain. In any office, a dialect, a prevailing set of values, rituals, and a power structure will develop to govern behavior. Such elements, interwoven rather than independent, together describe a firm's culture. Any new office member will need to make sense of the unknown, subtle aspects of the culture (like Paul in the vignette that introduces chapter 4).

DIALECT

The verbal and physical expression that is promulgated in an office is central to understanding its culture. In fact, some anthropologists and sociolinguists define culture as people in communication (see, for example, Cherry 1957), choosing as the unit of analysis linguistic groups. Before applying for work at an office, candidates study the office's oeuvre to gain a sense of its design standards and criteria. The applicant's portfolio gives members of the office an idea of the compatibility between the individual and the firm. The spatial expression of a firm through its buildings can only cohere if the individual firm members put that expressive dialect into practice.

Along with form-related expression comes a particularized form of verbal expression. The vocabulary extends beyond primarily formal issues to those of responsibility, procedures, and goals. In the statement "You figure out how to make this stair work" there is more ambiguity than is first apparent. There are several possible interpretations for what it means for the stair to "work": getting from one place to another while adhering to all codes and regulations; appearing useful and pleasing to the climbers; participating in the building's spatial composition; or being arranged in such a way that no square footage is wasted. In addition, the draftsperson must know when "this" stair has been so altered that it has become a different stair. Even simple statements can cause miscommunication with the uninitiated. As in any group's dialect or language, meaningful categories are assigned distinguishing labels. In an office where circulation is important, many subcategories are given names, such as perceptual path and primary, secondary, tertiary, formal, and informal circulation (see Cuff 1989b:87). As some researchers have noted, in the process of professional socialization practitioners acquire common vocabularies, so that they actually speak alike (Stelling and Bucher 1973). This occurs in the profession as well as in the firm whose members "speak the same language," and in that language lurks a set of values and practices.

VALUES

While a firm lives with a body of common values, not all the members of an office share a single set of values. Blau (1984) has shown that there are consistent differences between the values of rank and file and management in architectural firms, and there are presumably such differences between old-timers and rookies. Still, members of an office must share, or at least exhibit, common values or they must hold different values which complement rather than conflict with one another. In the earlier example, when Henry says to young architects, "We don't do it that way," he not only refers to acceptable behavior but also to what is good and right in the office's worldview. Unless the others share a part of his vision—his values—it will be difficult for him to delegate responsibility. He needs assurance that the group members are all heading toward the same goal.

In most architectural offices values are ambiguous because they cannot be enumerated or made explicit. Values are learned through experience and by example. The larger the office, the more ambiguous its values, and the more complex the transmission of those values to its members. Large offices are thus said to exhibit no set of values (see Dixon 1982), because internal coherence is difficult to achieve. To complicate matters, the values within an office change over time: the principal develops a new interest in urban design; an office's market for services shifts from hospitals to low-cost housing; within three years, there is nearly complete turnover in the office's staff. For the office as a working unit, such changes in values occur slowly. An office's values tend to be ambiguous and transient, with no clear boundaries. The totality cannot be fully known, because to freeze values in time and space is an invalid representation. However, at any given point in time, members of the office must act as if they know this stuff that cannot be known.[4]

PREVAILING PRACTICES AND RITUALS

If values concern things that matter in the office, then prevailing practices concern how the architect acts with those values in mind. As with its values, an office's prevailing practices (such as presenting a united front to clients) are rarely made explicit: one learns through experience. In larger offices, books of policy and procedures are sometimes developed. In my field work, I twice saw policy and procedures manuals being revised because firm members felt more consistency was needed between projects. Yet I never saw anyone use these manuals in a formal way; no one checked the proper procedure before acting. The act of developing the guidelines was more useful than the resulting document, and the document's existence gave management additional authority over the rank and file. More reliable as guidelines are the prevailing practices and rituals, but these cannot be learned by studying a book.

Not every action has an established precedent, nor is there only one acceptable way to act in most cases, but the newcomer to an office senses that there is a right way and a wrong way to do things. The only problem is to find out which way is which. The office develops acceptable and inappropriate patterns of behavior for most recurrent situations such as negotiating fees, moving projects through their various stages of development, and hiring and firing. Nevertheless, many architects make comments like "This is a manic, not a methodical office." Beneath the surface, such statements reflect a lack of control and knowledge on the part of the speaker, and, simultaneously, a belief in creative spontaneity. While senior members of an office may have a flexible set of procedures to invoke in various circumstances, these are cabalistic to others, especially newcomers, who explain such behavior as spontaneous.

Regardless of how manic or methodical an office is, there are certain rituals observed in nearly every architectural firm. Rituals are recurrent patterns of activity that carry not only a manifest meaning, but a latent, symbolic meaning. An architectural office has rituals involving its own members, and these go along with consistent ways of working with clients and consultants. There are rituals about how architectural ideas are generated; at the other end of the design process, there are charrette rituals about how projects are completed. Some rituals concern the value of group cohesion, such as retreats, baseball games, and picnics that symbolically establish an affinity within the firm extending beyond mere working relations. In a rational economic model, these cohesive activities are seen as the co-opting of labor toward management objectives, but since management in most architectural offices is not nearly so distinct from labor as it is in the corporate setting, the co-optation argument is only partially relevant.

In spite of professional rather than entrepreneurial relations between management and rank and file, there are significant relations of power existing in any architectural office. Power, here, refers to the ability to move someone or something within the organization in a desired direction (Zartman 1976). Power in the architectural firm can be achieved through a variety of means: persuasive ability, the strength of one's design ideas, decision-making authority that comes with status in the office, or support from powerful individuals. The culture of every architectural practice incorporates a power structure,

5.6 The elaborate model shop
in Frank Gehry's office shown
here is indicative of the significance placed on working in
three dimensions. The extensive use of models throughout
a project is a prevailing practice in the firm.

one version of which is formal, the other informal. The formal power structure is like the policies and procedures manual—in times of duress it may be invoked, and external relations are conducted through proper channels, primarily the hierarchy and seniority that form the formal power structure. Informal power, then, is far more effective in the day-to-day operation of an office and in the development of an architectural solution. It is primarily within the framework of informal power that decisions are taken about architectural projects. Informal power can be gained by attaching oneself to other members of the office who either will relinquish their assigned powers or will ooze power onto all those associated with them. For example, one young entry-level architect informally became the right-hand woman of the principal designer of a firm who delegated to her more authority than her formal status granted. Blau (1984) tells us that voice, a form of power, is also acquired in an office through esoteric expertise, such as knowledge of computer-aided design or lighting. She makes the point that those higher up in the organization will rely upon and listen to the individual with such expertise, not only about matters relating to that expertise but about others as well, since access to power is a form of power in itself. Another means to achieve informal power within the office is through experience. The greater the knowledge one has of the office's culture, its prevailing practices and values, its dialect, its power structure, and the possible roles one can assume, the greater the ability to achieve one's desired ends.

ROLES

Although every office is comprised of unique individuals, there are recurrent patterns of activities and values among offices that carry with them a particular significance in the overall practice of architecture. These recurrent patterns can be called roles. They are typified responses to typified expectations, important to office culture because they are plans for behavior governing the ways in which individuals will participate in the office (Berger 1963:95). In the theatrical metaphor from which the concept of role is drawn, it is as if a script is provided and actors take on the persona assigned,—acting, thinking, and feeling the part. Each role, therefore, has an internal structure that shapes both the action and the actor. We do not, however, "pretend" in these roles. According to role theory, we become what we play at, in an effortless and unself-conscious way, so that actions, beliefs, and relations are formulated within the context of roles. For architectural offices, such roles then can be seen as structuring the identities of the individual participants as well as composing a matrix of identities unique to the firm.

In architecture, the broadest level of roles include architect, client, contractor, and consultant. These categories of individuals imply and describe the expected ways people will act in a project, the values they will hold, and the significance they will attach to various aspects of the project. There are more specific occupational roles within the architectural office that we can name, such as draftsperson, project architect, designer, partner, principal, or model maker, but this categorization is somewhat misleading. Since architectural offices are characterized by a high proportion of professional staff (as opposed to a doctor's office, where there might be only one doctor with a staff made up of nonprofessionals and professionals other than doctors), many individuals will assume roles only temporarily. The model maker, for example, is unlikely to see herself as a model maker, but instead as a beginning architect who is working her way up. In this case, role and identity are not synonomous with job title. Naturally, the majority of individuals in any sizable office are still "on their way," and so do not identify with their current occupational status but with their intention of becoming full-fledged architects.

Another way to think of roles concerns the basic functions required to do the work of an architectural firm. Barker's (1968) analysis of behavior settings is applicable to architectural offices. He contends that every behavior setting (for example, the classroom, the bar, the firm) has a minimum number of roles that must be assumed if the setting is to be operative. In architectural offices, there are four roles that can be considered essential: getting and keeping work, getting it done, doing it well, and maintaining the organization. In organizational parlance, these roles might be management and marketing, technical expertise, quality control, and leadership. These roles can be fulfilled by a division of labor in large offices, where it is not unusual to find one principal whose primary role is to take care of business (get and keep work), another is the lead designer (doing it well, sometimes also getting it done), and another who is the symbolic or spiritual head of the firm (heroic founder or charismatic leader who maintains group solidarity). "Undermanning," in Barker's terms, can plague the small office, forcing each individual to assume several roles, including those for which they have no sympathy or competence. In Henry and Robert's story, these two men filled the roles of doing work well and leadership, but were not particularly good managers.

Regularly observable characters fall into one or more needed roles in the architectural firm. These include such types as charismatic leaders, entrepreneurs, creative eccentrics, wheeler-dealers, slaves, go-getters, technical wizards, it's-a-job types, rebels, and craftspersons. When architects speak of who they need to hire, they acknowledge unfulfilled roles in their practices. One architect, best described as a creative eccentric, wanted to hire someone to get the work done, complementing his own ability to get business and do it well. In his three-person firm, he said that he needed "one of those old guys in a button-down sweater who requires a reasonable salary and won't work overtime." Such roles have developed to govern certain activities that fulfill the office setting's fundamental needs.

ARCHITECT AND CLIENT   An architectural firm is a cultural microcosm, mediating between the individual architect and the public at large. Each office has its own programs for behavior, which help the collection of individuals operate as a unit as well as create a meaningful context for discrete actions. Firms, though varying widely in terms of their personality, have a common underlying framework that forms the social milieu of the firm itself. The second part of the social milieu of architectural practice, as significant as the firm's internal workings, is the architect's relation to the client. The practicing architect initially steps into the public domain in the professional firm, a relatively safe context of shared worldviews. Together with other like-minded practitioners, the architect moves to the boundary of that organization to meet the clients, taking a further step into the public realm.[5]

In the creation of any architectural work, there are no actors more important than architect and client, yet far more research is needed to understand their relationship. Patronage and its role in the arts have been widely studied, primarily in historical work related to painting. In architectural history, isolated works on specific architects and their patrons exist, but little has been written about contemporary patrons, or, moreover, about the distinct differences between patrons and clients (for a discussion of the issue, see Gutman 1989). Rather than patrons subsidizing the arts, the focus of this work is the clients of everyday architectural practice who, like the clients of other professionals, desire specific services that they pay for. The contemporary architectural client plays an active role with the practitioner, giving constraints, advice, and approval throughout the process, without which the appropriateness of the services is threatened. A frequent complaint among architects is registered against overly active clients who interfere in the process and prevent architects from doing their best work. As it turns out, there is some evidence tht the best buildings have clients who are very active but also willing to step back at crucial points in the design process.

Certain interaction patterns are evident in the concerted activities of individuals working together to create a building, particularly in their discourse. As will be shown in the next case, architects and clients design their interactions as carefully as they design their build-

5.7 Edgar Kaufmann, Sr., and
Frank Lloyd Wright at Taliesin
West. Kaufmann Junior was
briefly an apprentice at Taliesin, and his father, a wealthy
department-store owner, became one of Wright's great patrons, known primarily for
commissioning Fallingwater.

ings, that is, the meetings and the negotiations are themselves design problems. The specific conversation in any given meeting, while superficially disordered and impromptu, is more like jazz improvization: themes are raised, bantered, developed, resolved, bridged, and so on. Prior to examining dialogue at a microlevel, I examine the larger structure of relations between the architect and client within which conversations fit. The qualities of their working relationship are built over time and take the following forms: courtship, building rapport, unveiling boundaries, avoiding disputes, and constructing progress.[6]

The five patterns of architect-client interactions that I propose are interesting to compare to the five basic phases of architectural services prescribed by the American Institute of Architects (Doc B141, Handbook 1987) (see table 5.1). The AIA gives the sequential steps required to deliver competent professional services, focusing on actions required to produce certain objects, thus literally objectifying design. Those objects are drawings, contracts, and construction documents. My analysis "subjectifies" design, focusing on actions of subjects in relation to one another. The patterns of interaction are not sequential, nor do they concern competence or the production of specific objects; they concern the social construction of design.

To these subtle interaction patterns I have given labels like courtship and unveiling boundaries, although no labels exist among architects to distinguish between these different types of interaction. Since the patterns, once revealed, are widely observed, the labels may reflect "covert categories" (see Berlin et al. 1968) that, now labeled, can be more carefully scrutinized. In addition, although the five patterns are enacted by participants, they are not necessarily "strategies." Over time, with experience in design negotiations (as well as in everyday social relations), we learn to evoke certain responses from a listener (see Goffman 1981). Just as in everyday conversation one speaker does not plot, for instance, how to cut in on another and yet still finds a way to interrupt, design participants can engage in effective behavior that is nonetheless not strategic.[7]

DESIGN INTERACTIONS   Interaction is intense throughout the design process. Certainly the architect spends some time at the drawing board designing alone, but this is limited. One remarkable study found that architects on average have only one thirty-minute period of uninterrupted time each day (Rutland 1972). When I've recounted this information to architects, they generally think thirty minutes is an overestimate. If time-budgeting data were available for design participants, we could chart the interaction over the life of a project to summarize who works most closely with whom, and when that collaboration occurs. The models below are approximations, based on my own observations (but without

Table 5.1
PATTERNS OF ARCHITECT-CLIENT INTERACTIONS

	AIA DESCRIPTION	AUTHOR'S DESCRIPTION
1	Schematic design	Courtship
2	Design development	Building rapport
3	Construction documents	Unveiling boundaries
4	Bidding or negotiating	Avoiding disputes
5	Administration of the construction contract	Constructing progress

quantifiable data), showing that different participants phase into the process at points where their input is most needed and their interests are most vested.[8]

Because each of these graphs models the architect's dealings with another participant, their combination (the last graph) shows the intensity of interaction for the architect during a project's life. According to these models, the architect should experience slight "independence" or fewer "interruptions" at the end of schematics, and then again at the end of design development. As the process wears on, the focus of the architects' interactions shift from the client to other professionals, primarily consultants. The architect's total level of interaction is higher than any other participant's, which explains why architects are often heard wishing for greater autonomy. On the other hand, clients' participation decreases until they reinsert themselves (sometimes unwantedly) in the final stages of the process. Architects who keep their clients engaged at some level throughout design development and construction documents may have fewer problems with last-minute changes.

These graphs give an overview of design interactions in practice, but lack the depth and intrigue of actual architect-client relations. To understand the richness of those relations, captured by the five interaction patterns, I recount below the story of a mosque planned for a group of families and designed by a young architect with two assistants. Although this case is not typical—it is in fact quite unusual—it demonstrates that a wide range of collaborations falls within this analytic net. For each of the five categories that describe architect-client relations, I include an illustrative vignette from the project.

5.8 Relative levels of interaction experienced by architects throughout design and construction of a project. In the top graph: note surges of interaction prior to clients' final approval when the project moves on to a subsequent phase; interaction with clients generally decreases over life of a project. In second graph: work with consultants is most intense just before client approvals, in the middle of each phase. In the third graph: dealings with contractors vary, increasing over time if a contractor is brought in from the beginning and taking a dramatic leap during the bidding and negotiating phase if the project is sent out to bid. In the fourth graph, architects work together throughout the process, but most intensely as a phase nears completion and approvals are sought. The bottom graph shows how all these graphs combine to create the architects' experience of interaction. In combination, the level of interaction is consistently intense, with slight reprieves earned as each new phase begins.

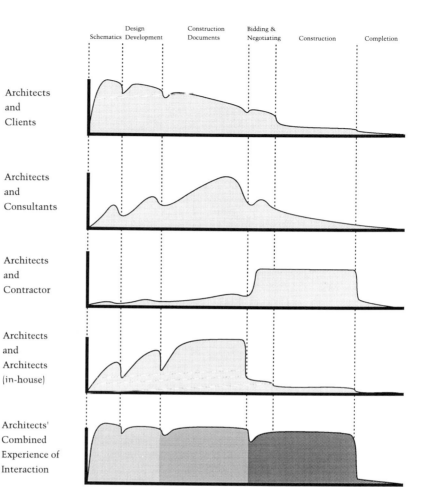

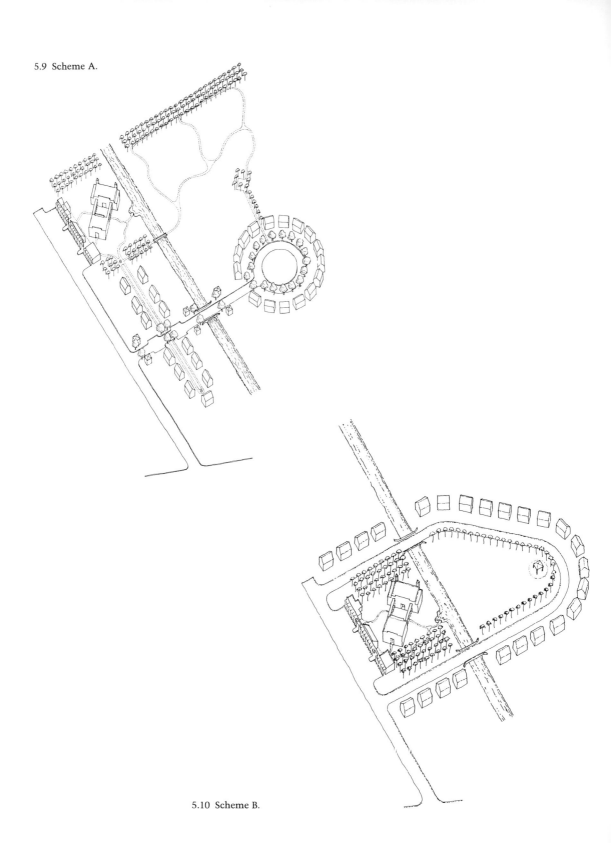

5.9 Scheme A.

5.10 Scheme B.

5.11 Final Solution. Schemes A and B are the two different alternatives for the neighborhood plan that were merged by clients to create a new and final solution. In this solution, the mosque and community center remain at the center-left of the site as in scheme B, with a small cluster of hosues added as in scheme A. The residential street is curved around an open space, providing a safe, single access community area (as in scheme A) but with a greater number of house sites.

In September 1984, a group of Muslim families hired Michael Underhill to design a low-cost, perhaps prefabricated, community center (estimated at 4,000 sq. ft., $35/sq. ft.) and to plat 30 housing sites on twenty acres outside Houston, Texas. In addition, they asked Underhill to plan for a mosque, a library, a priest's quarters, visitor's quarters, and an administrative office, all of which would be built in a second phase. Two leaders of the client group worked with the architect to explain their special requirements and rituals for this, the first mosque of their sect in North America. The architect and his assistants, enthusiastic about the project in spite of the limited budget, began researching traditional mosque forms and how these might weld together with typical Texan building forms. They developed two alternatives for the complex of buildings, including schematic plans, sections, elevations, and site plans, as well as five alternative residential plat maps. The two client leaders selected one of the building complexes for further development, but indicated that the final decisions about the mosque's form rested with a religious leader in India. A community meeting for all the families to decide on the neighborhood plan was called, and some twenty-five men, women, and children attended. In a raucous three-hour meeting, the group reached a compromise solution that combined the physical form of two different alternatives into a new and acceptable solution. Architect and clients continued to refine the schemes and to seek local approvals, yet the complex chain of decisions within the clients' religious sect and their lack of funds has placed the project on hold.

COURTSHIP

On the recommendation of the local American Institute of Architects' office, Abas F. and Mustan X., the client leaders, called to interview Underhill. At the time, they were also speaking to an Indian architect about the project. After meeting with the clients, Underhill enthusiastically prepared a proposal, suggesting a fee of $7,000 (including fees for consultants), reiterating the important cultural, historical, and budgetary issues, and enumerating steps to follow. After three months' silence, the clients invited Underhill to a contract signing ceremony: he'd gotten the job. While the other architect knew more about their customs and religion, he did not seem very enthusiastic about the project. The ceremony was held at the priest's house, where women and men were separated, and a meal was served to the men on a cloth spread out on the living room floor. Underhill never got a chance to read the contract before signing it. The next two meetings were set up to discuss the requirements: rituals of purification, preparing meals and dining, men's and women's quarters, sacred space, prayer rugs, religious ceremonies, and so on.

When architects and clients meet, their first efforts center on trying to assess and understand one another: they "size each other up." They send and pick up clues indicating what the rest of the design process holds in store, both in terms of their general attitudes and specific information such as budget, program, and schedule. The courtship phase is characteristically tentative: architect and client try to determine if their relationship has potential, whether they are compatible, if the future is promising. Like courting, it can be awkward and un-

comfortable, or titillating. The extent of discomfort is directly propor-
tional to the disparity between the two parties' interests in working
together. When one party definitely wishes to proceed while the other
is more tentative, mutual assessment is both uncomfortable and crucial. When both parties are pleasantly surprised with their initial encounters, as in the mosque project, courtship is an engaging process.
Underhill consciously displayed his enthusiasm for the project and his
willingness to learn the unfamiliar customs of his clients, which gave
him the edge over his rival. The clients had a special ceremony in
Underhill's honor, publicly sealing their agreement to work together.
As the clients admitted the architect into their community, he was
also made aware that he had much to learn about their culture. In
courting, factual inquiries are made as architect and client ask for and
present information about the project. Early on, Underhill found that
the clients did not have money to build the project and that a bank
loan was forbidden by their religion. He grew wary not only about
whether the project was a real one, but also about his fees, fears later
alleviated by the clients' reliable payments. These first impressions
between architects and clients will influence subsequent actions as
participants gather a sense of the issues they must define, argue for, or
relinquish, and when it will be necessary to coerce, convince, educate,
agree, or compromise.

The relationship between architects and clients does not begin
with a tabula rasa but with preconceptions, to be fulfilled or contradicted by ensuing interaction. The social stereotypes about architects
and clients (chapter 2) are most active in courtship. The mosque
clients knew nothing about Underhill except that he had the professional organization's recommendation; thus his enthusiasm was especially attractive. Simultaneously, architects hold preconceptions about
clients, as well as forming projections of their client's preconceptions.
These projections frame behavior; the architect responds to his or her
vision of the client rather than the actual client. For example, Underhill stated his willingness to work with a minimal construction budget to overcome the stereotype of architects' extravagant planning
without regard to the client's ability to pay. Underhill expressed interest in working with a prefabricated building, though he admits privately that his efforts were aimed at getting the commission for the
neighborhood plan, which was the part of the project that attracted
him most.

BUILDING RAPPORT

Soon after receiving the commission, Underhill's assistants began
studying mosques, the building type and its traditional architectural
elements, all of which research was presented to the client leaders.
Although the clients were not convinced they wanted a traditional

mosque, they were impressed with the office's interest in their building project. Underhill also brought in a programming specialist to help uncover the mosque's unfamiliar requirements; he learned the clients' terms for building elements and members of the religious community (for example, *kibla, sahn, dai*). In the design alternatives, Underhill went beyond the clients' stated needs: they could carve a piece of commercial property from the site to raise additional funds; he had considered the community's children in terms of school bus stops and safety; the community center complex could include an elegant garden. The clients, on their part, expressed their appreciation for the special interest Underhill showed in the project, praised his work, insisted on paying him at regular intervals, and took care to schedule meetings at Underhill's convenience. All such behavior helped architects and clients forge a congenial working relation.

In any linked negotiations, that is, those that extend over time as with ongoing professional-client relationships, building rapport is predominant activity, particularly in the early stages of the design process. However, rapport is not simply "established" at the outset; it must be maintained and strengthened throughout the period that participants work together. Good rapport contributes to effective communication, forging channels for reaching agreement and avoiding disputes, and is central to all negotiations, be it between hostages and terrorists, labor and management, doctors and patients, or architects and clients. Professionals are socialized, in fact, to believe the professional-client or patient relationship so central to their work that they define a failure in their practice as "somebody who can't work with you" (Stelling and Bucher 1973:670).

Rapport rests on assumptions about a standard architect-client relation that serves as a baseline; actions that go beyond baseline expectations effectively build comraderie. Architects and clients expect a working business association, however formal and impersonal, that is enhanced through more personal, informal interaction. As Underhill learns the clients' terms and traditions, the clients become more open about private and sacred rituals, which bond the actors in a more intimate relationship. Because clients must expose rather intimate information about their lives during the design process, trust is essential to creating appropriate buildings.

There are many means to build rapport between architects and clients. To overcome the clients' preconceptions about proprietary interests, architects will join forces with their clients, assuring them the design process will be a mutual effort. As such alliances are formed, there may be the discovery, and sometimes cultivation, of an "outsider"—a common adversary upon whom insiders can vent frustrations. At other times, actors push accomplishments back and forth across the table, each wanting to give the other the reward. Architects and clients exhibit their generosity by making comments to *mark* the favor, compromise, or any "other-directed" action. Underhill demonstrated he was working in the clients' interest by preparing two alternative building complexes in four days, meeting with clients for several hours after the regular workday, and hiring a programmer. The clients raised $1,000 from community members in a single evening to pay Underhill's bill promptly. It is clear that many of the elements in the story above concern building rapport between architect and client.

UNVEILING BOUNDARIES AND PREFERENCES

The clients presented Underhill with a book showing what they considered the most beautiful mosque, not at all a traditional building but a richly adorned modernist interpretation—quite unappealing to the architects. The architects' preferences for historical models stood in contrast to the clients' desire for a contemporary statement. On the other hand, the clients were not familiar with the specific physical forms for their sect's mosques; for example, they were not sure about which shape of arch was required, or the necessary location of the cleansing fountain. The clients intimated that such details in any event would need approval from the Dai in India, and he would let them know what was acceptable: how many arches they would be allowed, how many windows, and so on. The constraints from the Dai were difficult for Underhill to grasp. For instance, the Dai's assistant had blessed a part of the site for the mosque and community center, and much later, Underhill discovered that only a tiny corner of the building needed to sit on the blessed land. Later still he learned that the assistant would come back and bless another parcel if necessary.

Besides comraderie, architects and clients establish certain values, as preferences or limits for the design process. Participants need constraints in order to bring the process to a close, yet these limits are established in process rather than a priori. The client must assure the architect that there is only so much money and no more. An architect asks for written client approval to avoid future alterations to work already completed. As the project proceeds, architect and client slowly unveil the limits and preferences that guide design, generally after some amount of rapport has been established. In the example, the clients revealed their aesthetic by showing Underhill the mosque book, which convinced him he would have to argue well to incorporate traditional Islamic building elements. From the architect's perspective, the mosque project was plagued by a lack of clear constraints particularly related to authority: who made what decisions when.

Constraints and preferences divulge the values that architects and clients uphold in design collaborations. Because this is such a significant part of any architectural undertaking, three commonly observed means of establishing values are described: nonnegotiable declarations, barbed remarks, and a show of strength. Sometimes architect or client will present a bottom line, which is to remain undisputed, a line that cannot under any circumstances be crossed. A developer-client says,

"All financing is based on 21,000 square feet of leasable space. If that changes, we lose the project." Underhill employed what I have called the "structural defense" when he explained that columns were structurally necessary in the community center (although a more costly alternative was possible, the columns retained the traditional aesthetic he preferred). In fact, bottom lines are not necessarily absolutes, but attempts to establish constraining limits that are nonnegotiable.

A persuasive way to set constraints is the barbed remark, which is a veiled boundary since it has two intended interpretations: at the surface the statement is relatively acceptable, while underneath is a message about limits. The statement is phrased at once to get that latter point across and to keep the actors away from heated debate or disagreement. Architects say things like "That's been done on every tract house from here to Los Angeles" or "You don't want a tacky little lobby." On one level, the architect insinuates the client has good taste (that is, taste similar to the architect's), but at another level, the architect intimidates, cutting off options. It is a rare client who will say, "What do you mean? Of course I want a tacky little lobby" (Cuff 1981).

Lastly, a show of strength is occasionally invoked to maintain one's desired relationship with the other participants, most dramatically through desperate options. This is a last resort, since invoking such options undermines rapport and puts the project at risk. During the planning of a new civic park, one group of dissatisfied neighbors threatened, "If you to ahead with these plans we'll take it to city council, to the *Times*, and to Channel 5 if we have to." The architect's main bargaining chip is to threaten to quit, but its use is highly unusual. There is a paradoxical relationship between flexibility and integrity, for although flexibility is essential to a good working relationship, so is having a firm commitment and standing by it. One client told me, "If Chris [the architect] obeyed my every whim I wouldn't trust her. She's stubborn and uncompromising sometimes, but she's got integrity—no question about that." Reciprocally, the ideal client, as one architect put it, "knows what he wants and what he wants is right." Both parties must balance principled action with open-mindedness to create fertile constraints.

With the mosque, the clients preferences were far clearer than their constraints, especially concerning approvals, rendering both architect and client somewhat powerless—the building was constrained in part by an unknown actor (the Dai) with unknown values. When architects and clients know the boundaries and values are shared or at least complementary, the process runs smoothly, but when they stand in opposition, the specter of conflict arises.

AVOIDING DISPUTES

The community meeting was a long and loud mêleé on the night the five neighborhood plans were presented for a group decision. In his introduction, the architect clearly stated his preferences, which influenced the client representatives who were, in turn, convincing the men of the community. The women on the other hand were sitting somewhat at a distance, deciding among themselves that one of the architect's least preferred solutions was most desirable. As the men hovered around the drawings in the front of the room, arguing about the pros and cons of several solutions, the women would buttonhole their husbands and send them back into the argument with new positions and issues. Many times the architect was called in for clarification, but the heated discussion took place primarily in the group's native language. Three hours later the room calmed, the Abas made an announcement to Underhill: with his approval, the group had reached a compromise solution that combined the physical form of two different alternatives into a sixth and acceptable solution. The architect agreed, and each male adult stepped forward, following the priest's lead, to sign an agreement that Abas drafted on the spot outlining the compromise solution. Both Abas and Mustan made public remarks about the commitment and fine work of the architects, and the meeting was adjourned.

However counterproductive it may be, one of the best-obeyed unwritten laws of everyday architectural practice is: Avoid confrontation whenever possible.[9] Despite the careful and well-meant establishment of rapport between actors in the design process, the inherent disparity in their interests, responsibilities, and preferences leads to disagreement. Direct conflict is a serious matter, for it can destroy long-term rapport, color subsequent interactions, or force a decision at an inopportune time. One architect describes his "well-timed explosions," when he unleashes his displeasure before the client. He thinks that this can be effective only a few times; it should therefore only be invoked for very important issues in any design project (Cuff 1989b:79). When actors take up sides in a kind of stand-off, the flow of negotiations is upset. In the community meeting, Underhill avoided confrontation even though the clients were settling upon a compromise less acceptable to him than his preferred alternatives. Because the architect found no easy way to enter the clients' negotiations, he was left outside the decision-making process. The resulting solution did not have the integrity embodied in the initial alternatives, according to some critics.[10] Instead of embarking on a serious dispute, Underhill chose to accept the compromise scheme and slowly modify it through design development into a stronger scheme.

There are times when both parties were unable to avoid serious conflict, which I observed only twice during my field research. In both cases, the project was in the final stages of construction documents, making a complete halt unlikely, thus reducing the ultimate risk. Both cases also followed a long deterioration of rapport, undermining the basis for more affable interchange.

The most obvious means to avoid conflict is to refrain from taking sides and evade the stand-off. Having perceived the upcoming conflict, an actor retreats from a strong position to one that is more agreeable to the other, either by compromise or by admitting a mistake. Likewise, rather than meet issues head-on, especially those that appear directed toward conflict, architect or client commonly try to orchestrate the issue's discussion. Again, this is a means to control the conversational ball and thus direct negotiations; it can be done in words or drawings, as the following example demonstrates. An architect wanted to put a turret atop an already carnivalesque house, but he felt the client would be reluctant. At first the turret was not mentioned, though it appeared in several (but not all) drawings; but at the next meeting, the two spoke of the turret and gradually it appeared in more drawings, until finally it appeared on the house itself. Issues are frequently orchestrated to alter the timing of design negotiations, particularly when it appears that biding time will effect a more favorable outcome. One architect explained an interesting strategy she used to bide time. She holds many more client meetings than necessary at a project's outset, so much so that clients feel time is wasting away, at which point the architect snaps out of a holding pattern and leaps into design. She claims that the clients are so anxious to see some "architecture" that they rarely slow the process with disagreements or changes.

CONSTRUCTING PROGRESS

Underhill worked constructively with the two client leaders, who clearly stated needs and preferences leaving the architect to resolve problems. Decisions about specific architectural issues for the mosque and community center could be made in manageable meetings, at regular intervals. In contrast, it was difficult for the architect to work with the entire community, since once his initial presentation ended no one seemed to run the meeting. He wasn't sure how agreements were hammered out among the members, when consensus was needed, or when the client representatives could decide. Progress in this project, like many community projects, was difficult to stage and complicated further because no one knew who would finally approve the plans or who would finally pay and how much. Final authority rested in India with the Dai, but he was inaccessible. At one point, an architect claiming access to the Dai interjected himself to make new design proposals, and while neither architect nor client was impressed, it appeared that they had to accept some of these recommendations.

Constructing progress is probably the core activity when people meet together about buildings. In the mosque story, progress was swift and manageable during the first three weeks when all the schematic alternatives were prepared. Thereafter, the process was complicated whenever authority other than the client leaders' was needed, be it the authority of the community group or the Dai. Although this case seems somewhat exotic, the same problems can arise with indirect authority or large-group decisions in corporate clients, public clients, or multi-agency clients. Such blocks to progress are procedural, in that they concern the way agreements are reached rather than the subject of the agreements themselves.

Progress toward project completion can be insured through various types of procedural strategies. In the first place, each party attempts to discover the powers that be, making clear within the decision-making hierarchy whose approvals are needed to proceed with confidence. In addition, because fleeting words are easily forgotten, particularly when it suits a participant's purpose, approvals are sealed by asking the other to commit it to paper, either in words or drawings. The paper trail well known in bureaucracies is also present in architecture, especially since liability has become a central concern among practitioners. Clients receive memos summarizing the decisions of recent meetings, and if no corrections are made, agreement is presumed. In fact, meeting notes are often far more definite than the meeting itself, so that the memo becomes a tool for expediting progress.

In terms of objective progress, architects and clients constantly search for the direction toward a final building. The process is one of both discovery and invention, which is productive when participants are engaged in open-minded exploration, wherein issues and alternatives may be freely considered. When biases and preconceptions are suspended at least temporarily, conceptual directions can be tested without risking anything more than the time involved. A regular component of objective progress is education. For example, Underhill exposed his clients to historical examples of mosques, so that they would recognize their own cultural tradition in the buildings he was designing. Such education is at best instructive and expansive; at its worst it can be patronizing and coercive.

IMPROVISATIONAL TALK

This chapter's examination of the social milieu in architecture began with the office, then moved in more closely to view the architect-client dynamic. If we look for an even finer grain of that dynamic we encounter the specifics of conversation, which is improvised somewhat like jazz, following a structure of timing, tempo, rhythm, sequence, response, and theme. Although design participants do rehearse for particularly important encounters, in general architects and clients do not plan their conversations to any great extent. Like jazz, the performance is emergent, depending on how the players are constellated and on their interactive rapport, but it is not a matter of chance. Just as the building's form emerges over time, reflecting its dynamic social and material context, so does spontaneous conversation.[11]

One of the most interesting reasons to examine the architectural conversation is its apparent lack of order: sitting in on a meeeting, the observer may wonder what is going on. The following excerpt from a meeting between three architects, three clients, and one cost consultant (hired by the clients) will help demonstrate that conversations are guided according to the actors' goals in a relatively orderly fashion that is nevertheless difficult to perceive. The meeting takes place during design development, when the overall agenda is to negotiate final agreements about a dormitory.

CLIENT 1: We put the bathrooms too far away on every floor. This would be a logical place [pointing to plans] but we don't want to put a bathroom on the south side where the light's good for [dorm] rooms.

CLIENT 2: We should change this study room into a one-room double. The studies don't need great views—they're mainly used at night.

ARCHITECT 1: Okay [changes study room on plans]. In order to get the baths more central, we'll have to rethink this stair. Or maybe we could add another bath on each floor.

COST CONSULTANT [part of client team]: It costs a lot to break up baths.

CLIENT 1: It's not a good idea for social reasons either. It's better to have only one bath per floor, or the kids will be divided.

COST CON: Rather than multiple, complete baths, how about separating toilets from showers?

ARCH 2 [after measuring distance with a scale]: Walking 120 feet to a bathroom really isn't drastic.

CLIENT 1: But it's the psychological distance. Walking around three corners to get to the bathroom is bad.

CLIENT 3: The Committee feels the baths are not centrally located and that this is a serious problem.

[Arch 3 works with clients 1 and 2; sketches a new solution.]

By the time this meeting occurs the building's design is well defined, so that issues like bathroom and study-room location do not threaten the scheme's overall integrity. On the other hand, these are design issues and not merely programmatic problems. It is clear that the main topic in this part of the meeting is bathroom location, but why one statement follows another is not so apparent. This example shows that any utterance can have multiple meanings and most have more than one possible interpretation, based on preceding conversations, the roles each actor plays, the power relations, the upcoming events, and the expectations of participants. For instance, the second architect is in charge of overseeing the drawings back at the office. She makes an effort to avoid the difficult task of finding a new solution satisfying to all participants and then redrawing the plans and sections: "If you'd just agree that a long walk to the bath isn't drastic, there wouldn't be a problem."

Another aspect of conversational analysis concerns sequencing, which influences the interpretation of any single statement. By the time the clients bring up the subject of bathroom location for the fourth time and resort to absent authority ("the committee") for strength, the third architect realizes a new solution is unavoidable. Repetition of an issue, raising it first or last, indicates significance. Although meetings rarely appear to be the place where decisions are made, in this instance the third architect's actions are decisive, since, as the senior partner in charge, he officially acknowledges that a new solution is needed by sketching alternatives.

Early meetings are dominated by the client, who initially has the most information to impart. It is the client who initiates a discussion of limits and preferences in words and sometimes sketches or photographs, creating the framework with which the architect must contend. Later the encounters are dominated by the architect, who must explain and guide consideration of the design. With the mosque, the shift occurs after the third meeting between architect and client. In the first meeting, clients interviewed the architect; in the second meeting, they explained how the mosque and community center would be used. Because this project was highly condensed at the outset (for various reasons), the architect prepared preliminary schemes for the third meeting, concretely exposing his understanding of the clients' requirements. The basic form of architectural meetings—conversation about drawings or models that define a building—carries from the middle of schematics through the end of design development.

Before proceeding to an analysis of the explicit verbal interchange between design participants, I want to consider some special qualities of graphic dialogue.[12] In the initial encounters with the architect, clients often contribute visual images to guide the project. Some clients bring a sketch plan of their preliminary ideas about the future building and its spatial organization. Some, particularly residential clients, bring magazine photographs that portray the feeling, ambiance, materials, or style they prefer. One architect explains that she goes through architectural magazines with clients, flipping through rapidly to prevent the client from deciding on "one like that" or locking into anything specific. "I try to make it clear that picking and choosing is not in order. All I want is reactions; a good building isn't a collection of bits and pieces. It's hard to get clients to respond like this, but the more photos and drawings, the better. Then it's harder for them to pick and choose." Architects want to stay away from something like grocery shopping, in which clients select this kitchen, that window treatment, this entry, and those colors, with no notion of the overall composition.

The understanding one gains from looking at magazine photographs is ambiguous and reading the client's clipped photos and sketch plans is problematic. Consider the difficulty of reading the clients' images in the case of one client building himself a home. The three photos described here are a small fraction of the number the client brought his architects in the shoebox of clippings he collected over several years. Among these were Rockefeller's Japanese "villa," a woodbutcher, rough-sawn redwood house, and Noguchi's rehabilitated thirteenth-century samurai house. From the architect's viewpoint, few places could have been further apart in terms of sense and quality, yet the client saw some similarity among the settings. Although the architects concluded that the client liked natural wood interiors and a loosely "Japanese" aesthetic, it is easy to see that such an interpretation is highly ambiguous.

Architects contribute the lion's share of the graphic dialogue, starting with images of their past work, which speak constantly from the walls and model cases around the office. In early meetings, architects employ loose sketches to explore tentative visual ideas with the client. One architect explains that the advantage of a scribble sketch is to move from words to images, beginning with images that are non-specific. Since clients usually have little experience with visual conversation, architects are afraid they will misinterpret diagrammatic images as having greater specificity. By keeping sketches (or early models) murky, architects hope to raise issues or confirm impressions that will later inform the building design. Such drawings, while representing an approximate building to the architect, are easily misread by the client, setting a misleading direction for subsequent work. Plans, sections, and elevations, the conventional means to represent a building, are difficult images for most clients to interpret. Much of the talk surrounding such drawings is meant to clarify what is in the drawings, but in the mosque case, not until the architects drew perspective sketches did the clients grasp how the building would look. Models often serve the same function.

DESIGN TALK

The protocol of a complete meeting, selected in part for its brevity, will serve as an example for the remainder of this chapter. In the following three-person conversation over drawings, a recently hired kitchen consultant is being introduced to a project: the lodge of a new ski resort in Colorado. The architect has told the consultant a little about the project prior to the client's arrival. The project is well into design development, and the basic form of the lodge has been determined. The kitchen consultant is needed to make specific recommendations for the eating and cooking areas. The client, a wealthy restauranteur, is particularly concerned about this aspect of the lodge. Here, the client is trying to give the kitchen-man a sense of the basic intentions (the ambiance) without wasting any time (focus on "back of house"). (The numbers in the text refer to issues raised, and will be discussed later.)

CLIENT: I want to focus on "back of house." [To the kitchen consultant] Leon, take notes. I'd like to see a nice, generous door here [pointing to set of schematic drawings]. I want to be able to bake here, make our own breakfast breads, doughnuts, pastries. As a reference point, I'd like it to be like the NutTree—I can arrange for you to see that (1). I want to be able to warehouse some food items (2).

ARCHITECT: I think we should do that somewhere other than in this building (2).

CLIENT: We need a spacious storeroom (2). I want to stay away from frozen foods—I don't like frozen foods. We'll have fresh soups, poultry, salads. And I'd like a butcher shop operation (1).

ARCH: Can we fit all this in (2)?

CLIENT: As long as we have 50% in back-of-house operations (2).

KITCHEN CONSULTANT: So it's a hofbrau? With big twenty gallon pots of spaghetti? If we make chili, we make it from scratch, and there'll be charbroiling, maybe a rotisserie (1)?

CLIENT: Yes, yes (1).

ARCH: Let's show some of this cooking excitement. Maybe an opening through this wall . . . (3)

CLIENT: It can get pretty messy. We shouldn't open it up entirely (3).

ARCH: Well, maybe just a glimpse (3).

CLIENT: No, I don't think this is a good idea (3).

ARCH: Let's try it and see if it will work (3).

CLIENT: The food has to be assembled very quickly. This is good cooking but fast serving, like short order but with good food (1).

KIT CON: What about employee dining (4)?

ARCH: Daniel [the client] wants a nice one (4).

CLIENT: I don't want these people with our guests. We're going to treat our guests like luxury hotel guests. You don't find a bushoy getting his hair cut in the barber shop with Gerry Ford sitting in the next chair (1).

ARCH: Let's get back to the eating area. How about something like this [sketches basic adjacencies between circulation, employee dining, and service access] (4).

CLIENT: Yes, yes (4). [Client goes to make a phone call.]

KIT CON: I should give as much space as possible to food preparation and storage. Maybe we'll need a mezzanine; this is going to take up a lot of square footage (2).

CLIENT: I bet this is something no one's addressed: parking for employees should not be visible to guests. It makes them mad. I don't want this to get lost. [To the architect] Will you make a note of it (5)?

[Client announces he has to leave; some final discussion of tasks and responsibilities.]

An examination of this protocol reveals at least five different topics being discussed (noted in the dialogue above):

1
The looks and the ambiance of the lodge-dining, including the type of food

2
Food storage and the general square-footage requirements to which storage issues are tied

3
Opening cooking area to view

4
The nature of employee dining

5
The location of employee parking

From this brief excerpt, we glimpse the undulations of these topics throughout the conversation, like objects that keep bobbing back to the surface. Beyond reaching agreements on these issues, the general objective of a conversation like this one is mutual understanding (see Forester 1985). Here, the client wants all those who work with him to share his vision of the ski lodge as a luxury resort. He wants to assert who's boss, and he does so by laying out the topic for conversation ("back of house"), by assuming personal responsibility for positions (I don't like frozen foods; I don't want employees mixing with guests), by ignoring the conversation when he chooses (making phone call, cutting meeting short), and by telling the architect and the consultant to take notes on important issues. The architect also establishes his primary role in the threesome by speaking more frequently than the kitchen consultant, by speaking for the client, and by steering conversation ("Let's get back to . . ."). In some sense, this conversation is between the architect and the client, even though the meeting is called to brief the kitchen consultant, who speaks only three times. His introduction to the project is a vehicle for architect and client to realign themselves. There is a sense from this interchange that the kitchen consultant must learn to accompany the pas-de-deux between architect and client if he is to enter the stage.

The overall development of this conversation can be diagrammed as follows. First, someone lays out a starting point, after which discussion ensues about topics related to the general theme, proceeding with no immediately apparent logic. Topics are raised, dropped, ignored, reviewed, but few subjects are treated with any continuity; no issues are resolved. The speakers test whether they understand one another—

whether they have made sense of their situation together (Forester 1985).

In figure 5.12, the squares stand for turns taken in the conversation to raise a topic. By reading across rows, a topic can be traced through the conversation. The most general issue, for example, concerning ambiance and cooking style, is raised by the client repeatedly. Neither of the others pursues the subject, but even after they've gone on to another topic, the client will raise his chief concern again, an intermittent fixation.

Interchanges between participants in design follow a basic pattern of crescendos and interruptions. Various parties state their opinions, potential conflicts are revealed, challenges are sometimes issued. This is the crescendo, but it does not entail resolution. While the primary topic of conversation has moved to another subject, members of the discussion enter their final comments about the first issue, out of phase, as if they had needed time to think it over. The issue of square footage and storage, above, follows this pattern of concentrated consideration followed after an interruption by final words. In this particular case, the kitchen consultant, much later in the conversation, summarizes his sense of the storage/square-footage issue and how he will respond to the problem. The issue of opening the kitchen to public view embodies another pattern: here, architect and client doggedly stick to and express their positions in disagreement. The last topic, employee parking, is a "bomb" that the client drops with no further discussion.

DECISIONS, AGREEMENT, AND SENSE MAKING

We might assume that progress in this system is advanced by decisions taken in the meetings among participants, yet decisions in design dialogue are difficult to trace. Though one might expect an issue to be raised, debated, and decided, this is not common. In the above analysis, an issue is raised, discussed, a related issue is raised, then a third, and none is decided—some are not even debated—as participants try to make mutual sense of the situation.

Since design conversations, unlike a debate or a bargain, are not clear win-lose situations or decisive settings, power in the situation is gained through subtle means. Controlling the conversation is one means of gaining tremendous authority in design. Above, the client raises three issues (1, 2, 5), while the architect and the kitchen consultant raise only one topic each (3 and 4, respectively). Another means of gaining authority is to challenge the other participants. In this passage, the architect finds three ways to challenge the client: first, move food warehousing to another building; second, show the food preparation; and third, make the employee dining area "nice." The last case is the most interesting, since the client never mentions that he wants the employee area to be nice, only that he wants it separate from the

Ski Lodge Conversation

Topic 1: Ambiance

Topic 2: Storage & Sq. Ft.

Topic 3: View to Cooking

Topic 4: Employee Dining

Topic 5: Employee Parking

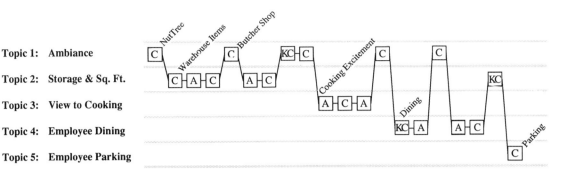

5.12 Ski Lodge Conversation. C = Client, A = Architect, KC = Kitchen Consultant.

guests' dining. The architect makes his statement "Jim wants a nice one" somewhat unrefutable, since Jim is unlikely to admit he wants an ugly dining room for the employees. This is a subtle means of manipulating the client, through dialogue, into a position that is actually the architect's.

The obvious question this portrayal of design conversation raises is: When and where then do design decisions occur? An architect will likely say that this uncertainty only confirms the fact that design decisions take place at the architect's drawing board, away from clients and consultants, but this view is too simplistic. Looking back at the protocol, we can uncover future decisions embedded in the statements: for example, the client is likely to remain convinced that the lodge will be a luxury setting, with fresh food, and that guests and staff will be separated. Each of these is a position (not a decision) with spatial implications. The meeting is an important place for actors to display their positions and to understand the positions of the others, and it is only in light of the collected positions that the emergent order of the design is revealed. In the section of the conversation where the architect displays a determination to open the kitchen to view, the client counters with his own preference. The architect verbally adjusts his physical solution accordingly—rather than a view, a glimpse of the kitchen. The architect stubbornly maintains his position, risking a minor dispute but at the same time acting with conviction. Another comment from each concludes the discussion of this issue and a tacit agreement is drawn that the architect will explore the idea, since the client chooses not to add a final word. Such tacit agree ments are far more common in architectural dialogue than explicit decisions, but they accomplish the same basic purpose of constructing progress.

Another characteristic of design conversation is apparent in the protocol above: the linked nature of issues can be seen. For example, one position is used as a litmus test for subsequent issues, as when the architect demonstrates a kind of never-say-die attitude about the view into the kitchen even when the client quite clearly disagrees. It is nearly impossible to find an issue in architecture that is not linked to many others. This is one primary reason why decisions are not simple, and are rarely made directly in meetings.

We can categorize the collective, though undecisive, movement of conversation under several headings. First, certain issues are emergent, such as the feel of the place or the nature of employee dining. They will not be determined in a single meeting but will emerge over time, as a series of understandings modified by new information and opinions. Second, there are straightforward issues that could be settled quickly but are not for various reasons (parties prefer biding time to compromise; the issue is linked to others that actors do not want to predetermine; the implications are unclear). Third, an issue is raised and an agreement is reached not about the solution, but about how to approach the problem. Agreements then can be methodological or substantial, linked or independent, emergent or simple.

There are certain points in a conversation when someone attempts to bring all participants together in understanding, as when an example is raised. Hack and Canto (1984) suggest that three types of exemplars bridge barriers of perspective and experience among participants in a design project: literal examples (the NutTree), analogies (like a luxury hotel), and metaphors (it's a hofbrau). There is no intention of reproducing the example exactly, whether it be a luxury hotel or the NutTree (a roadside attraction with homemade candy, bread, and other goods). But together the examples help the client paint an approximate picture of his mental image of the ski lodge. The examples are like mental drawings, or clients' photo clippings and sketch plans. They are intended to make explicit and clarify otherwise vague conversation about spatial entities.

The other primary means to establish mutual sense of the situation is to play out a possible life in the building. Playing out the life of a building entails imagining people acting in the future environment— a typical day at the future office, a party at the future house, lunch hour at the future school. In the above transcript, the client plays out a possible future that he does not want to occur: a bus boy gets his hair cut in the barber chair next to Gerald Ford. Such an example is used effectively because it not only incorporates physical place (as do literal examples like that of the NutTree) but also actors and events. Such imaginal theatre is very common in the early stages of a project, when there are no drawings to describe things that cannot be described verbally, and even afterward as a means of understanding further implications of the drawings, making something abstract more tangible.

The purpose of examining conversation in architectural practice is to see how the social context influences progress toward a design solution. In architecture, with the exception of idle talk, all conversation, both verbal and visual, is aimed at developing the final design solution. Yet little structure and order are manifest in the meetings between architects, clients, and consultants. These meetings do, however, have an order, though it is not one of logic and decision making—the material being considered is too complex and dynamic. The participants cannot decide on something they are actually in the process of creating. Instead, there is a subtle yet powerful structuring of relations between people who work together to create the building, within the architect's own office, and between architect and client. The constellation of individuals, as they make sense of each others' requirements and desires, moves toward a specific scheme that will be mutually agreeable.

The meetings between architects and clients, and the firms in which architects practice, are the primary components of the social milieu of design. That social milieu exerts certain influences upon the developing design solution. Now it is appropriate to ask whether those influences have a positive or negative affect on the building's final form. Can design be a social art *and* create excellent architecture?

Everyone has heard the well-worn joke that a camel is a horse designed by a committee. Behind it lies an accusation that has implications for architectural practice. In the past five chapters, I have analyzed a number of patterns demonstrating the extent to which design is a social art. If we recall Briggs's (1927) statement that every building of merit has a single architectural genius behind it, then by implication those buildings of lesser quality (the camels) must have committees and organizations as their makers. This chapter directly confronts the conventional wisdom that collaborative design processes produce a lesser architecture. By looking into the evolution of several exceptional buildings, we will see whether a single genius or a committee was responsible.

To consider design as a social act does not deny the role of the individual nor the individual methods that have been documented in prior research. Indeed, every collective process in architecture is made up of individuals representing the architects, clients, consultants, regulatory bodies, and sometimes the occupants. In each project the weight of the various roles differs, except that architect and client remain central to the process. These participants will be the focus of the case study inquiries.

DEFINING EXCELLENCE   If we want to examine the underlying social processes out of which excellent buildings arise, then we need to start with a definition of excellence. According to the most popular management theory in architecture today, a firm can do good work in various ways: it can be strong in ideas, service, or delivery (Coxe et al. 1986, 1987). The Coxe Group also distinguishes the "business centered practice" from the "practice centered business," which differ primarily in terms of the bottom line, the former's being quantitative while the latter's is qualitative. One feature shared by management literature and the professional organizations is that they take as their object the delivery of services, rather than the services delivered. Within the everyday world of architectural practice, doing good work implies more than making a profit (quantitative bottom line) or feeling good (qualitative)—it also means designing good buildings. This shift in focus is central to my analysis of the cases that follow.

The architectural management field has exploded over the past two decades, growing from virtual nonexistence into a blossoming discipline in its own right. A review of the literature indicates that architects have faced the same problems since the profession was born: getting and handling clients, making money, running an office, doing good work—with new dilemmas occasionally added to the list, such as liability. There is an abundance of writing, but not theory, on marketing, management, and legal issues, all of which has arisen out of law and business and not from architecture itself. An extensive review of the literature reveals a big gap in our knowledge: doing good work has not been studied systematically.[1]

When *In Search of Excellence* was published in 1982, the book's potential applicability to architecture seemed promising. From their study of America's best-run corporations, Peters and Waterman extracted a number of principles that these organizations shared that offered guidance for others struggling to improve. A stream of related texts followed this first look at corporate excellence. Some commentators declared that the corporations held up as excellent models were not so excellent after all, others celebrated "passionately" excellent examples.[2] The idea of learning about excellence from the best practitioners has contributed significantly to the burgeoning management literature. Are any of Peters and Waterman's principles at the core of excellent architectural practice, or do the profession's special qualities suggest yet another set of guidelines? Or, as architects often argue, perhaps each architectural firm and project is unique, thereby defying the sweeping generalizations that Peters and Waterman and their successors were confident enough to make about corporate America. It was obvious that much more remained to be known about architectural practice and its excellent firms.

The design quality debate is a controversial issue. Rather than take on the philosophical question of whether design quality can ever be absolutely determined, I define design quality as a phenomenological entity perceived by individuals, not as an inherent quality of the object or building. Thus, design quality is dependent upon those who make the judgment of quality. I maintain there are three principal evaluators of any building's quality and these are the consumers or the public at large, the participants in the design process, and the architectural profession. For present purposes, an excellent building is one perceived to be excellent by all three of these groups.[3]

Determining whether a building is appreciated by all three groups of evaluators is obviously quite complicated. Most ambiguous is the public perception of quality, since there is no single group representing the public, which encompasses visitors, regulatory agencies, many occupants, neighbors, and so on. Without conducting a full-scale post occupancy evaluation, however, it is possible to use a variety of indicators to point to public appreciation. These depend upon the project, but include the general response of the lay press, community reaction, number of visitors, reports from staff, leasability, and so on. In the case of the San Juan Capistrano Library, for example, the librarian tells stories that indicate how popular the building is with the community: more library cards issued than citizens in the community, the use of the library for weddings, the high number of building tours given each year, and income generated from renting the auditorium. It is important to note that positive public response to a building does not isolate design quality, if by that we mean an aesthetic evaluation of physical form, but takes a holistic perspective that includes need, function, management, fashion, and location.

Next is the problem of determining the opinions of participants in the design process. Compared to the public, evaluations by client, architect, and consultant are simpler to determine if we rely on their self-stated reports of satisfaction. However, the client and the architect are usually organizations, comprised of many individuals with very different opinions; key members of client and architect groups must, therefore, be singled out. Besides self-reports, there are additional indicators of the maker's evaluations: whether architect, client, and consultant have worked together on subsequent projects, if there have been post-construction technical problems, if the occupants have made alterations to the building, and if the client has recommended the architect to others.

Lastly, the profession's evaluation of quality is distinct from that of the actors or the public at large, and perhaps the closest to what is commonly meant by "design quality." Again, a number of measures can capture the professional assessment of design quality, but the most important are publications and awards in the professional press. While one article about a building is no evidence of excellence, there are some buildings which are published in nearly all the major journals, and receive several awards. These are the projects to which the profession attributes high design quality, and when the buildings are also well-liked by their makers and the public, then they would be called excellent in this study.[4]

It is my observation that the professional evaluation of quality, not the public's or the maker's, is challenged by the conception of design as a social act. When architects argue that great buildings are designed by creative individuals, working in relative isolation as an artist might work, they refer to those buildings that are generally accepted as great within the profession—those widely published, included in critical architectural histories, taught in the schools, and awarded prizes. This study confronts that common belief about the design process underlying highly regarded works of architecture.

To determine the social processes underlying design quality, I decided to undertake a set of three case studies focusing on excellent buildings rather than architects or practices. Based on the evaluative criteria above, the selection of case studies was a complex matter. To qualify as a case study at all, the buildings had to be widely published in professional journals and recipients of professional awards, as well as liked by their makers and by the public. Thus evaluations of all these groups needed to be known prior to conducting the study. I also wanted to capture the widest possible range of excellence within architectural practice, which meant selecting projects that differed dramatically. The variety I sought included architectural office size and organization, building type, and client type.[5] The three projects selected were: the Bergren House by Morphosis architects (1986), the San Juan Capistrano Library by Michael Graves (1983), and the Monterey Bay Aquarium by Esherick Homsey Dodge and Davis (1984). All publications about these buildings were collected, folllowed by visits to the buildings and interviews with key participants, including the primary architect and client.[6]

This concluding study, like any other, is prone to certain biases and distortions. Projects in this study are confined to California, albeit different regions; if significant differences in design excellence are distributed geographically, they will not be uncovered by this work. There are also no developer or corporate clients in the cases, so there is no information about their particular status as excellent clients. Likewise there are no buildings of certain common types: those with repetitive units (as with high-rise offices or housing), those where the clients' money really matters and strict economic constraints are imposed (as with low cost housing and private investment property), and those built on speculation, although relevant recent studies indicate no significant differences from the present findings.[7] Another concern is the architect's financial record: I do not have reliable information about the cost of services relative to fee. Finally, negative issues were under-reported in the interviews, and all reported material is distorted to appear more positive. All these case studies confound aspiration with actuality, creating a problem of validity.

In the following pages, I examine several buildings that are excellent by many standards and that most certainly exhibit a high degree of design quality. These buildings each have their own underlying social process, which can be described and analyzed to characterize their making. The question posed is: What is the intricate, underlying human equation out of which excellent buildings arise? (See Kostof 1970:60.)

BERGREN HOUSE/VENICE III

Venice, a small coastal town in the Los Angeles basin, is known as a free-spirited community in which roller skaters, art dealers, homeless people, body builders, and chic westside yuppies co-reside. On a modest residential street lined with bungalows, some strange canvas contraptions peek over the ridge of a 1920s house belonging to Ann Bergren, a classics professor at UCLA. There behind the house is the three-level, 800-square-foot addition known as the Bergren House or Venice III.[8] It was designed by Morphosis, a small firm (generally under ten people) headed by two principals, Michael Rotondi and Thom Mayne. The two architects do not specialize within the office and the design for any project is the work of both. With firms so structured, there is always great speculation as to who actually does the design, reflecting the belief that only one architect really designs any one project. For this building, both Mayne and Rotondi worked on the design; then because of the limited budget, Rotondi and the client together acted as the owner-builder, he directing construction and she doing the accounting.

The project has been widely published in the major architectural journals, winning a prestigious citation in the 1985 *Progressive Architecture* awards and a National Honor Award from the American Institute of Architects. Bergren herself even wrote an article about the building for *House and Garden*, describing the house and the relation between her house and her work. As for her role in the project, she states, "All I wanted was for Michael and Thom to build what they wanted to, and they did" (Bergren 1986:128). In our interview she continued:

Potential clients come to visit me all the time, so I do this little spiel, and I say just this, that the key moment was this moment in which I saw their [Mayne and Rotondi's] work disembodied from anything and recognized it, and that was an authorial moment. That's why I got this thing that was so quintessentially theirs and yet reflective of myself at the same time. . . . The initial choice of them is the authorial moment, because you're authoring your own thing by choosing people who, if they do what they want, will give you what you want. That's the key to it. And then you stay out of it, because you're not the architect.

Bergren implies that she removed herself from the process, but that isn't exactly the case. She says at one point, "I have the feeling that I did nothing, that I had nothing to do with the design of it at all, but I know that Michael and Thom have said to other people that I was very active." Rotondi contends that she was an active and valuable contributor. Perhaps what is most striking about Bergren is that she is intrigued with architecture beyond function. Her strongest contribution to the design was her constant challenge to the architects: they

6.1 Bergren House/Venice III. View from the street showing bungalow at front of site with Morphosis addition behind.

6.2 Bergren House/Venice III. Plans.

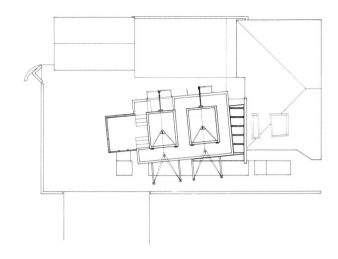

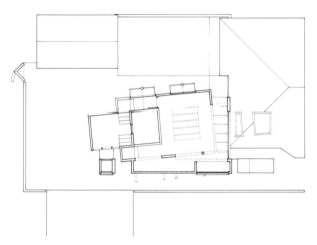

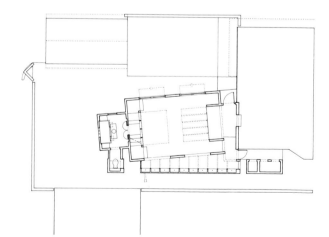

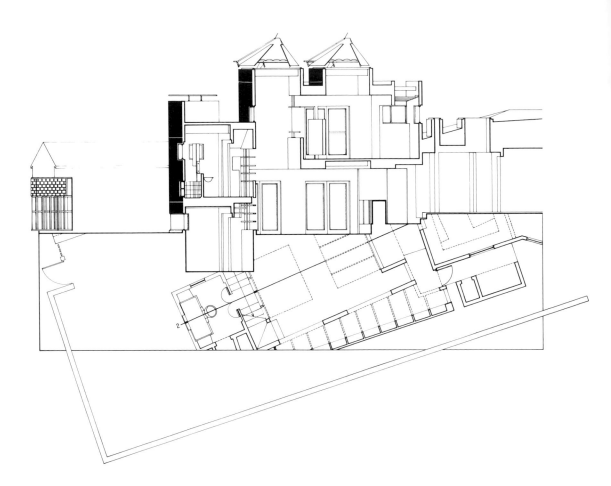

6.3 Bergren House/Venice III.
Section with plan (bungalow is
at right).

must do their best work. Clearly, her intense interest in architecture, in understanding it, learning about it, made her an active participant in the design process.

With such close cooperation between architects and clients, it might be assumed that they shared a specific notion about what the building ought to be—a common vision. In spite of the client's intense interest in the architect's reading of the building, architect and client perceive Venice III very differently, correlating to the different roles the building plays in each participant's life. The architect explains that the building was seminal in the development of his own work, and moreover, in his thinking about design.

For us, this work is seminal in the body of our work. Some projects are transitional, some projects are generative. . . . It allowed us to explore ideas in a way that we hadn't to that point. We discovered things that we hadn't discovered yet. The house once again showed us the power of architecture as an idea and that you can convey ideas regardless of the size or the scope of a project. . . . Specifically, it allowed us to explore sequential movement in a way that we hadn't before. It was very processional. It allowed us to deal with the relationship between a visual axis and an organizational axis (as opposed to one of movement), which had to do with the rational ordering systems that we lay on the world in order to comprehend the world, but then beyond that, the circumstance of everyday life. . . . We had an objective to set up certain datums through the building that would allow you, as you move through it in a circumstantial way, to understand that it was ordered in a very specific way.

By contrast, the client has a romantic view of the building, and a very personal view. She makes a remarkable statement to dramatize how strongly she feels about the building: "The building is such that somebody living in it every day is taught just exactly what he said, and experiences it over and over again. And there's an additional thing . . . which comes from the experience of living in it, and that is that if you've ever had the fantasy of perpetual pleasure, of having the perfect mother there to give you everything you ever want or need, every protection, every warmth, every pleasure, every everything, the building does that."

This kind of hyperbolic statement is not as uncommon as one might think. Sophisticated clients who work with well-known architects they admire, and who end up with buildings they very much like, sometimes express this extraordinary degree of adulation.

The collaborative spirit between architect and client was strong with Venice III. When asked if their architect-client relation would continue indefinitely, Bergren replied "As long as they're alive and not too busy, I would certainly consult with them before I did anything to the building (*laughing*): I don't have the shoes of the building shined without consulting them, because it's our piece." Rotondi added, "The way we figure it, we have joint custody." Out of this intimate collabo-

CHAPTER 6

6.4 Bergren House/Venice III. Living room looking toward lower level study and bath at middle of stairs.

6.5 Bergren House/Venice III. View of bedroom and skylights (beneath canopies visible in figure 6.1).

ration, we can distinguish the unconventional from the more common. Giving the building anthropomorphic qualities, its own life, and employing the metaphor of the house as child, are not unusual expressions. That the child is held in joint custody, however, meaning that architect and client both admit an ongoing role in the life of the building, *is* unconventional, and reflects the intense relationships on which this building is based.

Money was problematic throughout the project because it was in short supply. When asked about this, Rotondi replied: "We put a lot of time into the project, and instead of taking a fee (Ann was spending as much as she could), what we were investing into it was our time. She provided the land. Basically, she said, here's my back yard, do something with it. It wasn't a project that you do for business reasons. It's the kind of project that you do when you want to finally live the way you imagine an architect should live." The last sentence captures the ethos of this project, and the ideals that the architect holds. Those ideals include design freedom, total involvement in the entire process, but not profit. Although the architects did not make money on this project, its wide publicity and the client's writings about the work may have long-term, lucrative consequences. Also, it should be remembered that Morphosis is a successful firm by many measures: they have received a tremendous amount of recognition, they have a talented professional staff working in the office, and they have attracted good commissions, increasing in scale. It may be that "taking a bath" on an excellent project, while difficult in the short run, is a reasonable long-term strategy. This resembles the principle of the loss leader, where something is sold at a loss in order to attract customers.

Regarding the process of making this building, both architect and client say they are still working on it. Design took about a year, as did construction, and now the participants are spending another year fine-tuning the project and completing "punch list" items (unfinished or unacceptable work in a building). Throughout the first two years they met frequently. Very early on Bergren was tentative until the architects presented six study models and convinced her to actually go ahead with the project. They began by getting all the functional matters well in hand, according to Rotondi: "We'd show models and drawings. We'd analyze a plan that was based on function, and then [we] reached a point, I remember, when the conversations extended from the necessities of resolving the problems of programming to discussing the ideas that were in the building." In this process the architects assured the client that her fundamental requirements were considered before moving explicitly into the more conceptual development of the building, which as Rotondi states, was always there. This wasn't a mirroring of the client's requirements, as might be inferred. Again,

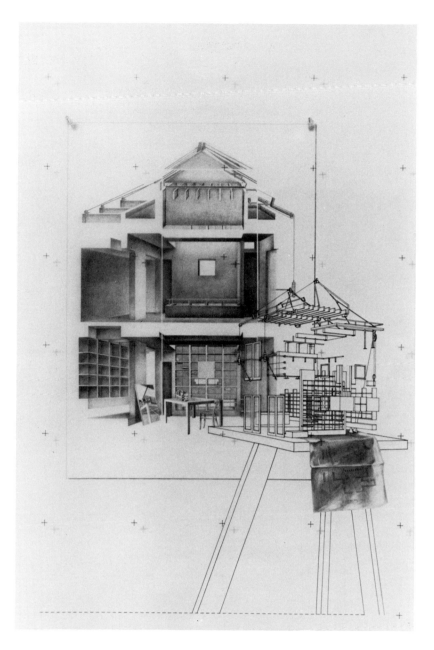

6.6 Bergren House/Venice III.
Analytic rendering.

EXCELLENT PRACTICE

6.7 San Juan Capistrano
Library. Aerial view.

Rotondi: "We would say, 'We have these spaces; this is how they function,' making sure that everything was in there, but it was never purely functional. We would describe how we thought the house would be used, because it certainly wasn't exactly the way Ann had imagined it." What should be noted is the specific deviation from the stereotypical process: the architect begins with function, but not in a conventional manner, since he *adds* to the client's requirements his own conception of a living house to be occupied imaginatively. These conceptions of the future life within the house are part of the scheme from its earliest manifestation, guiding the fundamental organization of space (related to Rotondi's earlier discussion of procession and organizational axes).

The Venice III project carries out a complex conceptual order with great integrity, something that may have been possible because of the relatively simple context for decision making. With only three primary actors and two other young architects who helped to build the project, there was a relatively direct way to handle even complex problems.

SAN JUAN CAPISTRANO LIBRARY

About sixty miles south of Los Angeles is San Juan Capistrano, a small city generally known for just two things: the swallows that keep coming back each year and the Mission. For centuries the Mission has been the heart of the city, which grew rapidly in recent years from a farming community to a commuter suburb of Los Angeles. At a time when old-timers were squaring off with hordes of newcomers, the new city planning department decided to sponsor a design competition for a public library, with aspirations for a work of architecture that could hold its own with the nearby Mission. This was a shift from the local concerns of a sleepy little town to dreams of something much greater. From an impressive group of finalists that included Charles Moore and Robert A. M. Stern, the scheme by Michael Graves was selected in 1981. Three years later, in December of 1983, the city of San Juan Capistrano and the county of Orange opened the doors to their new library, which remained true to the competition scheme, except for the location of the doors themselves. Although initially controversial, Graves's design has become the darling of the city.

This project is interesting in light of the last case, for like the Bergren house the library has received much acclaim from the profession through awards and numerous publications, but it is even better loved by the clients and community. This is possible because the library is a public building, while Venice III is private. The clients differ dramatically: a single individual with private funds, as distinguished from a set of organizationally complex public entities with public funds. In contrast to Morphosis, where two architects with a small

firm share credit for design, Michael Graves is the classic hero-
architect who does all the design, supported by a large staff—about
fifty-five people at the time of this study. Finally, the close relationship between Bergren and Morphosis contrasts with the distant dealings between the library clients in southern California and Graves in
Princeton, New Jersey. Naturally, these distinctions contributed to
fundamental differences between the two projects' evolution, yet there
remain similarities all the more remarkable for their contrasting
origins.

In a discussion with six of the lead representatives of the various
client organizations, it became abundantly clear that they believe the
library is a prominent chapter not only in the history of San Juan, but
also in their own lives. Emily Jackson, the head librarian, is filled with
stories demonstrating the place's significance:

> The first thing I noticed was that the chain-link fence got beaten
> down while [the library] was still being built. There were all these
> people coming in to see it before it was open and that was exciting.
> The painter had his paint chips stolen twice and we had a full set of
> plans disappear. Yes, there was controversy in the community, but al-
> ready we knew something special was happening here. . . . The kids
> kept haunting us, wanting to come in. The first time we let them in
> they were so excited, they said, "This is like Disneyland" (*laughter*). It
> was the only exotic, exciting location they could think of to compare
> it to. It looked kind of like a fairy tale place. . . . There have been 30
> to 40 weddings here. . . . We've had this incredible number of volun-
> teer hours just because people like to be here, like to work here, and
> want to feel a part of it. . . . Physically, we [who work here] find
> ourselves less tired at the end of the day here than when we occasion-
> ally have to work at another branch; maybe it's the light, the colors,
> I don't know what. People from all over the world and all over the
> country know about the library in San Juan Capistrano and that gives
> the people here a lot of pride.

The pride that these individuals feel swells as they talk about the
building. Steve Julian, the city manager, says, "In your public career,
you don't always have the opportunity to do something different, and
to have that chance is a lot of fun." The head of county libraries who
was instrumental to the project's success, Elizabeth Martinez-Smith,
adds, "You're right. It's the only building I've wanted my name on."
This sense of ownership, fundamental to privately developed projects,
may be unusual for public undertakings, but common to those that are
excellent.

The clients are amused by the fact that Michael Graves refers to
it as "my library" (in a recent magazine article), but also pleased, because their respect for Graves is great. They seem to take special pleasure in the fact that they have a personal relationship with someone
so well known, but they make clear that they did not follow the master's wishes unquestioningly, and in fact successfully argued their own

positions. The assistant city manager and local historian, Pamela Gibson Hallerin, said, "[I] sat in the office next to Steve [the city manager], and heard him on many occasions talking to Michael in rather loud tones (*all laugh*). . . . [But] Steve never told him what he should do, he just said, this isn't going to work from a practical point of view, we need to have a change. Michael then was free to change it in the way he saw fit." The library client was a complex entity, made up of both county and city representatives, and the clients themselves admit they weren't always sure just who the client was. Nevertheless, an informal division of coordinated labor arose among them, with Julian, the city manager, designated the point man to negotiate with Graves, Raymundo Becerra, from the city planning office, as the design expert, and Martinez-Smith making sure the county did not put up any roadblocks. There were also problems arising from the particular situation. Since Graves was only one person, working a long way from Capistrano, he sent people from his office to manage the project in his absence. These functionaries were anything but popular with the clients. Unlike Graves, who could respond immediately and authoritatively to their requests, the project architect tended to be less flexible, defending Graves's original ideas. The city manager articulately expressed the group's feelings about the architects' representatives:

I think because of their "follower complex," they really couldn't conceive that anybody would question what the architect was doing, [especially] us mere civilians (*all laugh*). . . . All of us made real distinctions between Michael and Michael's staff. All of us took delight in working with Michael; with the staff it wasn't the same. The staff people weren't as curious—Michael's a pretty thoughtful person. In the magazines he's always portrayed as the egotist, and he certainly has a big ego, but he's a very soft person and pleasant to be around. He's intellectually curious and pulls things out of you in terms of what you want. There was a tension that existed between Michael and myself and a lot of that was created because his staff played this interpretive role. But interestingly enough, I think the tension produced some good results.

Graves managed to keep his distance, geographically and otherwise, from the day-to-day problems that arose, and yet was able to resolve problems the project architect brought back to the solitude of his Princeton office. When I asked Graves whether this was an intentional strategy, he said he was not conscious of it at the time, but since the work on the library he has seen how effective a strategy it might be. On a big project, a particularly powerful client uses the tactic himself: "[He tells people below him, 'You go negotiate the fee.' So that when he meets me at the ballet, he can say, 'There've been no problems—it's so wonderful working together.' And everybody's happy and just like brothers and it's just terrific. I hadn't realized that [way of working] until quite recently." The distance between the architect and the site was problematic, but Graves thinks less so than in other projects, because from the competition the clients had "this artifact of the building in hand: a model and drawings from which they could discuss whatever was important to them."[9] Problems of distance were also overcome by the fact that on-site affairs were managed by the structural engineer, Bob Lawson, a key local consultant highly respected by everyone involved. The problems engendered by Graves's assistants stem from the fact that Graves maintains singular design control over the work in his office. "In my practice, I'm the principal designer of all the projects, and the character of all the schemes is given by me. I have a real interest in it, unlike a larger or another kind of firm where there are partners and if A can't go to the meeting, B does. I go to the meetings." This way of working offers an advantage and a disadvantage with regard to decision making: Graves's singular control creates the possibility of an intimate, one-to-one relation with the client that smooths out decisions for a coherent project, but he cannot delegate authority to anyone else in the office, and in fact, cannot go to all the meetings.

There is one feature of the building that has been faulted by numerous critics: the entry to the building off the long gallery axis, as proposed in the competition scheme, was shifted to the less dominant, less dramatic axis of the reading rooms (compare figures 6.8 and 6.9). Such problems can teach more about excellence than things done well and approved by all. There are conflicting stories from the architect and clients about how this evolved, but everyone agrees it was initiated by the clients. The new placement of the entry, according to the clients, was requested for functional reasons and presented no problem for Graves. "He was able to modify that elevation, that entrance, but he still maintained the basic principle about how a building is organized on axis on all the series of rooms. It wasn't just shifting the entrance anyplace." Graves, on the other hand, remembers no functional rationale for moving the entry. He believes that decision, which caused the complete reworking of that side of the building, was a detriment to the project. He tells this story, similar to the one told by the clients, about the compromise:

There's a wonderful story. We were meeting in the then city hall and it was the time when they were talking about the central axis or the side axis which was so dominant in the building, and we had solved that problem. I had lost [the axis debate] and one other minor point came up which we were discussing. Everything got very quiet, and the table started to shake, and the light fixture started to shake. It was my first earthquake but I didn't know it, so I hadn't noticed that everything had gotten very quiet. It was my turn to say something, and they said, "Michael, will you just be quiet, we're having an earthquake and if you can produce one of these every time you're intent on a point, you can have the point."

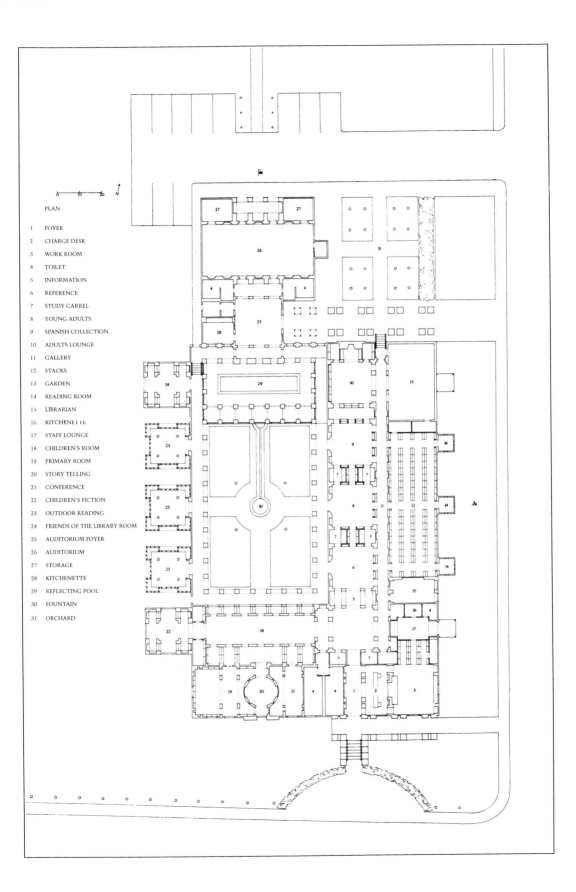

PLAN

1   FOYER
2   CHARGE DESK
3   WORK ROOM
4   TOILET
5   INFORMATION
6   REFERENCE
7   STUDY CARREL
8   YOUNG ADULTS
9   SPANISH COLLECTION
10   ADULTS LOUNGE
11   GALLERY
12   STACKS
13   GARDEN
14   READING ROOM
15   LIBRARIAN
16   KITCHENETTE
17   STAFF LOUNGE
18   CHILDREN'S ROOM
19   PRIMARY ROOM
20   STORY TELLING
21   CONFERENCE
22   CHILDREN'S FICTION
23   OUTDOOR READING
24   FRIENDS OF THE LIBRARY ROOM
25   AUDITORIUM FOYER
26   AUDITORIUM
27   STORAGE
28   KITCHENETTE
29   REFLECTING POOL
30   FOUNTAIN
31   ORCHARD

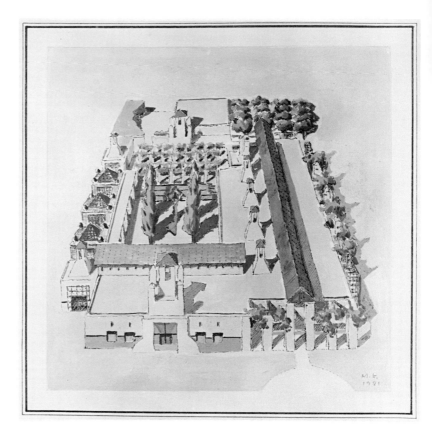

6.9 San Juan Capistrano Library. Early perspective rendering, showing long gallery axis oriented to building entry (shown by dark roof at right). Compare to aerial photo and plan (figures 6.7 and 6.8) where entry has been shifted to the left.

6.10 San Juan Capistrano Library. The gallery axis through building.

Graves said he lost the debate because one client was intent on the reading room axis and would not consider alternatives. The story, having become something of a legend in the building's evolution, indicates the intensity of the argument, and symbolizes the significance both architect and client place on the negotiations. While there are gaps in the facts, it is my interpretation that this was one case where the clients demanded a specific design solution instead of presenting an issue to be resolved with the architect.[10] The solution had no apparent negative effects on the public's or clients' assessment of design quality, but lowered the project in the eyes of the profession, if written criticism is the measure.

With the San Juan Capistrano Library, as in the prior case, architect and client perceive the basic strengths of the building in different terms. The clients talk about the building standing strong in relation to the Mission, healing rifts between county and city, newcomer and old-timer. They talk of the excitement people feel in the place, the light, the low-anxiety atmosphere. There is another oft-told story about the building that the librarian recounts, which captures something of the clients' evaluation of the place:

The first thing that happened that made me realize what kind of public response we were going to have was when this woman came and said "Could I please come in?" (just before it opened). She walked in and she started to cry and she said, "This building is so beautiful, it makes me feel wonderful." I think people are really starved for beautiful buildings. For me, that's the strength of the building, is how it makes people feel. It inspires people. I don't think it's just a good building or a nice building, I think it's a great building.

This story has the same exaggerated overtones as Bergren's comparison of her house to the nurturing mother. Such comments are extreme because they reflect the depth of emotion clients feel about their buildings.

The architect, on the other hand, has a relatively objectified view of the building's strengths, rather than an emotional, experiential, or political one. Graves says:

What was important to me was the courtyard—the idea that you could have all these disparate parts from the children's wing, to the adult wing, to the auditorium, to a fourth side that wasn't to be completely built out but would give them room for expansion later, which we're doing now. (We're building a new building on the gazebo side that's just in preliminary drawings now [1988].) I was interested in the quality of light that you could get in a library both from top light and from the side that would be filtered by virtue of the courtyard. . . . The precedent was already there, in the Mission—not a stylistic preference on my part but a model for gathering the various parts of the Mission together, from the church to the chapel to the refectory to the sleeping quarters. All of those were gathered around a central place and that seemed to make a lot of sense to me.

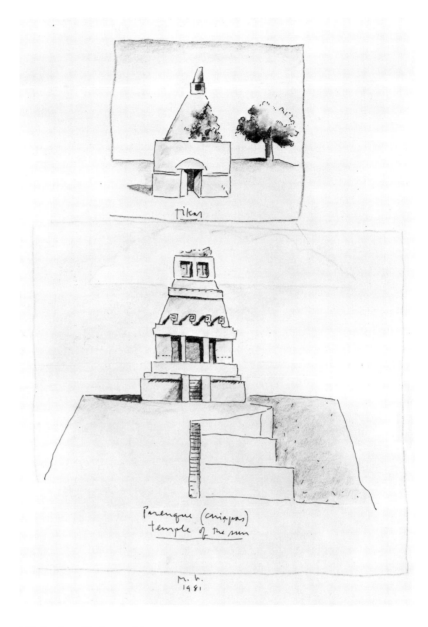

Tikal

Palenque (chiapas)
temple of the sun

m. b.
1981

6.11 San Juan Capistrano Library. Referential sketches of Tikal and Palenque.

6.12 San Juan Capistrano Library. View of the courtyard.

While each reads the building by highlighting the same elements such as light and courtyard, the similarity ends there. Again, these contrasting images of the building developed in complementary rather than conflicting ways, and once constructed, the building fulfills both visions.

Was the San Juan Capistrano Library not only a successful building, but a successful business proposition? Graves is vague: "I don't know. If you asked a lawyer, 'Did you lose money on this?' he would say 'absolutely.' But I probably didn't put any of my personal time in the mix of money, so all of that was free. If I can live, and if I can buy the groceries, then I'm fine, or if I can pay college tuition, then I'm okay. But making money is another thing. If we can buy this building (where the office is), put a new toilet in—everything like that becomes an issue for us because we're not rich."

Graves avoids a strict businesslike approach to his architectural projects and to the running of his office. Instead, he adopts a genteel pragmatist's attitude: he is not trying to "make money" per se, but to pay for the necessities of daily life. When I asked about his unusual and widely discussed appearance in a magazine advertisement for shoes, he said, "For all the people who say 'You shouldn't have done it,' I have to tell you that it paid for my daughter's wedding. And, it's not immoral. Therefore, I'd do it again." Which he may, for American Express and a sum of $25,000. This is not exactly a business plan, as I pointed out.

We don't have a marketing plan at all, except to say yes or no to the things that come in. We have never gone out to get anything—not because that was the plan, it's just that there hasn't been time to do that. . . . If we get an RFP today in the mail, Karen [the marketing person, de facto, for architecture] will come to me and say, "Do you want to go after this museum in Tucson? Here's the rap: you have to have a local architect, it's $30 million, its schedule is that, you have to go for three meetings, you have to do this and that. Should we go after it?" I'll say yes or no. If that's a plan, that's as serious as it gets. But it isn't: "The fees will be that; we will make X dollars; we will operate in a way that will net the office [so much]." Maybe we should, but as long as we can stay above that we will.

It's not quite as frivolous as that because as the office gets older, and the people in it get older, we want them to stay desperately. [We] want the office more or less as it is, with the kind of talent we've got. . . . And if somebody makes X dollars with me and can get 2X across the street, then it becomes very real to me. If that person is very valuable to me, I've got to make sure that the office makes enough money so that that person isn't going to make just 2X, but 2X plus something. . . . You have to have continuity. You can't afford to have people come and go.

Like other "good" professionals, architects think it impolite to discuss their desire to make a profit. Just as Rotondi says he put in his time for free and lived "as an architect should live," Graves wants to "stay above" an income-oriented business plan. Both express the belief that good work and a profit motive are incompatible.[11] But the concerns Graves raises also make a strong connection between doing good work and fees earned (translated into salaries and office improvements). It seems, given the continuing life and growth of Michael Graves's office, that he is in fact managing his practice well. In spite of his apparently casual attitude, he employs two people to run the business side of his practice, one for architecture, the other for products. He is engaged in a range of activities, from appearing in the ad, to the design of teapots, to high-rise buildings, to giving public lectures. Michael Graves is a study in contrasts, for just as he nudges a dog aside and cleans a place for a visitor to sit in his cluttered personal office, one realizes he has an intercom that connects him to all the ongoing activities in the large, rambling building his firm occupies. In his blue workshirt and cords, he tells you exactly how much he makes with the sale of each teapot, and how the manufacturer could do better marketing. This tension between the calculated and the casual, and the fine balance that Graves has struck, may be fundamental to his success.

MONTEREY BAY AQUARIUM

After the once plentiful sardines inexplicably left Monterey Bay in the 1950s, the Hovden Cannery, like others on Cannery Row, fell into disrepair. The rambling, ramshackle husk of a building sparked the imaginations of marine biologists working at Stanford's nearby Hopkins Marine Station. The group, dedicated to the unique and diverse ecology in Monterey Bay, got the idea sometime in the mid-1970s that the old cannery could house a modest aquarium facility to educate visitors about the bay. Among the biologists were Nancy and Robin Burnett, daughter and son-in-law of billionaire David Packard, founder of Hewlett-Packard. About the same time, another daughter, Julie Packard, was completing her studies in marine biology at the University of California, Santa Cruz (UCSC).

The Packard Foundation, a private charitable organization, had recently challenged its board members to develop new projects deserving major contributions. Julie and Nancy, both on the board, together with their fellow biologists asked the foundation to fund a feasibility analysis to explore the aquarium idea. This document, prepared by the Stanford Research Institute, described an aquarium to be housed in the rehabilitated cannery, with an exhibit concept, square footages, about 300,000 visitors per year, and a cost of five to seven million dollars. Mr. Packard agreed to hire an architect and to foot the capital outlay on the assumption that the aquarium would have to carry itself.

6.13 Monterey Bay Aquarium.
Aerial view.

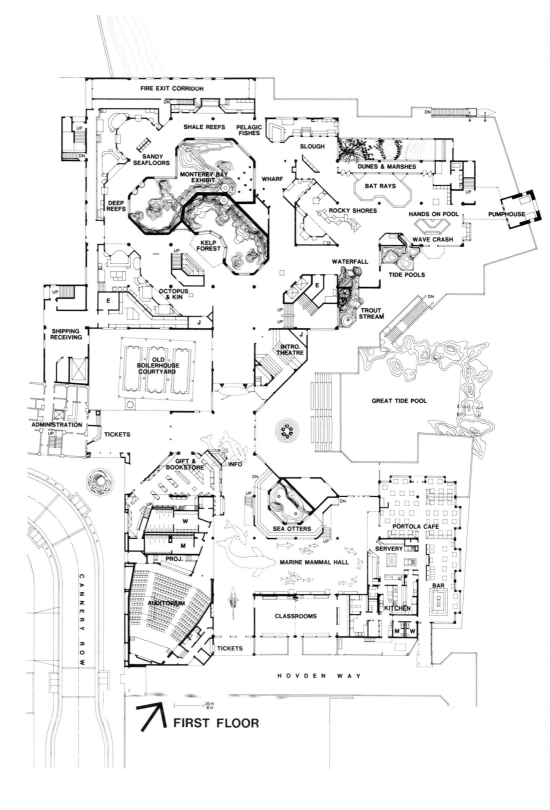

FIRE EXIT CORRIDOR

SHALE REEFS   PELAGIC FISHES

SLOUGH

DUNES & MARSHES

SANDY SEAFLOORS

MONTEREY BAY EXHIBIT

WHARF

BAT RAYS

DEEP REEFS

ROCKY SHORES

HANDS ON POOL

PUMPHOUSE

WAVE CRASH

KELP FOREST

WATERFALL

TIDE POOLS

OCTOPUS & KIN

TROUT STREAM

SHIPPING RECEIVING

INTRO. THEATRE

OLD BOILERHOUSE COURTYARD

GREAT TIDE POOL

ADMINISTRATION

TICKETS

GIFT & BOOKSTORE

INFO

SEA OTTERS

PORTOLA CAFE

SERVERY

MARINE MAMMAL HALL

BAR

PROJ.

KITCHEN

AUDITORIUM

CLASSROOMS

TICKETS

HOVDEN WAY

CANNERY ROW

20 ft
6 m

FIRST FLOOR

As coincidence would have it, the San Francisco architectural firm Esherick Homsey Dodge and Davis (EHDD) was just completing a marine laboratory building for UCSC when project architect Linda Rhodes learned from the client that an aquarium at Monterey was being considered by Packard family members, one of whom was a student at the university. By this point, Rhodes had left EHDD to open her own office. Along with structural engineer John Rutherford she spent several months doing background work on the project, talking to people and finding out what was going on informally. When they determined the cannery could not be rehabilitated, the handwriting was on the wall: this prospect was far beyond Rhodes's one-person operation. She associated again with architect Charles (Chuck) Davis and EHDD.

No one could have imagined opening day six years later in October 1984, or the eightfold increase over the early estimates: the aquarium's final cost was $40 million and attendance exceeded 2.2 million in the first year. Today, the 180,000-square-foot aquarium teems with sea life and its admirers. The building itself was inspired but not straitjacketed by the original cannery. Pieces of the early structure—the boilerhouse, the pumphouse, the old sea wall—anchor the new building around three acres of enclosed space. The volume is fragmented ("train wreck architecture" jokes the architect) to reduce the overall scale, and to recall the cannery's ad hoc form. It is made of tough, enduring materials like concrete, metal siding, and steel sash. Inside, the building recedes to form a backdrop for the dramatic exhibits and the hordes of visitors who meander freely from regions flooded with natural light, to more typical back-lit tanks, to the tidal pools out on the deck. Technically the aquarium is the most advanced of its kind, with innovations in the flow-through seawater system, plastics for the tanks, corrosion protection, and naturalistic exhibitions.

The architects for the building were chosen in the fall of 1978 when four teams were interviewed, but EHDD/Rhodes actually had little competition. EHDD is a large, established firm that has grown from about 35 persons when the aquarium was underway to nearly 70 persons today. There are four principals, as the firm name implies, led in spirit by senior partner Joseph Esherick. Each project in the office has one partner in charge, with Esherick acting as design critic for nearly all projects. The firm is so stable that the lead partner for the aquarium, Chuck Davis, has been with the office for twenty-six years—and he is the newest of the partners.

Armed with experience from the UCSC marine facility and its technical requirements, the architects and engineers made their bid to

6.15 Monterey Bay Aquarium.
North elevation.

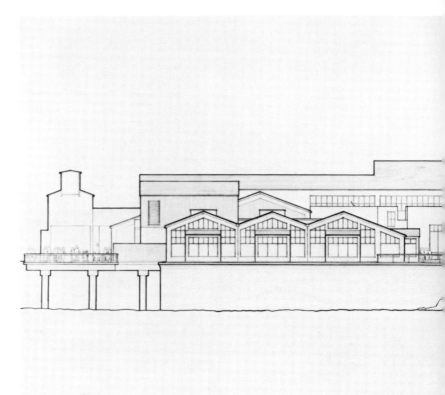

Mr. Packard and the planning committee (made up of five biologists, including the Packard children). This is how Chuck Davis describes the interview:

I'll always remember this because it's the only time it's ever happened. At the end of the interview, Linda and I thought they would retire to chambers, deliberate, and then get back to us. That was my first introduction to who clearly was going to be running the process, because Mr. Packard stood up and said, "Well, Chuck, when can you go to work?" I kind of blinked and said "I can be down there next Tuesday," and he said, "Fine, I'll see you on Wednesday." So Linda and I, plus three people from the office [and Rutherford, the engineer], rented a house and we all moved down there. This is all still very vivid in my mind because it was really exciting. We had this empty lab at Hopkins to make into a drafting facility so we bought a bunch of plywood and saw horses. The biologists were going to set up shop in the next room over, talking about the exhibits and ideas they had. So Wednesday this pick-up drives up—I was outside sawing up plywood—and out steps Mr. Packard in his boots, baggy pants and a big, red workshirt. He took a look around and said, "Well, Chuck, let's go take a walk." When we got out to the point, he said, "The kids have got this idea, and SRI's written this report and I don't know whether there's anything to it. It may all be a bunch of baloney. But my deal

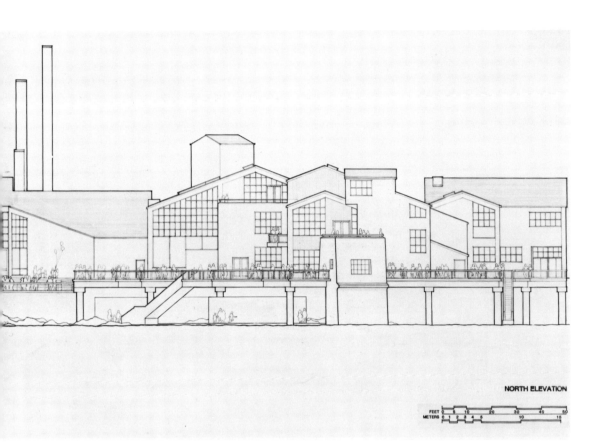

NORTH ELEVATION

FEET 0 5 10 20 30 40 50
METERS 0 1 2 3 4 5 10 15

with you is going to be, I'm going to come up here every Friday, and if
I like what you do, we'll work another week and if I don't, I'll pay you
off and send you home. Is that a deal?" I was very excited about the
project, so I said "Sure, that's fine. As long as I get paid for what I do,
I don't have any problem." He said "Okay, fine. I'll be here Friday to
see what you've got." It quickly developed that we'd work like hell
until Friday, then we would have these meetings with Mr. Packard and
his wife, Lucille, and sometimes some of the [planning committee].
We'd work during the week usually until eleven or twelve at night,
Thursday night we'd work till three or four in the morning, and then
Friday the whole group would come. On Saturday we'd take what
pieces we had left and start over. Basically, that was our schedule.
It was a killer.

This early phase, which Linda Rhodes calls "pre-schematics," lasted
until one Friday in July. "Every Friday he would shake our hands and
say, 'Keep going,' and on that Friday he shook our hands and said,
'You did a really good job and it's not your fault, but bye-bye, fold up
your tent, and send me a bill.'" Rhodes has a clear recollection of the
pivotal events of that Friday and the ensuing weekend:

We started in September of 1978, and by July 1979 we knew enough
about the project to know that it was going to be a $15–$20 million

6.16 Monterey Bay Aquarium.
View of exterior and Great
Tide Pool.

project, it was going to involve a new building, we weren't going to be able to put parking on the site so that was going to be a big issue in terms of permits, and we had some pre-schematic drawings of the building. At that point, the project was far enough along for Mr. Packard to see that it really was going to be quite a monumental undertaking. It was not going to be the kind of project he originally assumed it was going to be, so he . . . basically laid us all off, though it didn't last long. He realized he needed a bigger, better organized management team. It was being run on his side by an informal group, and . . . there was never a consensus among all of them [referring to the biologists, Mr. and Mrs. Packard]. I think Mr. Packard felt strongly that it was going to be very difficult to control the project minus that consensus. He needed a structured decision-making process. At that point, he hired me to be project manager and to initiate a much more formal organizational structure, and secondly, he made Julie the project director. That was very sensitive, [because the biologists] wanted a cooperative board where they were all equally involved and equally responsible. They saw it very much as a consensus building process, whereas Mr. Packard, representing the board, concluded that the project was going to go much too slowly and much too erratically. . . . From my perspective, in terms of keeping the project going, it was a very key decision.

Of the many legends kept alive in memories about the aquarium's evolution, the majority revolved around a lionized Mr. Packard. He was demanding, decisive, uncompromising, and intelligent. His engineering background allowed him to challenge even the most technical recommendations. He could (and did) recalculate the air exchange rate for the entire building volume on his pocket calculator, and suggest that the ducts were 30 percent oversized. He informed contractors they would be fired if he ever again saw re-bar out of position in a concrete pour. He gave prospective exhibits a supposed share of the entrance fee, and used his figures to keep the consultants' efforts prioritized: "Well, now, you've got your admission charge, and the kelp forest exhibit is going to be worth maybe $1.50 or so, and I'd say that sand dollar tank is worth about ten cents." When I asked Julie Packard, now the aquarium's executive director, how the client contributed to the aquarium's excellence, she gave her father the credit, corroborating opinions voiced by the architects:

Working with my father, having one person to make the decisions, no bureaucratic process to go through . . . obviously is a dream for a consultant. [He] was willing to pay for high quality, and had a real commitment to excellence in the materials and in the execution. To have the client ask, "How can we build this so it will last 50 years?" and the architect say, "Use this and this material" and the client say "Yes," all in one meeting, even though it meant going over budget—I imagine that's pretty unusual, to be able to do something right. As a client, [he] was intelligent and totally conversant in all of the engineering details. They could communicate with him on their level, and not only that, he made some very astute contributions to improving the building and its systems. The key to the success of any process is partly to have someone in charge, who can make decisions, who

6.17 Monterey Bay Aquarium.
Sections.

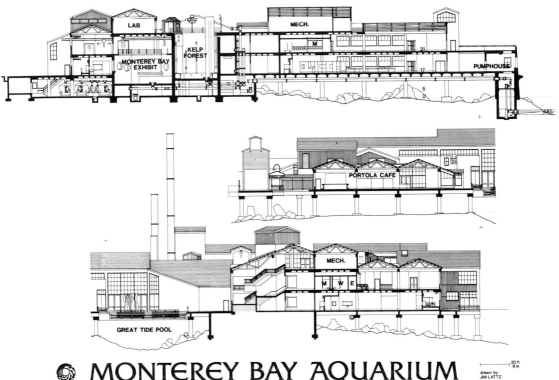

CHAPTER 6

knows what needs to happen, who can tell everyone, "We don't get to talk about it anymore, we've decided about it, so let's go on to the next thing."

Such leadership was essential in a project that boggles the mind with its complexity. By Rhodes's calculations, there were some 200 separate consultants on the job along with 16 governmental review boards. The building straddles the boundary between two cities, and had to meet California's strict coastal commission demands, which had not approved a building since 1966. Politically, the local population was hot against development, nervous about traffic, skeptical of outsiders. The aquarium, as conceived from the very beginning, had virtually no precedents, either in terms of exhibitions, their organization, or technical systems. To build the immense and complex facility required construction documents that included over 250 sheets of basic drawings for the building, and another 200 sheets for the exhibits. The project spanned many years, and for architectural projects time is not only money, but complexity: rules change, actors change, values change, and all become more complex in the process.

Somehow the aquarium emerged from this morass an excellent facility by standards of the public, the client, and the architectural profession, winning its most recent award from the national AIA in 1988. There are several factors that, in varying degrees, have contributed significantly to its success. First, there were several strong rallying points, in both aesthetic and functional terms. All parties involved agreed that the form of the new building should be loosely guided by that of the original Hovden Cannery, that the circulation through the aquarium should be unstructured, and that the aquarium would have an educational mission focusing on Monterey Bay. The clients also disliked other aquariums that were entirely dark inside; they wanted well-lit space that offered a more pleasant experience. Everyone felt the site was spectacular, and wanted visitors to be able to enjoy it. These points gave guidance and stability to an inherently complex undertaking, though some of the requirements have been the target of professional criticism.[12]

Second, among the consultants there was a significant degree of shared knowledge about essential concerns along with basic priorities: both the client and the architect had an informed interest in the building's engineering problems; engineer and architect had a long history of collaboration; seawater issues involved a concern for building materials, exhibits, the heating and cooling system, and structure. No one specifically intended the aquarium to be an award-winning building; as Davis says, "I always thought of the building as being this great proscenium of a stage where the exhibit people could do anything they

wanted and we were going to provide an armature." There was general
agreement that the exhibits, the visitors, and the technical problems
were going to guide the building, not the other way around.

The relations between primary consultants, that is, architect, project manager, structural engineer, and mechanical-electrical engineer,
were long term, preceding and extending beyond the actual designing
of the aquarium. Trust and respect were already established among
them. Moreover, all key participants lived at least part-time in Monterey, including the architect, project manager, structural engineer, and
project director Julie Packard. Especially for the consultants sharing
the rental house, this proximity kept them in close face-to-face interaction and away from the everyday business of their home offices.
Such intensive focus was perhaps fundamental to the project's success,
for it facilitated steady negotiations, close participation, and a sus-
tained awareness of the overall project rather than just the subele-
ments with which any single individual may have been involved.
Davis aptly characterizes the interactions as like those of a family. He
describes his working relationship with Linda Rhodes thus: "We certainly had our differences, but we're kind of like brother and sister: we
quarrel sometimes. We had some very tough arguments, but we both
really respect each other and more than that, there's a real genuine
friendship. So, while we quarreled a lot, we also used to go out and
have dinner, defuse the situation, and work out our differences." Indeed, the consultants' relations paralleled that of the clients, who were
in fact a family. Such informal yet powerful bonds between actors
made conflicts both difficult to avoid and difficult to leave unresolved.

A third element of the project's success was the capabilities of the
key players: Mr. Packard's demand for quality and business sense, Julie
Packard's high standards for the programmatic integrity of the aquarium, Chuck Davis's approach to architecture (avoiding the imposition
of form, finding architectonic resolutions to technical, social, and con-
textual problems), and Linda Rhodes's managerial and political competence. There was a general recognition of the expertise involved; the
client group believed in allowing the experts hired to do their own
work. As Julie Packard put it: "At some level, clients have to figure
out if they're going to step back and trust their consultants or not. . . .
If I'm buying services from you to design a wonderful building, I
should stay out of it and let you design your wonderful building. . . .
We tended to have a hands-off approach with our architect on the aesthetic details of the building, but the functional details led to a lot of
discussion." These three sources of architectural strength—rallying
points, shared priorities, and exceptional individuals in close relations—are observable in the making of the Monterey Bay Aquarium.

The scale and complexity of this project distinguish it from the Bergren House and the San Juan Capistrano Library, making the aquarium's underlying order of excellence somewhat unique. As with the other projects, no one got rich rendering services to design and build the aquarium. Participants do, however, believe the aquarium was a significant event in their careers, one that has gained them further commisions and consulting positions. In fact, the client is hiring the same team of architects and engineers to design a new addition to the aquarium.

EXCELLENT CLIENTS, ARCHITECTS, AND PROJECTS

These three cases of architectural excellence are best understood within the larger context of this book. In preceding chapters I have portrayed everyday architectural practice without evaluating the quality of the buildings produced. I described the characteristics of design problems in practice and the relationships formed to resolve them without attempting to distinguish which, if any, of these characteristics were tied to the quality of the resultant buildings. The preceding cases analyze the evolution of three outstanding buildings, particularly in terms of how the project was managed and organized, who made what decisions, how the key individuals worked together, and what those people thought of the building itself. These studies thus can shed light on basic issues of architectural practice in relation to the evolution of good buildings. They go beyond the assumption that design quality results from the right firm with the right client and the right project; instead they examine what "right" means in context. With this understanding, it is possible not only to recognize the potential for excellence in an architect, client, or project, but also to act in a manner that will promote rather than stifle excellence.

Clients who participate in excellent projects clearly distinguish themselves from the general run of clients for whom architects work. Such clients begin with an exacting attitude; what they exact is quality. Mr. Packard is a good example. As in everyday projects, clients come equipped with budgetary and functional requirements, but these do not outweigh the concern for a building's final quality. More specific in their vision of the eventual building than the average client, excellent clients also bring expectations about its form. They have an aesthetic precedent in mind, and select their architectural office on the basis of its past work, which they perceive to be closely related to their expectations. Thus, there are no true "shoppers" in excellent projects, as there are in everyday practice, because the clients demand more than inexpensive fees and tight scheduling from their architects. Even for the Capistrano Library, which was decided by competition (a legitimated means for clients to shop for architects), the clients began with strong images of an appropriate building based on the Mission and selected the architect based upon the competition entry, a sample of the architect's design approach to their own project.

After choosing the architect for a commission, excellent clients, while demanding and ready to stand their ground, remain open-minded and flexible. Unlike ordinary clients who may be more rigid or in some cases spineless, the clients who produce outstanding buildings have a clear set of guiding values. Simultaneously, they are willing to take advice, add to the budget, and remove themselves from the architect's intimate area of expertise, the manipulation of physical form. More than their counterparts in the everyday practice of architecture, excellent clients are curious about architecture as architects themselves conceive it, which helps them to grasp the designer's goals. When the building is complete, these clients get even more than they bargained for.

The excellent architects such clients choose also have a particular profile. Like their clients, they are principled individuals who remain flexible, embracing the inherent dynamics of the design process. Unlike the stereotypical prima donna, they are attentive to the clients' interests yet also willing to argue strongly for their convictions. Many architects have either weaker convictions or less ability to gracefully argue a point; some exceptionally principled designers maintain an inflexibility that rebuffs most actual clients. In excellent projects architects may or may not operate independently of other designers, thus disproving the idea that good buildings are only designed by autonomous artist-architects. Some are; some are not.

In the practices that produce excellent projects, architects approach each problem as part of a larger body of work, connecting past ideas and future undertakings. Thus no project stands alone, which helps designers avoid the idiosyncracies and fashion consciousness that critics condemn. Along the same lines, in the three cases above none of the architects tried to squeeze a profit out of the project; they did, however, try to break even. If their reports are accurate, it may be that architects cannot live on excellent projects alone, necessitating income from some other source (such as designing products, bread-and-butter projects, teaching, and so on.)[13] The excellent project exists, then, not only because of a particular cast of participants who contribute to its design, but also because of other undertakings that afford the architect an opportunity to ignore certain financial constraints. The architect who does not monitor billable hours closely will spend as much time as needed on a project, rather than as much time as the fee will pay.

Even though we can describe the excellent architect and client, in no case do these individuals consistently produce excellent buildings. Morphosis, Michael Graves, and Esherick Homsey Dodge and Davis have all designed buildings that would not be included in a study of excellence, as have Mr. Packard and the City of San Juan Capistrano. It is a significant point, because it reminds us that excellence is not the product of exceptional or heroic individuals, but the result of a *team* of exceptional individuals who have developed an appropriate means of working together on a project that holds potential. In general, it makes more sense to talk about excellent projects than excellent architects or excellent practices.

The design process for outstanding projects is generally characterized by warm, almost familial relations among actors, as well as by conflict and, at times, tension. In all three cases, there was a strong personal relationship between the key participants. Though this was not necessarily established through frequent meetings. Even though Graves and Packard were somewhat removed from day-to-day operations, both found means to develop strong ties to the other core participants. The process in these cases did not involve a series of formal, businesslike meetings in which issues were raised and resolved systematically. It was more energetic and impassioned, both architect and client hammering out the design for a building that would strongly influence their futures. Nor was the process straitened by a set of billable hours rigidly observed. These projects were not driven by budgetary concerns, and in fact frequently upset the orderly mechanisms of financial planning. There was no extended period of rapport building needed, since the client came to the table with informed respect for the architect, who was then predisposed to respond positively. Limits were clearly set by each party, but there appeared to be greater flexibility in all but the most central constraints when compared with ordinary design processes.

The excellent project that emerges is based on a strong architectural concept understood by the principal actors in their own terms, by which it retains its integrity through the complex machinations of the design process. The project stimulates a sense of ownership among the people involved in its making and even among its subsequent occupants. Beyond pride of ownership, clients, architects, and consultants speak of the building lovingly, expressing the intimate connection they have to the building. The building spawns new work, and the principal players continue working together on new projects.

It is also possible to describe the office's characteristics as they relate to and perhaps fuel excellence in architecture. Briefly, the excellent architectural office (or hub-office, in the case of project team working out of Monterey) appears to have strong leadership, a loose organizational structure, a respect for the creative genius, a clear set of values, informal, face-to-face communication, and a high standard of quality (these characteristics are closely related to those Peters and Waterman garnered from corporate models). The architect whose name is on the door is actively involved throughout the project, acting as head designer and manager without substituting an impenetrable layer of management between the head and those who get the work done. In all three case studies, the principals who played the leadership roles in the projects are known as talented, strong-minded designers.

DYNAMIC FORCES AND PRINCIPLES FOR UNCERTAINTY

I have characterized excellence in architectural practice by examining the architects, clients, processes, and buildings that are part of excellent projects. But the description above is fairly static, characterizing singular "components" of the undertaking in isolation. My own criticism of much management literature, including that applied to professional practice, concerns its tendency to avoid the very dynamics, fluctuations, complexities, and uncertainties that characterize the everyday life of the practitioner.

From the interviews I have conducted, there appear to be a set of contradictory forces at work that frame the development of an outstanding building.[14] These opposing tendencies embody tension and opportunity: the tension generates a high level of energy among participants; the opportunity is to create an excellent work of architecture. Such dialectics arise from the individuals who described their roles in the three building projects. Blau (1984) found that design practice is characterized by contradictory forces that present dilemmas to practitioners. The dialectics I describe are related to Blau's, for they are the architects' attempts to resolve dilemmas by means of mixed strategies, reflecting the complex contradictions of the circumstances involved. These dialectics are:

1
Quality demands
2
Simplicity within complexity
3
Stereovision
4
Open boundaries
5
Flexibility with integrity
6
Teamwork with independence
7
Exceeding the limits

The order of the items follows their likely appearance during a design process; practitioners, consultants, and clients aspiring to design excellence can thus see the tangible clues of an outstanding project in the making, from the first interview between architect and client to the relationship that develops thereafter. The dialectics are contrasted with the parallel observations from everyday practice, which serve as a baseline from which the excellent projects depart. For each of the seven principles of excellent practice, I have listed the specific observations from the case studies that helped formulate the category in appendix C.

QUALITY DEMANDS

In everyday architectural practice, early meetings between architect and client resemble the early throes of courtship, a phenomenon elaborated in chapter 5. But the ordinary encounter is analogous to a blind date when compared to early stages in the relations between players in excellent projects. Ordinarily, architects and clients know little about one another, yet they may be anxious to establish a business relation, and may use fee or schedule as the decisive factor. The everyday practice of clients who shop for architects, looking for cut-rate fees, is mirrored by architects who accept any project that helps subsidize the office. Those projects may be presented by clients as a set of functional requirements and budgetary limits, without professed interest in other architectural objectives. In everyday practice, clients demanding quality (and willing or able to pay for it) are rare, as are architects unwilling to compromise their standards of design at any cost.

By contrast, in excellent projects the client demands an architectural quality that architects themselves are accustomed to demanding from clients. From their very first encounters, architects and clients hold each other in high mutual esteem because they have done their homework. In each of the three case studies, the clients selected the architect based on knowledge of previous design work, and not on cost of services, convenience, or a friend's recommendation alone. In addition, the client comes with a formal precedent in mind, and thus begins with not only functional but physical and aesthetic concerns. That precedent may be the architect's past projects, as was the case for Bergren when she chose Morphosis; or it can be part of the project's context, as was the Mission for the library and the cannery for the aquarium. The precedent, interpreted for its structural underpinnings by the architects, does not unduly restrict design freedom, but because the client begins with some vision of the final outcome, a certain level of uncertainty and anxiety is avoided. Conventional assumptions about roles are defied, each seemingly adopting the other's position. Architects feel fortunate to work with the clients, demonstrating sincere concern for the clients' needs, requirements, desires, and interests.

Perhaps the simplest yet most significant clue as to whether a project has the potential for excellence is a client's early and informed demand for quality. Strong architects and clients demand quality while respecting one another's interests. The careful mutual assessment observed in everyday practice is certainly part of excellent projects, but it goes beyond sizing each other up, to the decision to exact design quality.

SIMPLICITY WITHIN COMPLEXITY

Normally, architects and clients spend a great deal of their time together establishing a rapport, based upon rather generalized foundations such as conversational ease, shows of kindness, and so on. In excellent projects, rapport is built primarily around issues related to the task at hand. In each of the three cases, those identified with needed expertise are relied upon throughout the design process. This arrangement creates a relatively efficient organizational structure to carry out any task, permitting each consultant to contribute his or her best work. It also reduces the ambiguity that plagues everyday practice, because knowledge and authority are more clearly associated with a particular individual. In excellent projects, as in all projects, that expertise is occasionally challenged by other participants. Nevertheless, unambiguous expertise provides one form of simplicity within the inherently complex context for design.

Under normal circumstances, a large client organization with a complex project seeks a large architectural firm whose structure may in fact mirror that of the client. According to data presented in chapter 2, this is increasingly the case. When the architect's organizational web intersects with the likewise tangled client web, chaos threatens. Managerial skills then take precedence over design quality, coordination over intense individual efforts, moving things ahead over doing them well. These are the dilemmas that growing firms face as they try to maintain a high standard of practice.

The three case studies suggest that excellent projects do not result from multilayered complexity, but from responding to complexity with simplicity, which itself takes various forms. There is, in each of the cases, a dialectic between simplicity and complexity such that the project's success appears to depend on an appropriate blend of each, since too much complexity can overwhelm the potential for excellence and too much simplicity may preclude the rich texture of outstanding work. Since architectural projects have grown more complex in recent years (see Gutman 1988), the problem is typically how to create some simplicity within the complexity. Of the case studies, the aquarium is by far the most complex, with over 200 consultants, 16 review panels, and a 200-page set of working drawings. The requirement that consultants move to the project site assured face-to-face interaction and close contact between architect, client, and consultants, helping to simplify the process. The client's structure, although it began as a complex, consensus-building group, was simplified in midstream.

Faced with complexity, architects and clients in the case studies streamlined some aspects of the operations, either by simplifying decision making through an insistence on face-to-face interaction, or by simplifying the organization's structure so that decision making was concentrated among a limited number of people, as happened at both the aquarium and the library. By contrast, the 800-square-foot, single-client Venice III project offered enough simplicity for two designers to work cooperatively to develop a sophisticated and intricate concept.

STEREOVISION

In everyday architectural practice, there are frequent mismatches between the architect's and the client's understanding of what is being designed. For example, architects often complain that clients' demands are completely inconsistent with the building's basic idea. Clients have similar complaints. In some cases, architect and client appear to aim for entirely different outcomes, as when the architect for the Texan mosque project sought historical allusions while his clients desired an ornate contemporary design. In some cases, the architect's and client's concerns emanate from opposed and exclusive interests, so that one's triumph is the other's loss: the client who insists upon minute functional requirements prevents the architect from achieving conceptual integrity.

In light of the mismatches between architects and clients in everyday practice, I imagined that the participants in excellent projects held a shared vision of the design outcome. I was mistaken. Instead, the architects and clients saw the building in what I call "stereo-vision," in that their separate views, though different, combined to make up a single composite. The client and architect portray the project in very different terms, appreciating different aspects of the design: Rotondi speaks of visual and organizational axes, Bergren about the house's nurturing effects; Graves describes the courtyard as a structuring device, the clients talk about its openness, the light, and the special place it creates in the library. These perspectives are not the same, and what characterizes excellent projects is that they do not conflict, but complement one another, dovetailing to create a strong bond between two sets of interests.

Rather than sharing their architect's vision, the clients in excellent projects understand the architect's goals in their own terms, and take a special interest in the view through the architect's glasses. In everyday practice, clients often make physical design demands or request specific architectural elements. In the case studies, clients generally avoid stepping into the architect's role, keeping an arm's length from formal design. This appears to counter the notion of design as a social art, so I want to clarify this observation. In the excellent projects, clients were actively engaged in the design process, but when it came to architectural expertise they trusted their consultants. During the design process, clients discussed their requirements, opinions of the architect's proposals, and ideas for better solutions, but they removed themselves from the actual manipulation of physical form.

OPEN BOUNDARIES

Much of what transpires in everyday architectural practice is directed toward establishing limits. Architects and clients take defensive positions, making sure the other party understands their own constraints, boundaries, and bottom lines. This structures the design process by defining what constitutes an unacceptable solution and mapping the realm of acceptability. Declarations about limits are absolute and close-ended, framed in negative rather than positive terms. Such boundaries are frequently based on stereotypes, such as the tightwad client or the impractical architect. Architects, constructing such an image of the client, may show examples of their most costly past projects to entice the client to higher quality construction. Or clients will insist upon hiring their own project architects, cost control specialists, and space planners to keep the architect in line. Here again, Argyris and Schon's (1974) observation, that espoused theory produces its own results, is pertinent.

In the excellent projects, however, architects and clients established limits at the same time as they set goals. These goals were open-ended and positive, rousing participants to perform to their best ability. Excellent clients demand excellence from their architects and set them a challenge: Bergren wanted the architects to do the best building they had ever designed; the library clients wanted a building that would rival the Mission; Mr. Packard expected the aquarium to be built to last fifty years. These challenges are upper limits, rather than bottom lines, positing an ideal to guide individual actions.

If the client in excellent projects is demanding, the architect is principled. The building design develops in the hands of someone who holds a particular philosophy about architecture, for example as multi-layered experience, as idea, as problem-solving, as figurative rather than abstract. The particular philosophy guides and underlies actions, so that the architect behaves in a more or less consistent, principled fashion. Perhaps the most significant expression of these principles for action in the case studies is the strong architectural concept behind each excellent project. Each architect maintains that the building's idea was strong enough to protect the building's integrity even after the inevitable modifications during planning and construction phases.

In contrast to the one-shot commissions found in ordinary practice, the architects for excellent buildings view projects within the overall development of their thinking, responding to past work and leading to future explorations. Their goals for a specific building go beyond the immediate project; any established limits are challenged in light of this larger context for the work. By combining provisional limits with long-term goals these architects reduce the ambiguity that plagues everyday design processes, since the actors in excellent projects not only know where unacceptability begins but also the direction toward desired ends.

FLEXIBILITY WITH INTEGRITY

Those architects and clients in everyday practice who busily set limits are at the same time demonstrating a high degree of determination, and sometimes integrity, about the project undertaken. There are other architects and clients who seem to express a high degree of flexibility in one or more areas crucial to a successful project; for example, an architect who does not protest a committee's revisions to his or her original plans, or a client who worries only about the construction cost, leaving appearances to the designer. There are ordinary projects at both extremes, in which participants are either uncompromising or highly malleable, but this is rarely the case in outstanding projects.

A certain intensity as well as intimacy characterizes the excellent projects I studied. The intimacy that develops between active participants includes not only positive regard for one another, but strong disagreements and battles of will. Davis compares his relation to Rhodes to a brother-sister relationship in which there are quarrels as well as the necessity to resolve them. The fundamental connection between participants, the building they are trying to produce, underlies the instabilities caused by conflict. Unlike everyday undertakings in which actors expend great effort to avoid conflict, participants in these three cases recall great arguments during the design process. Davis talks about nearly getting fired for trying to save the boilerhouse of the old cannery in the new aquarium; at the library, they argued about shifting the axis; during construction, Bergren decided she needed a way to see out of the bedroom and would not accept a quick solution that the architects were not completely happy with. Around key decisions, actors voiced their disagreement and confronted the concommitant risk; these buildings mattered enough for them to struggle energetically to find the best solutions.

Another distinctive quality of excellent projects is the flexibility both architect and client bring to the process. Since each respects the other's competence, each takes the other's opinions seriously. Participants' stories indicate that such open-mindedness comes from recognizing the other party's expertise while simultaneously feeling confident in one's own. Most issues are thus resolved relatively amicably, though this does not preclude the conflict that erupts when strong convictions are at stake.[15]

In excellent projects, the participants' flexibility is tied to their acceptance of the dynamic circumstances and the uncertainty inherent to the design process. Architects who are principled also embrace the ongoing evolution of any design solution, and are prepared to rethink their proposals. Demanding clients also adapt to changing circumstances, reconsidering program, budget, and design preconceptions. By taking the risk of giving up what was once thought necessary and true, architect and client become more invested in the overall process. Thus, for example, when the clients chose the Graves competition entry for the library, they actually contradicted their own recently established design guidelines. That they broke their own rules to select the Graves scheme represented a singular commitment on their part, one they did not want to later retract. In summary, excellent projects are characterized by both strength of will and flexibilty in attitude, by a complex intimacy among actors, by a high level of commitment to the project, and by the embracing of a dynamic situation.

TEAMWORK WITH INDEPENDENCE

Watching everyday practice I have often imagined collaboration, or even a cooperative organizational structure, to be the ideal form of working together to produce a building. I observed lead architects dominate a project in the design phase, only to lose control when it moved into production phases. I heard the complaints of younger staff members who felt alienated from the very projects they drew up and dissociated from the offices where they worked. Talented individuals often worked without the networks that would permit the full expression of their talent. In some instances, teams of professional staff together completed projects that provided satisfying work for the architects but did not necessarily produce exceptional projects.

The excellence cases, however, suggest a different model from the cooperatives I had idealized. Certainly a team-like sensibility bonded the central players who struggled together to create the excellent outcome, but these individuals did not necessarily participate equally or collaboratively. Instead, key individuals played key roles; their talent and authority was reported to be essential to the building's success. The teams I observed in everyday practice lacked these key individuals.

This is not to say that every building has a single genius behind it, but it does support the widespread belief that good buildings are not designed by committee. Instead, excellent projects are designed by a few leaders, who, working together, are able to move the project along and coordinate the group of contributors. For the library, clients complained of working with Graves's assistants because the latter could not make decisions on Graves's behalf. It appears that the ideal organization is a collaboration among a team of leaders who represent their respective groups; in the worst case, these groups are represented by a committee. Although the library client had no single authority, the architect provided the fulcrum for the project. This combination maintained a relatively simple decision-making structure until Graves's assistants stepped into the act.

When an excellent building is finished, its contributors all claim it as their own. A client talks about "my" library, and laughs when the architect says the same thing. The people involved recognize the important contributions that others have made, but feel their own participation was significant to the building's final form, and that it belongs to them. They are proud of their work, as parents are proud of their offspring.

EXCEEDING THE LIMITS

Ordinarily, when a project is finished it has usually exceeded the client's original budget, taken longer than expected to complete, and made less profit for the office than the architect hoped. In this sense, ordinary projects often exceed the limits set by architects and clients, as do outstanding ones. In everyday circumstances, however, neither architect nor client believes those excesses were entirely justified. Everyday practice also produces many pleasant surprises; the final buildings may go beyond what was imagined. Clients may see that the architect's insistence on a certain issue was well founded; architects find the quality of light exceeds their expectations. Between the excellent and the everyday, the difference is one of degree, rather than kind, when it comes to breaking limits.

When an excellent project is complete and ready for occupation, it exceeds the expectations of its makers, particularly those of the clients. The building goes beyond their ability to imagine, a direct result of giving the architect freedom to invent design solutions that the clients themselves could not conjure up. When these clients describe their satisfaction, there is a sense that the architect read their innermost dreams in order to design a building that captures what they themselves could not articulate: the library catalyzed the community's sense of place, the house is a nurturing mother.

In another sense, opening day reflects only part of the results of the design process. With excellent projects, architects, clients and consultants enter into long-term ongoing relations that do not end when the building is completed. Good work breeds more good work. A building can take the architects' thinking a step forward, establish their expertise in a particular building type, or provide a publicly visible recommendation for subsequent commissions. By contrast, in everyday practice I met architects who had never visited their completed buildings (even when they were nearby), and clients who never paid their final bill, indicating that neither held a long-term view of the working relation.

Finally, with regard to outcome, the basic rule of "give more, get more" pertains. Both client and architect appear to give more, financially, than they might have expected to give. The case study clients all decided to increase the construction budget in order to get the best building possible; none of the architects claimed to have made money on the projects. Yet none would say, after the fact, that they had made a mistake or would do it any differently.

IN SEARCH OF NEW EXCELLENCE

In Search of Excellence revealed that America's best-run companies employ eight basic principles. These they identified as: a bias for action; staying close to the customer; autonomy and entrepreneurship; productivity through people; hands-on, value-driven methods; a "stick to the knitting" style; simple form/lean staff structure; and simultaneous loose/tight properties. Although this study of architectural excellence takes a different focus, there are useful comparisons to be made. Rather than examine the internal organization of the excellent architectural office—the equivalent of the well-run company—I have started with the office's product: the excellent building. The task is to unravel the evolution of that project, to see how it became excellent.

Many of the characteristics that Peters and Waterman extract from excellent corporations correlate with qualities I have observed in excellent architectural projects.[16] The "action orientation" that characterizes excellent corporations is similar to my observation that excellent architectural practice involves a tension between complexity and simplicity. In business, the best companies proceed simply in complex circumstances, demonstrating a disdain for formal, bureaucratic structure and emphasizing the importance of face-to-face communication. These principles of action, simplicity, and communication are central to Peters and Waterman. They talk of the importance of project teams working out of project centers, which is exactly what Chuck Davis instituted to design the Monterey Bay Aquarium.[17] On a completely

EXCELLENT PRACTICE

different scale, Bergren and Rotondi chose an unconventional organizational structure to complete Venice III, but like the aquarium team, demonstrated their propensity for action, simple structure, and informal, immediate communication.

Excellent companies value autonomy and entrepreneurship, and the strong relationship between size and innovation is often cited: small firms are generally far more innovative than large ones, and the most creative large firms seem to have the ability to act as if they were small. Innovative companies recognize the importance of champions, creative leaders, aging heroes, and corporate rebels, much as the best architectural firms do, particularly in the dynamic of independence within a team. With regard to size, the small firm has long been considered the source of greatest architectural creativity, and Peters and Waterman's analysis hints that large firms like Esherick's and Graves's may remain creative because they retain small-firm structures. They are neither highly bureaucratized nor top-heavy with management, but are instead formed around design champions who run teams much like a small office.

In the best companies a strong central direction results from clear, shared values, which include an obsession with quality (for example, Caterpillar and John Deere), a bias toward informality, agreement as to what the company stands for, and so on. The same is true in excellent architectural practice, where design is guided by principles that the firm is known for, while other offices change styles as readily as their clients demand. As far as customer relations is concerned, however, the corporate and architectural worlds part ways. In the best corporations, staying close to the customer through excellent service is a universal principle. Since architecture, as well as other professions, do not ultimately rest on the brief wedding of customer to company at the moment of sale, architects' relationships to their clients are inherently distinct. The difference between the relationship of producer to consumer and that of professional to client creates fertile ground for a study of the social context of design. The relationship of professional to client in excellent practice, according to the present study, is one that includes intense interactions followed by respectful distancing, mutually high demands for quality, complementary but not overlapping visions, and the ability to engage in productive conflict.

This analysis has examined what the three case studies of excellence hold in common. To generalize from these three cases is useful for formulating hypotheses, but such generalizations can only be tentative at present. In architectural practice, excellent buildings appear to evolve from interactions that embody seven dialectical principles emerging out of a complex and dynamic set of circumstances. Some of these principles of architectural excellence are probably applicable to excellence in the practice of other professions such as medicine and law, but just how much of this analysis is unique to architecture will require comparative research. As noted in chapter 2, architecture has more similarities to its sister professions than is sometimes imagined, despite the greater remuneration associated with legal and medical services.

These principles of excellent projects outlined above depict practice in a radical new light, and provoke a number of questions. Is it possible to make a profit and design an excellent building? Could all everyday practice be turned into the practice of excellence? Can an excellent prospect be identified from the first architect-client meeting? If I generalize from this study, the preliminary answers are rather shocking. Design excellence and profitability may be incompatible. For this reason, some projects can be outstanding, but not all projects from any single firm. The architect should be able to recognize a project that has the potential for excellence from the client's initial stance. Excellence, however, comes not from a talented architect or exceptional client alone, but from an emergent chemistry among principal participants. Thus, we cannot speak of excellent firms or excellent architects—only excellent projects.

At this point, these are provocative hypotheses. There are broader conclusions to be drawn from this final study of the three cases, along with the extensive field work and interviews that preceded it. Perhaps the most basic discovery I have made during this research is that the mythical architect as lone genius-artist is a false image, insofar as it represents a simplification of actual circumstances. At the other extreme buildings can be created by committees, but not usually with the highest caliber results. Instead, individual talent, leadership, even genius are important to architecture when they exist in a social context that is conducive to such efforts—a context that consists of other demanding, talented individuals who operate as a team. What I have tried to demonstrate is that the context in which a building is developed is not a static entity but vital, dynamic, and actually formative. The cast of characters, the limits and goals they impose, the power they project, the expectations they hold, the organizations that structure their roles, the conflicts they endure, the intimacy they share, and the respect they are given—all compose a fluctuating constellation of possibilities. From that constellation, participants design a building, utilizing all available human material. It is in this sense that design is a social art, and that the practice of architecture is a culture.

During my second year in architectural graduate school, I started work on the first of three "real" projects—my initiation into actual practice. In all three projects, I was part of a team that developed the program, and translated that program into schematic design principles. Our goal was to predict the client organization's spatial needs over the coming years, laying the groundwork for a new building. Although each job was organized somewhat differently, in general the project architect would take over from us, working with the head of our programming team. All three projects had complex organizations for clients: a county health department, a large university administration, and an apparel manufacturer. For each job, we on the programming team interviewed individuals and facilitated workshops for scores of "clients," returning to our office to brainstorm about the potential conflicts among work groups, about who actually held the power, about what the clients were trying to tell us as they explained how their work meshed with their physical surroundings. We disagreed about what we saw going on in the places; the clients gave us conflicting reports about the organization's needs; there seemed to be no way of reliably predicting how certain aspects of the organization would change in the future.

Then, at some point, we wrote and drew an extensive final report, laying out our observations and recommendations, which included, in two cases, schematic designs for the overall project. Sometimes it was hard for me to follow the trail between our findings and our design recommendations. It was also difficult to trace the fate of our report once it was in the organization's possession. In two cases, the projects were built, and I wondered if I recognized any bits and pieces of my own contribution in the final form. The evidence was ambiguous, but I could detect a pale ghost of the concepts and recommendations in the buildings. Granted, my position on the project team did not afford an overview, but from this lowly vantage point it was easier to see than from above the complexity of designing for a complicated organization with a similarly knotted project team. I believed that what we were doing was of value, helping to create a building better suited to the everyday life it housed; at the same time, I knew I was part of the very "complexity" I had identified as problematic. I began to think my friends who had chosen to do small-house remodels for private individuals might have found a better avenue through the profession.

This book was born out of my own early experience in architectural practice. Experience is the classic foundation for all empirical research, in which a testable hypothesis is developed from the evidence of the senses. As with much social science research, experience leads not to an experimentally testable hypothesis but to a series of perplexing questions about what is going on in a given situation. The ethnographic research I began ten years ago, sparked by the three actual projects described above, has been a search to understand what is going on in American architectural practice today, that is, to grasp the culture of architectural practice.

In this book I have made a series of primary claims based on my field work in practice, interviews, historical analyses, literature reviews, and case studies. The most overarching observation is that the production of places is a social process. That is, a very basic task of architectural work is to collect all participants, both in the office and out, to develop a manner of working with them and to interact with them in order to create a design solution. This task, the social process, is significant to the form-giving task of architecture, for it is from this human constellation that the building's final form emerges. The simple but radical proposition is that design itself is a social process. This is a broadening of the definition of design as that activity which occurs at the drawing board, usually in the early phases of a project, to include all those human activities that contribute to and shape the final form. From office staffing to client relations, from telephone calls to negotiating a contract—all relevant activities become part of design.

A related observation is that while architects know quite a bit about the crucial part of "drawing board design," there is widespread ignorance about the social art of design. In many instances, I believe, when a project is criticized for lacking integrity or quality or when an architect is considered a "hack," it is often because he or she cannot design in the social sense. "Strong service" firms, as they are sometimes called (see Coxe 1986), give experienced and reliable service with the primary goal of satisfying their clients.[1] This approach only partially realizes the capabilities of the profession, for rather than engaging the client in a collaborative context, the architect to some extent subordinates his or her own contribution. A "strong idea" firm that tends to dominate its clients has the same problem, only reversed. Both are missing pieces of the broader picture of design. It is my contention that only by laying claim to the entire design process and becoming good at it can architects participate fully and successfully in the creation of good places. Here I will break with ethnographic method to propose ways to reform the object of my study—surely anthropological blasphemy. But because I myself belong to the group I have studied, I feel a responsibility to go beyond a description of the problems to offer tentative suggestions for how they might be overcome. How, in fact, can architects lay claim to the entire design process and become good at it? This is the question that concerns me here.

This research has revealed that the profession explicitly deals with only part of the design process at present. To understand what architectural practice is all about, I have found it appropriate to apply a

7.1 Howard Roark in *The Fountainhead* is the epitome of the solitary, uncompromising architect. He abhors the social process that architecture engenders, choosing instead to work out his frustrations as a laborer in a granite quarry. The movie glamorizes the myth that all collaboration leads to mediocrity.

model that portrays the design process in practice as a series of dialectics. Sets of dualities embody a tension or contradiction within the profession. From my research, I have concluded that in four key dualities the profession favors one pole while neglecting the other, and that this bias creates its own new dilemmas. First, through its emphasis on the traditional role of the creative individual, the profession masks the growing significance of collective action. Second, design is believed to sprout from a series of independently made decisions rather than from the emergent sense made of a dynamic situation. Third, design and art have been separated from business and management concerns, in spite of the fact that the two domains are inextricably bound in everyday practice. And fourth, the image of the architect as a generalist—a Renaissance man—is countered by the challenges facing practicing architects who specialize in their market for services. These four dualities, raised throughout the preceding chapters, form the basis for the changes I recommend within the profession. The neglected elements can be found alive but struggling in the architect's everyday work world. It is my contention that only by bringing practice back into the conception of architectural design can we strike the necessary balance, or, to put it in different terms, reconstruct the vital, dialectical tension.

In order for recommendations to be made effective, they must allow architects to reconstruct their vision of their own task within the agencies that create and sustain the professional vision: the schools, the professional organizations, and the press. This is no small task. The logical site to concentrate upon is the schools, since they play a significant role in an architect's training, and since they, as institutions, have a relatively centralized structure for implementing change. Secondarily, I will make recommendations for changes within the professional press and for the professional societies. The three institutions together form the wellspring of beliefs within the culture of practice, maintaining professional unity around those core beliefs. (This is not to say that they stand in full agreement with one another, as explained in chapter 3.)

The following recommendations are guided by an analysis of the current state of practice, and do not intend to tinker with *or* revolutionize the existing system. My overall strategy is to suggest changes within those components of architecture's institutions that are strongest as well as those that are weakest. Enriching strengths and redressing weaknesses will increase the stability of architecture's institutions, and doing so with everyday practice in mind will relieve the tension between ideology and action in the profession. My aim is to help architecture develop "controlled diversity." By that I mean to reinforce the profession's role in unifying and standardizing its practices, an important source of professional strength. Rather than promote a single approach, however, I argue that changes within the field demand greater diversity. The profession thus maintains its control over standardization within architecture, but what is unified and standardized is a diverse set of options. For example, the professional licensing exam is highly unified, but might profit from adding self-selected tests in various fields of specialization. By contrast, the diversity in architecture curricula today could be more highly structured, specifically to serve professional purposes of integrating beliefs and practice.

THE INDIVIDUAL AND THE COLLECTIVE

If the goal is to more closely align the institutions of the architectural profession with practice itself, one of the first items of propaganda that must be challenged is the primacy of the independent practitioner working with relative autonomy. This myth, as I have indicated, is not unique to architecture but is embedded in the cultural system of all professions. The point is not to undo the role of the individual in architecture, which would be both undesirable as well as impossible. The individual professional will always remain central to design; we must recognize, however, that the individual acts in the context of a larger and increasingly significant social environment. As such, the cult of the individual should not dominate our beliefs about practice any more than the collective or team. How can this transformation in thinking be accomplished?

While the preeminence of the free practitioner is inculcated through various channels, the most effective point for intervention is the architectural academy. Within the schools, the core belief in individualism over collaboration is bred in the studio. This is counter-intuitive, since the studio depends upon group spirit and cohesion among its members, as well as upon a close working relationship between instructor and student. The problem resides in the fact that these in-use principles of design are not part of the espoused theory. Collective aspects of designing receive virtually no pedagogic attention and generate little reflection, nor does the importance of architecture's social context, even though it plays a definitive role in the studio.

Looking back to the atelier model offers some direction for contemporary studios. In the atelier, students at various levels worked together on competitions according to their ability. Older students helped train younger ones, who in turn chipped in to help produce the older students' competition entries, and all worked under the direction of the atelier master. A mutual dependency was established in such bands of students, which, at the same time, had a clear hierarchy very much like the situation in offices. Certain studios or exercises could be structured in a similar manner, vertically integrating students in the different years of a program.

In any studio, it is possible to bring conscious attention to the interactive aspects of design. If students keep a journal of their thoughts about and responses to the instructor's critiques, this will help them see the role that such interaction plays. When group projects are given, students can participate in guided discussion to critique their own team's organization, considering the opportunities and problems it afforded.

In addition, the nature of studio work can be revised to better prepare students for collaborative practice. Specifically, studio problems that require teams to solve them and studio problems that require negotiation with actual clients or consultants will help teach collaborative skills. Elsewhere, I have developed a sequence of studio problems that begins with what I call a pas-de-deux, a collaboration between two students, and advances in complexity through a final problem with many contributors and political implications (Cuff 1982; see also Cuff 1989). At present, after design solutions are complete, they are evaluated by elder professionals, usually academic architects who sit on juries at the end of each term. These juries should be augmented frequently with individuals who represent client and consultant points of view, thereby reinforcing designing from multiple perspectives while reducing the implied significance of individual professional evaluation (as from the instructor and his/her peers) over all others.

Besides the studio, other areas of the professional curriculum need modification. Our professional practice courses typically focus on contracts, financial planning, project management, and marketing,[2] which should be complemented with teaching about client relations, personnel issues, consultant negotiations, and team and leadership skills. Part of the reason these are so infrequently taught is that there is little supporting literature on these subjects. A new emphasis must be placed on developing the history not only of architectural heroes, but of heroes and heroines as leaders rather than isolated figures, and also of the teams, firms, and clients that make buildings. The well-documented collaboration between Louis Kahn and the structural engineer August Komendant (see, for example, Komendant 1975), or Fruges's patronage of Le Corbusier, are examples of the new histories that need to be written. Similarly, stories about firms must augment what we know about individuals, with models such as Boyle's analysis of Skidmore Owings and Merrill (1977).

Finally, it should be apparent that the evaluation of buildings by those outside the profession needs a forum. More and more, the public

7.2 Aline Barnsdall and her
dog in Los Angeles during the
1920s. Barnsdall was an oil
millionaire and patron of art
and architecture, commissioning Wright to design her well-
known Hollyhock house and
smaller projects on her estate
by Schindler and Neutra.

is inserting itself into the architectural process via design review boards, the slow-growth movement, and citizen advisory committees, but it is time the profession took greater initiative. Consider the possibilities if magazines published buildings with stories about the public reaction and various participants' critiques. Or if a prestigious award program decided its winners according to the evaluation of a jury that included clients, engineers, and prospective tenants as well as architects. These models are not the only ones to adhere to; we need to develop a controlled diversity of options, allowing the profession to respond to complexity while retaining its privileges and fulfilling its obligations to society.

DECISION MAKING OR SENSE MAKING?

The dominant belief, elaborated earlier, is that design is a kind of problem solving involving problems that can be defined, are determinate, and can be solved. There is a concomitant emphasis on *decision making* as the primary skill an *individual* needs in order to successfully give form to a project. Based on this research, the more accurate description of the necessary skill is not decision making but sense making, which corroborates Forester's work on planners and architects (1985, 1982). "If form giving is understood more deeply as an activity of making sense together, designing may then be situated in a social world where meaning, often multiple, ambiguous, and conflicting, is nevertheless a perpetual practical accomplishment" (Forester 1985:14). The notion of sense making implies a collective context in which we must make sense of a situation, inherently social, interpret it, and make sense with others through conversation and action in order to reach agreements. How do we possibly train future architects in something as esoteric as sense making? Again, if we start with the studio, it is easy to find modifications that will contribute to this end.

Studio problems are typically reduced in complexity from their real-world counterparts in order to make them manageable by novices in a short period of time. Although this reduction is pedagogically necessary, there is no need to eradicate the same issues from every project while leaving formal manipulation of the site and building problematic. Some studios should focus on the social, economic, and political complexities of building that are presently eliminated. In such studios, projects, like those in practice, will incorporate negotiations with clients whose program is not rigidly set and who change their minds in midstream. Other projects will require student teams to design around conflicting interests; for example, of a corporation that wants its identity displayed in a high-profile image versus environmentalists who want a building that blends with the landscape. To deal with these kinds of issues will require that the instructor bring more than a program to studio; representatives of the participants or well-developed case studies are needed. This shift will lead students to focus on making some sense of the situation before decisions can be made, and then to refine their sense of the situation as it goes along. Although the building design will not be as developed for this type of problem, solutions should be more sophisticated in terms of how well they resolve conflicting interests or reflect client concerns.

There are two fundamental alterations to studio activities that must occur to shift the focus from decision making to sense making. First, we must repopulate the studio with the people we meet in practice: clients with their shifting ideas about the project, and engineers with their own professional values, for example. Similarly, if students engage in actual design negotiations with each other on team projects, they will develop the skills that will be valuable when they must collaborate in an office. Second, it is critical that reflective attention be paid to sense-making activities, to ensure that they are consciously considered, analyzed, and internalized by students and faculty. This can be accomplished by discussion, keeping a journal, student evaluations, readings, and testing.

Again, there must be a body of literature developed to support the teaching of design as making sense of a situation. Studies such as Forester's, Schon's *Reflective Practitioner*, and this research need to be augmented with additional contemporary cases and also by historical studies of the evolution of particular buildings. Ackerman's (1949) description of the making of Milan's Duomo in the Middle Ages is an excellent example of the kind of study we could use as a model. In it, he recounts the decades of changes in the church political structure and the string of architects who were placed in charge of the project, along with a myriad of details about fee, budget, and construction problems. Similarly, current project descriptions that we read in the professional press must include the tracking of a building's evolution. The catalogue for the show *Processes in Architecture* is a good standard. It describes the dynamic evolution of three large projects, explaining how the building design changed within its shifting context. Documents that record making sense of situations offer models for action and an alternative mental construct for the design process.

DESIGN AND ART VERSUS BUSINESS AND MANAGEMENT

The classic schism between art and business embodied in architecture and promoted by our institutions must be bridged using a variety of strategies. With few exceptions, we concentrate on drawing-board design alone in studio, in history courses, and in the journals. Management and business issues of practice are relegated to professional practice courses, AIA documents, and privately offered seminars clothed in business school garb. This enforced separation in thinking is detrimental to practice, where the results are that great designers

7.3 In school, group projects
such as this are a means of developing skills for collaborative design work.

cannot make ends meet and well-run offices cannot win design awards. At present, the proposition that good business practices can be integrated with excellent building design is greeted with a fair amount of skepticism.

Many of the previous recommendations will aid the integration of design and business concerns (such as problems engendering negotiation and therefore management skills). In addition, we should rely more heavily on case method teaching to bring an integrative view of practice into the classroom. The case method, developed at the Harvard Business School, is an effective means of bringing the messy issues of the real world into the more rarified academic setting. Students are presented a problem with background information, positions, relevant data, but without resolution. Their responses to the case form the basis for structured discussion. Architectural cases exist and new ones are being developed (see, for example, Joroff and Moore 1984; Marmot and Symes 1985). In these case studies, both art and business concerns can be raised along with the specific effects of their interaction.

With reference to the architectural studio, it is obvious that management and business considerations need to be added to some school projects. Team problems could simulate, as part of the project, the creation of a firm, setting up its organization, staffing, salaries, schedule, and so on. Each "firm" then would solve the building design problem, and comparisons within and across teams of the firm-related decisions could be made as the work progresses. More simply, a single management problem could be interjected that forces students to alter their drawing board design activities. For example, a new office policy is instated, requiring weekly review of projects by a design committee; or a budget review has led management to cut the schematics phase short. Clearly, such simulations of practice management will not hold all the implications that they hold in actual offices, but this does not diminish their validity. We accept the equally problematic simulations of building design, and we must now develop acceptable, integrated models of business and art.

At the other extreme, professional practice courses and the American Institute of Architects must determine how best to bring design concerns into their domains. Until recently these settings have been bastions within architecture for project delivery, marketing, office management, and contracts, ignoring building design.[3] The management concerns must be tied to their impact on the work the office produces. This simple connection, between process and outcome, has been elusive in schools, the press, and the AIA. Within the AIA, the separation of interests is solidified in the organizational structure that distinguishes a "practice" committee from a "design" committee. A more apparent manifestation of the distinction can be found in the journals, which publish recent architectural work and award-winning projects. Rarely do these publications go beyond visual description and analysis in their discussions of the finished projects. To reunite outcome and process, journals might augment their visual description with how the office organized itself to produce the work, how key decisions evolved and among whom, and how the fee was distributed across the life of the project. Beyond that, architects and their investor/developer clients will in some cases open their books to report their profit, overhead, and expenses, showing where the fee goes. Magazine readers would then get a much fuller picture of the project and how the business of architecture created design opportunities and constraints. The key is to tie creative production of buildings into the knot of art and business.

SPECIALISTS AND GENERALISTS

In architecture, as in other professions today, the debate continues over the issues of specialization and generalist training. Should we be preparing the next generation of architects to be able to cope with the vast and complex array of issues that will confront them? Or should we accept the increasing specialization within architecture and train experts in the relevant subdisciplines? The response, both institutional and ideological, has been to train generalists, as is evident in the broad standardized curriculum that architectural schools offer in order to receive accreditation and in the multisectioned architectural registration exam that all architects must pass.

Gutman (1988:42), in his analysis of current trends within the profession, implies that the increasing complexity of architectural projects is producing a dumbbell effect upon practices; that is, firms are becoming either more comprehensive or more specialized. This trend could be better reflected in the structure of architectural training. While it makes sense to give all architects a broad, sound basis for professional competence, schools perform much less adequately when it comes to the specializations that many architects employ in their practices. At present, the ACSA lists nine specializations offered by schools of architecture in North America, the most common being urban design, preservation, theory and history, energy, and computer-aided design (McCommons 1989:xxiv–v). And while many schools offer one or more specialized tracks through their curricula, the vast majority of students have few options in the particular school they attend.

Only with years of experience do architects become experts in, say, hospital design, or development projects. Experience will always play a significant role, but it need not be the only means to gain expertise. We could collapse the learning time, without denying the importance of practical experience, with various kinds of academic preparation. Popular specialities might be touched upon in regular professional degree programs; but since a particular specialization is usually determined once in practice in the context of a particular market for services, continuing education is the best opportunity for specialized training.

This divides the educational mission fairly neatly. First, professional degree programs would provide generalist training and broadly based preparation for competent practice, introducing students to the next phase of their education with overviews of common tracks for specialization. The Intern-Architect Development Program (IDP) serves as a bridge, where recent graduates might begin with a "general residency" and then move on to a specialized internship of their interest—for example, in an office that works extensively with computer-aided design, solar energy principles, office buildings, or wood-frame construction. This already happens on a highly informal basis, unlike medical internships, which are nationally coordinated. In architecture, the majority of information that interns have about offices comes by word of mouth and from the magazines, so that they may be acutely aware of a firm's formal orientation yet completely unaware of the other specific strengths it offers. Greater governance of internships, so that offices and interns could be matched more systematically, would benefit all parties. Internships will be more effective learning contexts if there is a reflective component added to complement the in-office training, such as periodic focus groups among interns or regular sessions with a mentor.

The IDP is a bridge between academic preparation and practice, but it is also the first step into a professional's life-long learning experience. Throughout their practicing years, architects find the need to refresh their knowledge and skills, as well as stay abreast of new developments. Once in practice, architects find they need to know things that seemed irrelevant while they were students. Specialized interests are culled from everyday experience; these should be supported by continuing education opportunities. According to Houle's (1980) analysis of continuing education in seventeen professions, the most effective programs will have both self-directed and institution-based components, relying on multiple designs for learning. These include self-monitoring, intensive study over long periods, concentrated impact study, and mentorship, to name a few. The development of serious continuing education programs in the office, in schools, and through independent organizations, will promote not only specialized expertise, but more qualified generalist foundations.

Finally we should reconsider what it means to train the "generalist" architect. Our current system concentrates attention upon the studio experience, which is viewed as an integrative or generalist activity. The studio is typically surrounded by courses that provide breadth—structures, history, graphics, professional practice—but studio is the core. If, however, building design itself has become a specialized track within architecture, as I and others have argued (see Gutman 1988) we could be preparing many more design experts for a profession that can handle only very few, and among whom only a small fraction are talented designers. An alternative model follows from this examination of everyday architectural practice. The schools should retain their generalist orientation, but instead of training students to become the best designers, they should train them to become the best leaders. For architects to be qualified leaders of complex design teams, they must surely be competent designers, but we must broaden their abilities in new contributing areas. Those areas might include: urban issues, political processes, negotiation, leadership skills, and development economics. These combine with the present overviews given to regular consultants' fields such as landscape architecture, mechanical, electrical, and structural engineering, interior design, land planning, and so on. Our existing academies fare well in some of these areas and not so well in others, but none systematically trains architects to take the knowledgeable lead in the complex collaborative settings where design evolves.

AREAS FOR CHANGE

THE STUDIO. Modify existing options by incorporating attention to reflective teamwork, socially realistic problems, and the integration of design with management issues.

PROFESSIONAL PRACTICE COURSES. Recompose professional practice course offerings to reflect the complexities of everyday architectural work, emphasizing case studies and design-business interaction.

THE INTERNSHIP YEARS. Further formalize the internship period, through greater oversight, centralized coordination of internship opportunities, and the development of specialized training options.

CONTINUING EDUCATION. Create an extensive continuing education system that offers practitioners opportunities for lifelong learning about new fields, specializations, advanced training, and practice-relevant information.

PROFESSIONAL RECOGNITION. Expand existing awards programs and publications of outstanding work to recognize that design is a social art, emerging from the complex interests of and interactions among diverse contributors.

BODY OF KNOWLEDGE. Through historical and contemporary studies, develop a body of knowledge that reflects the full story of architectural practice, not only its artifacts.

SOCIETAL TRUST. Rebuild the necessary trust between the profession and society by engaging members of the public and nonarchitectural design collaborators in all aspects of architecture.

7.4 Skidmore, Owings and
Merrill's project for the Washington Mall (circa 1974)
spreads before then-President
Richard Nixon, Nat Owings
(far left), and David Childs (far
right), who had just joined
SOM and is now a partner
with the New York office.

Practicing architects regale willing listeners with tales of woefully unprepared recent graduates whose lack of skills and architectural common sense make them near liabilities in an office. Their complaints are interrupted by academic architects who are committed to pushing the boundaries of current thinking without bowing to what they see as the self-interests of practitioners. The feud will not be resolved soon, but this work does suggest that advocating for or against "practical" training deepens the rift unnecessarily. What we need is a new definition of the "practical" that goes beyond technical skill building. I have elaborated upon the complex culture of practice, filled with crowds of architects and others who collectively grope toward hazy visions of a better place. We grope, in part, because we don't know any better. As architects we undergo years of arduous training, only to find ourselves naked in the land of practice. Our professional comrades—engineers, interior designers, landscape architects, planners—are probably in a similar state of distress, but our clients, with no preparation whatsoever, are even further disadvantaged. Clearly, the education of the general public—the pool of potential clients—should be a high priority, and is highlighted whenever architects debate their position in society. It is, however, both too easy and too ineffective to expect the public to change while we continue, self-satisfied, with business as usual.

After years of standing with one foot inside architecture and one foot out, scrutinizing how the world looks from both perspectives, certain dilemmas have become apparent to me. They seem to grow from a fundamental discrepancy between the stated beliefs of the profession and the everyday work world of architectural practice. Architects themselves live with this discrepancy; their tacit coping produces what I have called the culture of practice.

Unpacking the components of the architectural scene in contemporary American society, I have found that the profession's biases in certain dilemmas lead to unintended consequences that disadvantage architects and society alike: the role of the individual versus the collective in practice, the emphasis on decision making over making sense of the situation, the separation of the art and business of design, and the confusion about specialist or generalist architects. I believe the neglected side of these dichotomies can be addressed by reform within our profession, helping us not only to gain strength but to better serve society and to create better places. Targets for change that keep reappearing in our sights include the studio, professional practice courses, the internship years, continuing education, professional recognition, the body of knowledge, and societal trust. These seven areas for change, should they be addressed, will require reforms in the schools, professional organizations, and the professional press. These recommendations, together, invite no less than an ideological shift within the architectural profession, recasting its system of beliefs to take into account the culture of American architectural practice today.

APPENDIX A ORIGINAL RESEARCH

DATE	SUBJECT[1]	METHOD[2]	LOCATION	DESCRIPTION
1980	Firms(3) (79 individuals)	Observation	San Francisco Bay Area	Six months' field research in 3 study firms
1980	Architects(17)	Interviews(23)	San Francisco Bay Area	Architects in study firms
1980	Business developers(2)	Interviews(2)	San Francisco Bay Area	Marketing/management employees in study firms
1980	Project files(10)	Archival	San Francisco Bay Area	Reading files on projects observed
1980	Architects(10)	Interviews(12)	San Francisco Bay Area	Architects not part of study firms
1980	Clients(4)	Interviews(4)	San Francisco Bay Area	Clients related to interviewed architects
1980	Architect-clients(5)	Interviews(5)	Sacramento, San Francisco	Architects who also act as clients for large organizations
1984	Programming specialists(5)	Interviews(5)	Houston	Discussion of setting client program with specialists from 3 different architectural firms
1984	Firm(1) Project(1)	Observation	Houston	Following one project (6 meetings and numerous interviews with architect)
1984	Architects(7)	Interviews(7)	New York	Architect-stars discuss their conceptions of people in buildings
1985	Architects(3) and Clients(3)	Interviews(3)	Houston	Three teams of architects and their clients interviewed
1986	Firm(1) Architects(10)	Roundtable discussion and interviews(1)	Princeton	The Hillier Group: 230-person architect and development firm studied by team of researchers
1986	Architects(8)	Roundtable discussion	Memphis	AIA-sponsored group workshop on problems in practice
1987	Architects(14)	Roundtable discussion	Los Angeles	AIA-sponsored group workshop on problems in practice
1986/7	Architects(7)	Interviews(5)	Los Angeles, Houston	Discussion with leading architects about excellence in practice

1988	Architects(10)	Roundtable discussion	Princeton	Group discussion of problems in young, small practices
1988	Architects(4)	Interviews(4)	California, Princeton	Study of excellent projects
1988	Clients(8)	Interviews(4)	California	Study of excellent projects
1988	Architects(6)	Roundtable discussion	San Francisco	AIA-sponsored group workshop on problems of small firms
1989	Architects(6)	Roundtable discussion	Tampa	AIA-sponsored group workshop on problems of small firms

1. Numbers in parentheses indicate number of individuals participating.
2. Numbers in parentheses indicate number of interviews conducted.

TOTALS

  50 architects interviewed

  20 clients interviewed

   7 business developers and programming specialists interviewed

   5 firms observed

   5 roundtables on practice (52 architects participated)

244 individuals participated in study

  80 firms represented in study

APPENDIX B PARTIAL LIST OF ARCHITECTS INTERVIEWED[1]

Walter Brooks

John Casbarian

Kevin Daly

Charles Davis

Sam Davis

Peter Dodge

Peter Eisenman

Joseph Esherick

Tak Eshima

Richard Fernau

Anne Fougeron

Ming Fung

Chris Genik

Michael Graves

Jens Hansen

Hugh Hardy

Bob Hillier

Craig Hodgetts

Steven Holl

George Homsey

Jim Ishimaru

Jon Jerde

Robert Kliment

Richard Meier

Mike Murakami

Barton Phelps

James Stewart Polshek

Michael Rotondi

Peter Rowe

Stanley Saitowitz

Danny Samuels

Dolf Schnebli

Dan Solomon

William Stern

Michael Underhill

Johannes Van Tilburg

Tim Vreeland

Barry Wasserman

Tod Williams

[1]Those listed are architectural professionals, but not necessarily licensed practitioners.

QUALITY DEMANDS
Client wants quality
Architect selected on basis of past work
Client has aesthetic precedent in mind
Architect attends to clients' interests/needs
Strong individuals

SIMPLICITY WITHIN COMPLEXITY
Face-to-face interactions
Expertise: strong, clear, respected
Simple-complex combination (architect and client organizations)

STEREOVISION
Design quality emphasized
Client removes self from formal design
Client gathers architect's goals
Complementary visions

OPEN BOUNDARIES
Not a one-shot deal
Goals plus limits
Little ambiguity
Client demanding, architect principled
Strong architectural concept

FLEXIBILITY WITH INTEGRITY
Dynamics embraced
Project is significant to all
Intimate relations
Battles of will, conflicts
Architect principled and flexible
Client demanding and not single-minded

TEAMWORK WITH INDEPENDENCE
Decisions by key individuals
Leadership
Unity within a team
Ownership of the project

EXCEEDING THE LIMITS

No profit

Budget exceeded

Client gets more than expected

Spawns further work

Ongoing relations

Client expresses reaction in hyperbole

ACADEMIC PROBLEMS

1. DESIGN AS A MASTER VALUE
School projects take design to be a master value (see Blau 1984), requiring students to integrate it with some technical and social considerations. The projects are not burdened by business factors, economic issues, or power struggles.

2. SOLO OR DUET
The individual student works primarily alone, with guidance from the studio instructor in an expert-novice relation. Proposals are rarely considered from any point of view besides that of the architect (no outsider evaluation).

3. CLEAR PROBLEMS
Problems are designed to have a certain clarity and focus. Complexity is constrained and ambiguity is avoided.

4. CURTAILED PROCESS
Limits to the design process are set by convention, instructor, and academic calendar. There is never enough time to complete a project, but the deadlines are enforced and students are often encouraged to start over.

5. UNCERTAIN SOLUTIONS
Solutions are formal and technical responses based primarily on visual appearances (as opposed to functionality or economics). In school students may break the rules, challenge the program, and experiment.

6. SINGULAR STAKES
School intentionally provides a risk-free context, so that no one but the student is affected by the outcome. Qualities such as negotiation, altruism, compromise, and generosity are irrelevant.

PROFESSIONALIZED PROBLEMS

1. BALANCED PRACTICE
The qualified professional is skilled in both the aesthetic and business aspects of architecture, and is able to hold these in balance.

2. ARCHITECT AT THE HELM
The architect coordinates and guides the many individuals whose input is needed in an architectural project.

3. MANAGEABLE COMPLEXITY
Design problems are complex, requiring careful organization and management.

4. LINEAR SEQUENCE
The services of the architect are delivered in a regular sequence of phases. Services and their subactivities progress in a linear manner.

5. PREDICTABLE SERVICES

If clients and consultants provide thorough, accurate information, then the architect will be able to determine and provide appropriate services.

6. SIGNIFICANT TO MANY

Buildings are important to clients' lives but also to society at large, so architects must act responsibly.

PRACTICE'S PROBLEMS

1. DESIGN IN THE BALANCE

Architecture tries to unite ideologically contradictory forces in the union of art and business, so that at each step the primary professional activity, design, hangs in the balance.

2. COUNTLESS VOICES

The influence brought to bear on any project is distributed among numerous participants, each having a voice in the matter.

3. PROFESSIONAL UNCERTAINTY

The responsibilities, procedures, authority, allegiances, and expertise in any design process are ambiguous.

4. PERPETUAL DISCOVERY

Since the information needed to make decisions is never complete and every issue is potentially negotiable, the design process could go on endlessly.

5. SURPRISE ENDINGS

Although a single specific solution is expected, participants never know what that outcome will be, since the possibilities are limitless.

6. A MATTER OF CONSEQUENCE

Actors in the planning process are highly motivated, since the stakes are significant and the consequences serious.

1   **WHY STUDY THE CULTURE OF PRACTICE?**

1. This is the definition of culture offered by Clifford Geertz in *Interpretation of Cultures* (1973).

2. For a review of ethnography, see Gumperz (1971, 1982) and Geertz (1973, 1988). For a discussion of current debates about ethnography, see Clifford and Marcus (1986).

3. Ethnomethodology links phenomenology to linguistics, establishing the connection between everyday action and everyday language, as people go about constructing the meaningful, factual character of their social reality. For an overview of ethnomethodology, see Leiter (1980) and the seminal work of Garfinkel (1967). I have also relied on works in cognitive sociology (particularly Cicourel 1973) and social psychology, especially Alfred Schutz's work with the phenomenon of the social (see, for example, 1962, 1964).

4. The view of the world as a series of contradictory circumstances that when resolved create new dilemmas comes from theory of dialectics, and has been fleshed out in relation to architectural practice by Judith Blau in *Architects and Firms* (1984).

5. The four offices that refused to participate tell something about the types of firms missing from this study. One was a busy, socially oriented office that made little money on each of its jobs and could not afford to take any time from members' daily schedules to meet the needs of a researcher. The second was a "star" architect's firm, whose principal felt that I would be a tremendous intrusion: "I'd rather have you sit taking notes in my bedroom than in a client meeting." The third refusal came from a sole practitioner whose days at the office were divided between working on the one or two projects he had at any one time, writing his book, and designing a children's game about architecture. The last was a very large firm where I was unable to meet with the person in charge of making decisions about projects such as mine.

6. Like much information about the architectural profession, data about women architects is slim. Perhaps the best studies have been conducted by the American Institute of Architects, most recently in 1983 ("1983 AIA Membership Survey: The Status of Women in the Profession"). This study shows that the mean age for women, 35, is a full seven years younger than the mean age of male architects, and that a third of the women, compared to 10 percent of the men, are under 30 years old. In this study, when number of years experience was controlled, women still came out behind their male counterparts, indicating the effects of sex discrimination on advancement. For example, for those with 10 to 14 years of experience, 57 percent of men compared to 33 percent of the women had reached partner-level status.

7. According to Department of Labor statistics, in 1984, 2.4 percent of all architects were black and 3.6 percent were Hispanic. The AIA membership (1984) included 4.8 percent minorities, of which 2.3 percent were Asian, 1.3 percent Hispanic, .7 percent black, and .1 percent American Indian (reported in Greer, 1985).

8. The primary categories of missing data are: large architectural corporations, of which only two are included in this study, women in architecture (particularly at the principal level), and developer clients (the subject of my current research). Although very small firms were not among the three case studies, several roundtables have been exclusively made up of firms under five persons, so their issues have been included in the study.

9. Corbusier had problems with an incompetent contractor, a public water supply agency, the local community, and future residents. These stories are reported in Boudon (1969) and von Moos (1979).

10. From Vitruvius (first century BC).

11. This is what Horst Rittel calls "deontics." His theories about design problems and knowledge are central to the present study (see Rittel and Weber 1973).

2   BELIEFS AND PRACTICE

1. Magali Larson's (1977, 1983) sociological studies of professionalization and of the architectural profession provide foundations for this chapter, along with Eliot Friedson's excellent study, *Professional Powers* (1986). The contributions of two additional sociologists are important: Judith Blau's (1984) extensive investigation of architectural firms, and Howard S. Becker's (1974, 1982) writings about art as a collective enterprise, as well as his study, with Anselm Strauss et al., of medical school (1961).

2. The collection of historical essays on the architectural profession entitled *The Architect* (1977), edited by Spiro Kostof, is invaluable. Individual chapters by Boyle, Draper, Wright, and Esherick have been used in this study. Andrew Saint's *The Image of the Architect* (1983) examines the beliefs and ideals of architects yet offers little in the way of theory.

3. See Klegon (1978) for a critique of definitions that enumerate lists of characteristics for professions.

4. Historically, practitioners were never autonomous from clients and public, only from other professionals. Now, architects no longer act independently of other professionals, which is why I observed so many meetings with consultants during my field work. This is an unacknowledged source of frustration for architects who want more freedom; the frustration is often misdirected toward clients.

5. See Larson (1977:109–110). In the 1700s only sons were sent abroad for training, but there were women known for their architectural concerns by the mid-1800s (see Hayden 1981). The first woman to go abroad for formal study at the Ecole des Beaux Arts was Julia Morgan, who received her certificate in 1901 (Wright 1977).

6. Scully (1969) and Handlin (1979:90) discuss the great changes in the American building industry in the late nineteenth century. See Levy (1980) for an extensive discussion of the emergence of civil engineers. Larson (1977:122) raises the issue of new bureaucracies and their role in professionalism.

7. See Draper (1977) for a review of Americans at the Ecole. For discussion of women in architecture and Morgan in particular, see Wright (1977).

8. This is a complicated question dating back to Vitruvius. At least by the time of Palladio, architects were beginning to separate design services from construction and implementation. For a discussion of the evolution of engineering, see Levy (1980).

9. See Esherick's chapter in *The Architect* (1977:274) where he quotes Cret from the University of Pennsylvania's *Book of the School.*

10. For example, see the guidelines laid out by Cooper Marcus and Sarkissian (1987) and Franck and Ahrentzen (1989) on housing. Although there is a vast literature now available, integrating social and functional issues into the repetoire of architectural expertise, either in schools or in practice, has not been easy. Nevertheless, Montgomery (1989) makes the argument that social issues have so penetrated the profession that many architects now specialize in what he calls "people work."

11. The firm best known for its programming work is Caudill Rowlett Scott (now CRS–Sirrine, with headquarters in Houston), but most large firms offer some specialized predesign programming services, as do firms that do a great deal of interior office design or space planning.

12. This data comes from the AIA "Survey of the Profession—Individual Members" (August 1974). In general, the large surveys conducted by the AIA are among the more reliable studies of architects, but in the past they have not been conducted on a regular basis, nor were the same questions asked in each major survey; hence this rather dated attitudinal data.

13. For a discussion of the characteristics of design problems as "wicked" problems, see Rittel and Webber (1973). These characteristics are outlined in greater depth in chapter 3 of this book.

14. Gutman (1988) contradicts Ventre about shrinking architectural fees. His review of census data indicates that between 1972 and 1982, the architect's share of every dollar spent on construction increased almost one third, from 2 percent to 2.7 percent (see p. 7). Likewise, the most recent AIA Firm Survey (1989) finds that total billings have grown between 1985 and 1988.

15. I observed the "structural defense" in architect-client meetings. Architects will justify an aspect of the design scheme by convincing the client that it is structurally necessary. Since clients know little about the technical aspects of architecture, they are unable to refute the argument (for an example, see the Mosque case in chapter 5).

16. Along with the AIA, NCARB (National Council of Architectural Registration Boards), ACSA (Association of Collegiate Schools of Architecture), and NAAB (National Architectural Accrediting Board, for school accreditation) are the principal professional organizations for architects in America.

17. R. Schluntz and G. Gebert (1980:26–27). Estimates of membership are high due to the inclusion of student members in the figures. Only 21 percent of all respondents were members of the American Institute of Architects, and less than 1 percent belonged to the Society of American Registered Architects.

18. Based on personal communication with the head of NCARB, Sam Balen.

19. This census data, reported by Gutman (1988), undercounts the number of small firms, since the Bureau of Census does not survey sole practitioners but only firms with at least one employee. According to Gutman, of the 25,000 firms in the USA, about half are sole practitioners.

20. The profit rate comes from the work of Weld Coxe (cited in Gutman 1988:79) and is figured before distributions and taxes.

21. The number 30,000 is cited in Hirsch (1986:68), reporting 1986 enrollments. Correspondingly, Gutman (1988) estimates there were approximately 25,000 students in accredited and non-accredited architectural schools in the US in 1980.

22. Montgomery provides the 98 percent employment figure in a work that is forthcoming; for a general discussion of his findings, see his 1989 chapter in *Architects' People*, eds. Ellis and Cuff. Gutman (1988) corroborates the broad range of services now performed by architects in his estimate that 15,000 to 20,000 practitioners work outside mainstream architectural practice.

23. Similarly, a study of New York firms (where wages are generally higher than the rest of the nation) revealed that in 1982 only 20 percent of the architecturally trained personnel earned more than $35,000 annually (111 firms studied) (*Architecture* 1982).

3   **DESIGN PROBLEMS IN PRACTICE**

1. This is an actual transcript from an architect-client meeting, with minor details altered to protect confidentiality of the participating individuals and institutions.

2. The body of this chapter describes six characteristics of design problems in practice. These characteristics emerged from observation of and reports from design process participants. During the research period, I attempted an ongoing synthesis of the data. I compiled a list of more than twenty descriptive statements via content analysis, and eventually collapsed them into the six categories. The characteristics are dimensions rather than explicit features, since the great variation among design problems is best conceived as a continuum. Some problems, for example, will not involve very surprising endings (characteristic no. 5); the outcomes are relatively predictable.

3. A comparison of these characteristics with Rittel's ten characteristics of "wicked problems" (Rittel and Webber 1976) demonstrates their similarity. For example, my finding that design is a matter of consequence parallels Rittel's principle that designers have no right to be wrong; perpetual discovery is similar to Rittel's "no stopping rule," and so on.

4. Ninety-three schools in North America have accredited programs. This and other data about schools comes from the *Guide to Architecture Schools in North America*, edited by Richard E. McCommons (Washington, D.C.: ACSA, 1989).

5. See, for example, Martin's dissertation (1983) on approaches to design education and the *Architecture Education Study* vol. 1 (1981) for a close look at the design studio.

6. For two very different discussions of studio models, compare Joseph Esherick's personal account of his education (1977) and Martin's descriptive overview (1983).

7. The *Architecture Education Study* (1981) is a two-volume study conducted by a group of East Coast architecture faculty members. It contains a set of papers on design education (vol. 1) and two extensive case studies of specific studios (vol. 2). The data are richly textured, in-depth material based on case studies, but cannot be said to be representative of the larger educational population.

8. This is similar to the conclusion Bienart draws (1981:157). I would also note that architect-teachers are not representative of all architect-practitioners, since they do not survive on income from their practices alone but augment their practice (if they have one) with teaching salaries. They tend to be more interested in esoteric issues and may be less able or less motivated to balance aesthetic and pragmatic concerns.

9. The Intern-Architect Development Program (IDP), begun in the mid-1970s, is a welcome attempt by NCARB and the AIA to structure internships. However, only about half the states require IDP participation for licensure and only one quarter of all firms participate in IDP (AIA Fact Book 1988). Architecture still remains far behind medicine in practical training. The organization of medical internship, residency, rotations, and the teaching hospital prepares future doctors more systematically than any architectural model to date.

10. Although many professionals will argue that the AIA is of little value to them personally, or that it is an older, conservative organization that does not represent the younger, exciting firms, it nonetheless has an indirect effect on all practitioners. Not the least of these is the widespread but mistaken belief that the "AIA" after a person's name is equivalent to being a "real" architect. (In fact, the "AIA" only means that the practitioner is both a registered architect and has joined and paid membership dues. One can also join the AIA as an associate member if one works in a professional capacity under a licensed architect or has a degree from a school of architecture and intends to become licensed. Sixteen percent of AIA members are associates [AIA Fact book 1988].) In addition, the standard owner-architect agreement is commonly used by architects, at least as a model contract. The AIA is affiliated with other professional bodies that are virtually unavoidable if one wishes to become an architect, such as the NAAB, which accredits the academic curricula in architecture, and the NCARB, which establishes the requirements of licensure. The AIA lobbies for architecture's causes at the national, state and local levels. When conflict between parties or litigation arises, architects as well as the courts turn to the AIA for standards and guidelines.

11. A major revision of the *Handbook* was headed by David Haviland (editor), and includes a chapter I contributed entitled "The Architecture Profession" (1988:1.2). Many quotations in the present volume derive from earlier editions

of the *Handbook*. An interesting analysis remains to be done on the evolution of the *Handbook* as an artifact of the profession's changing ideology.

12. For further discussion of this paradox see chapter 6 of this book, also a collection of essays called "In Search of Design Excellence" (AIA 1989), and AIA *Memo* (1989). Blau (1984) demonstrates that the relationship between design quality, economic survival, and organizational structure is not a simle one. For example, she found that those offices that did best during economic crises were small and highly bureaucratized, regardless of the design quality of their buildings.

13. The connection between percentage of fee and hours spent is loose because fees also reflect pay scale. Front-end work is generally done by higher paid architects, while construction documents are completed by lower paid draftspersons. This tends to exaggerate the diagram further: even less time may be spent on schematics, and even more time on construction drawings and specs. In addition, the 20 percent figure for the construction phase may represent not only the time the architect spends in this phase, but a balloon payment received upon project completion.

14. See, for example, the article by Ackerman (1949), which documents the design and construction of the Milan Cathedral. Kostof (1977:15–16) also describes the coordination of builders and announcements to the public for architectural projects in ancient Greece.

15. Architecture firms based on collaborative practice, such as The Architects' Collaborative, Taft Architects in Houston, and Atelier 5, are plagued by inquiries about the "real" design genius behind the offices' work. For an example of shared authorship, see the discussion of Morphosis in chapter 6.

16. In particular, the attention paid to user satisfaction and participatory planning in the last two decades has encouraged clients and user input in the design process. Post-occupancy evaluations can hold architects accountable for the success or failure of their solutions (see, for example, Vischer and Cooper, 1986).

17. A good example of this type of discussion among architectural professionals can be found in *The Charlottesville Tapes* (1985).

18. Creating plans for a building that will have desired properties and will avoid unforeseen side- and after-effects is part of Rittel's definition of design, but he also points out that "there is no immediate or ultimate test of a solution to a wicked problem," so there will always be surprises (1973:163).

19. Although about 80 percent of all claims against architects and engineers result in no payments to the claimants by insurance companies (Franklin, n.d.), the threat of immense settlements keeps premiums high. The cost of insurance entices small firms to "go bare" (go without coverage). According to the 1986 AIA member survey, three quarters of the sole practitioners, but only 7 percent of the firms over 20 persons, go without professional liability insurance. This may be appropriate, given that only 3 percent of the sole practitioners but 43 percent of the over-twenty-person firms had at least one claim against them in 1986 (AIA Fact Book 1988; AIA 1987 Firm Survey Report).

20. Blau's (1984) data indicate that *repeat* clients are not a significant proportion of an office's clientele, but the connections among clients (referrals and recommendations) are difficult to trace. The experience of most architects is that a significant proportion of new work comes from client referrals.

4   THE MAKING OF AN ARCHITECT

1. Perhaps the primary linkages among high energy physicists are the linear accelerators, of which only a few exist, but where experiments must take place. Access to these accelerators is governed by the facilities themselves, and by the obtaining of funding (generally from federal grants) to conduct research (Traweek 1988). The centralization via funding and facilities establishes stronger conventions and standardization in the particle physicists' community than in architecture, where no such centralizing factors exist.

2. In Blau's (1984) study, she asked architects to indicate which of fifty names (architects, firms, and critics) they knew and liked. She found very clear patterns of "heroes and rascals," those who were well-known and liked and well-known and controversial, respectively (66–78).

3. The National Architectural Accrediting Board (1987) specifies four distinct areas of study that architectural schools must cover: technology, design, practice, and context (including history, theory, social sciences, etc.).

4. According to the ACSA, among students in accredited M.Arch. programs, 26.2 percent are female (*Peterson Guide to Architecture Schools in North America* 1982). That figure can be compared to the proportion of female faculty members in architecture schools, estimated at 10.3 pecent (*Architecture* Apr. 1985). Exacerbating the problem, a good share of women faculty teach in "context" areas rather than in studios, though no hard data on this exist at present.

5. For extensive discussion of the student-instructor interaction in studio (primarily the desk crit rather than the public jury), see the *Architecture Education Study*, vol. 1 (1981), particularly the papers by Schon and Argyris. See also Schon's *Reflective Practitioner* (1983).

6. The gender-biased overtone to the charrette was blatantly revealed by a male professor who told me, "I really was the one who opened the three-year program to women, since I was the one who organized the studio to meet five days a week from 9 until 5, with little or no work outside the studio. Before that, the women just couldn't compete with the male students, since they weren't able to lean over their drafting boards all those long hours, from being a bit top heavy."

7. According to the practitioners who participated in the AIA roundtable discussions from across the country (see appendix A), the oversupply of graduates and undersupply of jobs are more apparent in large metropolitan areas and less prevalent elsewhere.

8. The 40 percent of total fee breaks down thus: 18 percent general drawings, 6 percent structural drawings, 12 percent mechanical and electrical drawings, and 4 percent specifications. Since most architecture firms control the first and the last tasks, of the 22 percent that architects manage, only 7 percent of total fee is direct expenses such as technical salaries. But some of design development

(DD) is low-level staff production, and DD is estimated at 20 percent of total fee. (AIA *Handbook* 1969, 11:5.)

9. For example, the Intern-Architect Development Program specifies fourteen training areas that the entry-level architect must be exposed to in order to be eligible to take the registration exam (these are national guidelines that have not been adopted by all states): programming–client contact, site and environmental analysis, schematic design, building cost analysis, code research, design development, construction documents, specifications and materials research, documents checking and coordination, bidding and contract negotiations, construction phase (office), construction phase (observation), office procedures, and professional activities. (NCARB 1987.)

10. These are the definitions that were used to conduct the 1983 AIA Survey of Firms and are reproduced exactly as found.

11. The specifics about the registration exam change nearly every year, much to the dismay of test-takers. New portions are added (such as the site design section, which was added in the 1980s) and others are omitted. California decided to break from the national test sponsored by NCARB and to give its own test, which lasted for two years (1988–1989) before that state rejoined the flock. Now it appears that the national test will be given not once but twice each year.

12. Good data are not available at a national level, but in Blau's study of firms in New York, she found that small firms were more likely than large to fail in an economic crisis (1984).

13. This statement—that for a given project, design quality and profit may be incompatible—has caused a great deal of discussion at recent AIA panels on which I have served. Weld Coxe is its most vociferous detractor, stating that design quality *and* profitability can and do characterize architectural projects. Based on roundtable comments from members of "signature" firms (nationally recognized for their design quality), it appears that these top firms have become very good at negotiating healthy design fees for all their projects. They also admitted that the fee does not govern the amount of time they spend on design. In my own research, firms adopted what I would call a mixed strategy, in which firms perform a sufficient amount of bread-and-butter work to pay operating costs and to subsidize high-status projects. This argument is fleshed out in papers by Robert Shibley and James Franklin included in the collection "In Search of Excellence" (AIA 1989).

14. As one architect recently put it, "All those publications in the magazines get me fancy lectures in places like Sidney, Australia, but they don't get me any jobs in Los Angeles" (where he is located). However, Blau (1984) found that award-winning firms (those with recognition) are slightly more likely to succeed in economic crises.

5   **THE ARCHITECT'S MILIEU**

1. Statistics are taken from the 1982 Census of Service Industries, reported in Robert Gutman's study of architectural practice (1988). See chapter 2 for more demographic information about architects and firms.

2. Gutman (1988) makes the point that medium-sized firms can do quite large-scale work.

3. In Blau's study (1984) of 152 New York firms, nearly half of them went out of business during the economic recession between 1974 and 1979. Her data do not indicate, however, how many of those firms that "failed" were reconstituted under a different name or organizational structure.

4. When working with clients, for example, the architects within a firm rarely disagree with one another. By definition, the negotiations with clients over design, budget, program, or anything else, incorporate the values of all parties involved (Zartman 1976). It is on the basis of these values that acceptable solutions are developed, so when the architects do not share key values the negotiations become complex and confused.

5. Jerome Abarbanel, in his dissertation (1979), found architecture firms interact with organizational clients by way of what he calls "boundary units." In general, his study suggests that both architectural and client organizations show functional specialization with regard to interactions and negotiations among key players. However, the architectural firms exhibited only one such pattern of specialization, while client organizations exhibited a wide variety of organizational structures by which they represented themselves as clients in the design process (for example, facilities managers, ad hoc committees, and temporary divisions).

6. These qualities of architect-client relations are derived from my field work, described in chapter 1. Content analysis of the field notes yielded some forty interaction "bits" or groups of utterances that shared a basic intention, such as biding time, stating a bottom line, soothsaying, or educating others. These were then collapsed into five distinguishable but interdependent patterns representing the relations between architects and clients in everyday professional practice. These in situ findings have since been corroborated in interviews with architects and clients about their relations.

7. This portrayal of design discourse represents the architect's perspective better than it does the client's view. Hypothetically, for example, clients might have a more elaborate representation of design interactions in the courting phase, when they seek the appropriate firm for their project. Important research remains to be conducted on architecture's clients to complement this study, which follows architects through the various social settings of their normal practice.

8. The horizontal dimension, time, is adapted from Horst Rittel as presented in his annual lectures to the College of Environmental Design at the University of California, Berkeley, in his course on design theories and methods. The vertical dimension, "level of interaction," refers to the hypothetical amount of time spent in interactions with project participants (clients, consultants, in-house architectural team members) on a typical day.

9. Avoiding conflict at all costs is not a goal in excellent projects (see chapter 6), or, perhaps, outside North America, based on the reaction of foreign architects to my lectures on this issue.

10. This case was presented at a symposium at MIT, where several architects raised the point that the compromise solution was weaker than Underhill's initial schemes.

11. These ideas are paralleled in ethnomethodological theory (see Garfinkle 1967). Goffman views interactions as a staged sequence of "moves" by participants in a dynamic social context. A move, according to Goffman, is "any full stretch of talk or of its substitutes which has a distinctive unitary bearing on some set or other of the circumstances in which participants find themselves" (1981:24). In architecture, a move may be a turn taken in dialogue or a graphic image.

12. Architectural dialogue, unlike most discourse, entails two complementary conversations—a verbal conversation and a visual one. (A third and significant kind of conversation is paralinguistic: gestures, intonation, pauses, etc.) These two conversations can be conducted face-to-face or indirectly, yielding four primary types of architectural discourse: face-to-face verbal (talk), face-to-face visual (impromptu sketches), indirect verbal (memos), and indirect visual (conventional architectural drawings and models). The most interesting form of design discourse is face-to-face verbal and visual, which is the typical model of meetings between architects, clients, and consultants. Ideally, these are examined together as they occur in actual encounters (see Schon 1983).

6   EXCELLENT PRACTICE: THE ORIGINS OF GOOD BUILDING

1. Research for this chapter was funded by the National Endowment for the Arts. Part of the report for the NEA included an extensive review of writings about excellence in architectural practice. This bibliography, which includes books and articles at least tangentially related to the topic, can be found in my Final Report to the National Endowment for the Arts (Grant no. A-85-107078, 1990).

2. Companies cited in the book were tracked, and many were found to have serious problems in exactly the areas Peters and Waterman said they excelled (*Business Week* 1984 Nov. 5). See also *A Passion for Excellence* (Peters and Austin 1985).

3. Some buildings have no relevant public or consumer component, for example, commissions for private buildings such as a single-family house. The Bergren House, analyzed in this chapter, is such a building. Today, with the heightened activity of neighborhood design review boards, even private houses are being subjected to public evaluation.

4. An alternative explanation for the positive evaluation of a building by all three groups is that their reaction is a result of the "hype" surrounding a particular project (see, for example, Aronson 1983:291–329). Architect Ben Weese of Chicago first brought this to my attention after he reviewed this chapter.

5. Other selection criteria included: buildings that had been relatively recently completed so that the individuals would have fresh memories of the process, ready access to the buildings and actors, and a set of buildings that together represented no preferences about architectural style on my own part.

Based on a review of professional awards over the past five years, publications in major architectural magazines, the expert judgments of several architects and our collective informal knowledge about client and public reaction to projects, I arrived at a list of nine buildings. The original list of potential projects included Horton Plaza by Jerde, Mixon House by Taft, Loyola Law School by Gehry, High Museum by Meier, 72 Market by Morphosis, St. Matthew's Church by Moore, Bergren House by Morphosis, Monterey Bay Aquarium by Esherick Homsey Dodge and Davis, San Juan Capistrano Library by Graves. I conducted further research on each of these buildings to determine their appropriateness as case studies. A table was made to determine which three might capture the widest range of values along those dimensions mentioned above, while remaining a manageable research undertaking.

6. Interviews:
Bergren House
Ann Bergren (Professor of Classics, UCLA) (2/26/88)
Michael Rotondi (Architect, Morphosis) (2/26/88)

San Juan Capistrano Library
Raymundo Becera (then City Planner to San Juan Capistrano, now private planning consultant) (4/2/88, 4/5/88)
Pamela Gibson Hallerin (Orange County historian, then assistant to the city manager, now Assistant City Manager to the City of La Palma) (4/5/88)
Elizabeth Martinez Smith (County Librarian, Orange County) (4/5/88)
Steve Julian (City Manager to San Juan Capistrano since June 1981) (4/5/88)
Chris McSparren (Regional Manager of Orange County Public Library) (4/5/88)
Emily Jackson (Branch Librarian, San Juan Capistrano Library) (4/5/88)
Michael Graves (Architect) (5/16/88)

Monterey Bay Aquarium
Julie Packard (Executive Director, Monterey Bay Aquarium) (6/21/88)
Linda Rhodes (Architect) (6/20/88)
Charles Davis (Architect, Esherick Homsey Dodge and Davis) (6/20/88)

7. I have recently completed a study of the relationship between design and financing for the Urban Land Institute titled "Good Design/Good business in Real Estate Development." This report addresses some of the missing data issues by focusing on developer clients and projects with strict financial constraints.

8. The name Venice III derives from its position as the third and final member of a series of "alley houses," small buildings added to existing houses at the alley end of the lots, in Venice, California, by Morphosis.

9. The competition is a way to obtain both architect and building design simultaneously, thereby reducing the uncertainty and risk inherent to the design process (see chapter 3).

10. Another case, cited by the clients but not the architect, concerns the shape of the roof on La Salla building in the library complex. The architect wanted to change the roof form proposed in the competition scheme, but the clients insisted it remain the same.

11. This is a common belief within professions, neatly analyzed by Larson in her book on professionalism (1977). Indeed, these statements about losing money might all be espoused theory that does not reflect actual earnings. When the AIA gathered leaders of "signature" (star) firms together, they indicated that they make good profits in their offices (see AIA Memo 1989).

12. Critiques of the aquarium in professional journals have cited the confusing circulation through the building as a significant weakness (see, for example, Schmertz 1985).

13. It is not clear what architects mean when they say they are "losing money," "making a profit," or "breaking even." Without carful review of confidential financial documents unavailable to this study, reports about the economics of excellent projects must be regarded with some skepticism.

14. A content analysis of the interview transcripts generated a list of some forty statements that could be made about all three projects. These statements were sorted several times into different categorical groupings by the Q-Sort method, from which arose the primary and secondary organizations reported here.

15. According to Graves, for example, when the library's axis was called into question, the clients requested a specific solution—one that he did not feel was appropriate. He fought not to keep the axis exactly as originally proposed, but to have the opportunity to develop a new, more appropriate solution that met their requirements. This example is the exception; the client proposed a specific alternative rather than taking advantage of the architect's expertise, and the building suffered for it.

16. The eight principles of excellent organizations are so broad as to conceal the full range of Peters and Waterman's observations. For example, a bias toward action includes a disdain for formal organizational structure, the idea that even complex circumstances require simple responses, the effectiveness of small, short-term task forces, and so on. Likewise, their categories overlap far more than the labels imply, so that each of the eight principles seems to be based on certain more fundamental principles, such as informality, small-scale operations, and a service orientation (see Peters and Waterman 1982:302). At this more fundamental level, there is substantial correspondence between my work and theirs.

17. The idea was actually David Packard's; since Hewlett Packard was one of Peters and Waterman's excellent corporations, the correlation is not coincidental. Packard expected the architectural firm to perform as any other excellent organization under the circumstances.

7   **CONCLUSION**

1. The analysis of Coxe et al. does not focus on the dominance relationship between architects and clients, but rather on a 3 × 2 matrix that describes six distinct orientations for architectural firms. Coxe suggests that the organizational goals for each type are unique, whereas I argue that the organization of practice as a social process is fundamental to all firms.

2. This outline of typical subject areas for professional practice courses is based on responses to an AIA request for participation sent to all American architectural schools to develop a guide to teaching practice (1988). The NAAB criteria for the practice area of a curriculum explicitly requires coverage of each of the following areas: project process, project finance and economics, business and practice management, and law and regulations (NAAB 1987, "Criteria and Procedures").

3. Under the leadership of first Lou Marines and then Jim Franklin, there has been an effort to explore the relationship between practice and design in the AIA. Franklin initiated a program called Design/Practice 90s, looking specifically at excellence in architectural practice.

BIBLIOGRAPHY

Abarbanel, Jerome. "Architects and Their Clients: Interorganizational Decision-Making between Professional Service Firms and their Client-Organizations." Ph.D. diss., Cornell University, 1979.

Ackerman, James. "Ars Sine Scientia Nihil Est: Gothic Theory of Architecture at the Cathedral of Milan." *Art Bulletin* 31 (1949): 84–111.

Aiken, M. and J. Hage. "Organizational Alienation: A Comparative Analysis." *American Sociological Review* 31, no. 4 (August 1966): 497–507.

American Institute of Architects. *The Architect's Handbook of Professional Practice.* Ed. David Haviland. Washington, D.C.: The American Institute of Architects (AIA), 1988.

American Institute of Architects. *The Architect's Handbook of Professional Practice.* Washington, D.C.: AIA.
1969. Ch. 2: "The Construction Industry."
1969. Ch. 11: "Project Procedures."
1970. Ch. 9: "Owner-Architect Agreements."
1972. Ch. 4: "Careers in Architecture."
1972. Doc B551: "Statement of the Architect's Services."
1975. Ch. 5: "The Architect and Client."
1975. Ch. 10: "Interprofessional Agreements."
1982. Doc D200: "Project Checklist."
1987. Doc B141: "Standard Form of Agreement between Owner and Architect."

American Institute of Architects. "1983 AIA Survey of Membership: The Status of Women in the Profession." Special Report by the Women in the Profession Committee. Washington, D.C.: AIA, 1985.

American Institute of Architects. "1987 AIA Firm Survey Report." Washington, D.C.: AIA, 1987.

American Institute of Architects. "1989 AIA Firm Survey Report." Washington, D.C.: AIA, 1989.

American Institute of Architects. *Architecture Fact Book.* Washington, D.C.: AIA, 1988.

American Institute of Architects. "Code of Ethics and Professional Conduct." Washington, D.C.: AIA, 1987.

American Institute of Architects. "Ethical Principles." Doc 6J400. Washington, D.C.: AIA, 1981.

American Institute of Architects. "In Search of Design Excellence." Washington, D.C.: AIA, 1989.

American Institute of Architects. "Myths About Top Designers." *Memo* (July/Aug 1989): 5.

American Institute of Architects. "Report on the AIA Marketing Architectural Services Survey." Washington, D.C.: AIA, 1988.

American Institute of Architects. "Survey of the Professions—Individual Members." Report prepared by Case and Company. San Francisco, 1974.

American Institute of Architects. "Top Design Firms Keep Their Eye on Bottom Line: Good Design." *Memo* (July/Aug 1989): 5–6.

Anonymous. "No Academic Matter: Unconscious Discrimination in Environmental Design Education." In *New Space for Women*, ed. G. R. Wekerle, R. Peterson, and D. Morley. Boulder, Colorado: Westview Press, 1980, 235–253.

Aronson, Steven M. L. *Hype*. New York: Morrow, 1983.

Architectural Forum. "100 Largest Architectural Firms in the U.S." Vol. 120, no. 4 (April 1964): 14–16.

Architectural Education Study, vols. 1 and 2. Sponsored by the Consortium of East Coast Schools of Architecture and by the Mellon Foundation, 1981.

Architecture. "Survey of N.Y. City Firms Finds Income 'Woefully Inadequate.'" Vol. 71, no. 8 (July 1982): 21.

Architecture. "Decline in Design Firms' Profits Reported by Financial Survey." Vol. 71, no. 14 (December 1982): 16.

Argyris, Chris and D. A. Schon. *Theory in Practice: Increasing Professional Effectiveness*. San Francisco: Jossey-Bass, 1982.

Balfour, Alan. "Captive of Love and Ignorance: Architecture Education and Practice." In *Architecture Education Study*, vol. 1, 771–801. Sponsored by the Consortium of East Coast Schools of Architecture and the Mellon Foundation, 1981.

Bannister, T. C., ed. *The Architect at Mid-Century*. Report of the Commission for the Survey of Education and Registration of the American Institute of Architects (1950 survey). New York: Reinhold Publishing, 1954.

Barker, Roger. *Ecological Psychology*. Stanford: Stanford University Press, 1968.

Bate, P. "The Impact of Organizational Culture on Approaches to Organizational Problem Solving." *Organizational Studies* 5, no. 1 (1984).

Becker, Howard S. "Art as Collective Action." *American Sociological Review* 39, no. 6 (December 1974): 767–776.

Becker, Howard S. *Art Worlds*. Berkeley: University of California Press, 1982.

Becker, Howard S., B. Geer, E. C. Hughes, & A. L. Strauss. *Boys in White*. Chicago: University of Chicago Press, 1961.

Beinart, Julian. "Analysis of the Content of Design." In *Architecture Education Study*, vol. 1, 3–157. Sponsored by the Consortium of East Coast Schools of Architecture and by the Mellon Foundation, 1981.

Berger, Peter L. *Invitation to Sociology: A Humanistic Perspective*. New York: Anchor Books, 1963.

Bergren, Ann. "Interplay of Opposites." *House and Garden* (January 1986): 127–133, 174.

Berlin, Brent, D. Breedlove, and P. Raven. "Covert Categories and Folk Taxonomies." *American Anthropologist* 70, no. 2 (April 1968): 290–299.

Blankenship, Ralf. *Colleagues in Organization: The Social Construction of Professional Work*. New York: Wiley, 1977.

Blau, Judith. *Architects and Firms: A Sociological Perspective on Architectural Practice*. Cambridge: MIT Press, 1984.

Blau, Judith. "Beautiful Buildings and Breaching the Laws: A Study of Architectural Firms." *Revue Internationale de Sociologie* 12 (April/August, 1976): 110–128.

Blau, Judith. "Expertise and Power in Professional Organizations." *Sociology of Work and Occupations* 6, no. 1 (February 1979): 103–123.

Blau, Judith. "Where Architects Work: A Change Analysis, 1970–80." In *The Design Professions and the Built Environment*, ed. Paul Knox. London, Croom Helm, 1987.

Blau, Judith and K. L. Lieben. "Growth, Decline, and Death: A Panel Study of Architectural Firms." In *Professionals and Urban Form*, ed. J. Blau, M. E. La Gory, and J. S. Pipkin. Albany: State University of New York Press, 1983, 224–250.

Bledstein, Burton J. *The Culture of Professionalism: The Middle Class and the Development of Higher Education in America*. New York: Norton, 1976.

Boudon, Phillipe. *Lived-In Architecture*. Cambridge: MIT Press, 1979.

Boughey, Howard N. "Blueprints for Behavior: The Intentions of Architects to Influence Social Action through Design." Ph.D. diss., Princeton University, 1969.

Boulding, Kenneth. *Conflict and Defense*. New York: Harper and Row, 1962.

Bourdieu, Pierre. *Distinction*. Cambridge: Harvard University Press, 1984.

Bourdieu, Pierre. *Outline of a Theory of Practice*. New York: Cambridge University Press, 1977.

Boyle, Bernard Michael. "Architectural Practice in America 1986–1965—Ideal and Reality." In *The Architect*, ed. S. Kostof. New York: Oxford University Press, 1977, 309–344.

Briggs, Martin S. *The Architect in History*. New York: Da Capo Press, 1927. Reprint. 1974.

Bucciarelli, Louis L. "An Ethnographic Perspective on Engineering Design." *Design Studies* 9, no. 3 (July 1988): 155–168.

Building Design and Construction. "Owner Survey—How Owners Decide." Vol. 21, no. 1 (April 1980): 78–91.

Burke, W. Warner. "Conceptual and Theoretical Underpinnings of Organization Development." In *Organizational Development*, ed. Mark Plovnick, R. E. Fry, and W. W. Burke. Boston: Little, Brown, 1982, 210–222.

Business Week. "Who's Excellent Now?" Nov. 5, 1984: 76–88.

Byrne, John A. "Business Fads: What's In—And Out." *Business Week* Jan. 20, 1986: 52–61.

The Charlottesville Tapes. Transcript of the Conference at the University of Virginia School of Architecture, Charlottesville, Virginia, November 12 and 13, 1982. New York: Rizzoli, 1985.

Cherry, Colin. *On Human Communication.* Cambridge: MIT Press, 1957.

Churchman, C. West. "Wicked Problems." *Management Science* 4, no. 14 (1967).

Churchman, C. West. Gaither Lecture Series, University of California, Berkeley, 1981.

Cicourel, Aaron. *Cognitive Sociology.* London: Penguin, 1973.

Clifford, James. "Introduction: Partial Truths." In *Writing Culture: The Poetics and Politics of Ethnography*, ed. James Clifford and George E. Marcus. Berkeley: University of California Press, 1986, 1–26.

Clifford, James and George E. Marcus. *Writing Culture: The Poetics and Politics of Ethnography.* Berkeley: University of California Press, 1986.

Colman, A. D. "Notes on the Design Process: A Psychiatrist Looks at Architecture." *Journal of Architectural Education* 27, nos. 2 and 3 (1974).

Cooper Marcus, Clare. "The House as Symbol of Self." In *Designing for Human Behavior: Architecture and the Behavioral Sciences*, ed. Jon Lang et al. Stroudsburg, Penn.: Dowden, Hutchinson and Ross, 1974, 130–146.

Cooper Marcus, Clare, and Wendy Sarkissian. *Housing as if People Mattered.* Berkeley: University of California Press, 1987.

Coxe, Weld. "Can Design Leadership be Managed?" *Progressive Architecture* 65, no. 7 (July 1984): 55–58, 60.

Coxe, Weld, N. F. Hartung, H. H. Hochberg, B. J. Lewis, D. H. Maister, R. F. Mattox, P. A. Piven. "Charting Your Course: Master Strategies for Organizing and Managing Architectural Firms." *Architectural Technology* 4, no. 3 (May/June 1986): 52–58.

Coxe, Weld, N. F. Hartung, H. H. Hochberg, B. J. Lewis, D. H. Maister, R. F. Mattox, P. A. Piven. *Success Strategies for Design Professionals.* New York: McGraw-Hill, 1987.

Cuff, Dana. "The Architecture Profession." In *The Architect's Handbook of Professional Practice*, ed. D. Haviland. Washington, D.C.: AIA, 1988.

Cuff, Dana. "The Context for Design: Six Characteristics." In *Knowledge for Design*, ed. P. Bart and G. Francescato. College Park, Maryland: Proceedings of EDRA-13, 1982, 38–47.

Cuff, Dana. "Negotiating Architecture." In *Design Research Interactions*, ed. A. Osterberg, C. Tiernan, and R. Findlay. Ames, Iowa: Proceedings of EDRA-12, 1981, 160–171.

Cuff, Dana. "Negotiating Architecture: A Study of Architects and Clients in Design Practice." Ph.D. diss., University of California, Berkeley, 1982.

Cuff, Dana. "The Social Art of Design at the Office and the Academy." *Journal of Architectural and Planning Research* 6, no. 3 (Autumn 1989a): 186–203.

Cuff, Dana. "Teaching and Learning Design Drawing." *Journal of Architectural Education*, 33, no. 3 (April 1980): 5–9, 32.

Cuff, Dana. "Through the Looking Glass: Seven New York Architects and their People." In *Architects' People*, ed. W. R. Ellis and D. Cuff. New York: Oxford University Press, 1989b, 64–102.

Cullen, John. "Structural Aspects of Architectural Profession." In *Professionals and Urban Form*, ed. J. Blau, M. La Gory, and J. Pipkin. Albany: State University of New York Press, 1983, 280–297.

Cullen, John B. *The Structure of Professionalism*. New York: Petrocelli, 1978.

Davis, Douglas and Mary Rourke. "Real Dream Houses." *Newsweek* 88, no. 14 (Oct. 4, 1976): 66–69.

Deal, Terrence E. & Allan A. Kennedy. *Corporate Cultures: The Rules and Rituals of Corporate Life*. Reading, Mass: Addison–Wesley Pub. Co., 1982.

Dewar, T. R. "The Professionalization of the Client." *Social Policy*, 8, no. 4 (January/February 1978): 4–9.

Dinham, Sarah M. "Architectural Education: Is Jury Criticism a Valid Teaching Technique?" *Architectural Record* 174, no. 13 (November 1986): 51, 53.

Dixon, John Morris. "Design Quality in the Big Firm." *Progressive Architecture* 63, no. 2 (February 1982): 23–24.

Dixon, John Morris. "P/A Reader Poll: Compensation." *Progressive Architecture* 67, no. 10 (October 1986): 21–22.

Dostoglu, Sibel. "On the Fundamental Dilemmas of Architecture-As-Profession." *Journal of the Faculty of Architecture METU*, 7, no. 2 (1986): 51–66.

Draper, Joan. "The Ecole des Beaux-Arts and the Architectural Profession in the United States: The Case of John Galen Howard." In *The Architect*, ed. S. Kostof. New York: Oxford University Press, 1977, 209–237.

Eliade, Mircea. *Myths, Rites, Symbols*. New York: Harper & Row, 1976.

Ellis, W. Russell, Tonia Chao, and Janet Parrish. "Levi's Place: A Building Biography." *Places* 2, no. 1 (1985): 57–70.

Ellis, W. Russell and Dana Cuff, eds. *Architects' People*. New York: Oxford University Press, 1989.

Esherick, Joseph. "Architectural Education in the Thirties and Seventies: A Personal View." In *The Architect*, ed. S. Kostof. New York: Oxford, 1977, 238–279.

Fisher, Thomas. "P/A Reader Poll: Career Satisfaction." *Progressive Architecture* 68 (1987): 15–16, 20.

Fitch, J. M. "The Profession of Architecture." In *The Professions in America*, ed. K. Lynn. Boston: Houghton Mifflin Co., 1965, 231–241.

Forester, John. "Designing: Making Sense Together in Practical Conversations." *Journal of Architectural Education* 38, no. 3 (Spring 1985): 14–20.

Forester, John. *Planning in the Face of Power*. Berkeley: University of California Press, 1989.

Forester, John. "Understanding Planning Practice: An Empirical, Practical and Normative Account." *Journal of Planning Education and Research* 1, no. 2 (Winter 1982): 59–71.

Franck, Karen A. and Sherry Ahrentzen, eds. *New Households, New Housing*. New York: Van Nostrand, 1989.

Franklin, James R. "Toward a Standard of Care." Washington, D.C.: AIA, 1988.

Freidson, Eliot. "The Changing Nature of Professional Control." *Annual Review of Sociology* 10 (1984): 1–20.

Freidson, Eliot. *Professional Powers*. Chicago: University of Chicago Press, 1986.

Gardiner, Paul and R. Rothwell. "Tough Customers: Good Designs." *Design Studies* 6, no. 1 (Jan. 1985): 7–17.

Garfinkel, Harold. *Studies in Ethnomethodology*. Englewood Cliffs: Prentice-Hall, 1967.

Geertz, Clifford. *The Interpretation of Cultures*. New York: Basic Books, 1973.

Geertz, Clifford. *Works and Lives: The Anthropologist as Author*. Stanford: Stanford University Press, 1988.

Giddens, Anthony. *Central Problems in Social Theory*. Berkeley: University of California Press, 1979.

Goffman, Erving. *Forms of Talk*. Philadelphia: University of Pennsylvania Press, 1981.

Gorb, Peter. "The Business of Design Management." *Design Studies* 7, no. 2 (April 1986): 106–110.

Gordon, Douglas E. "The Ins and Outs of Specialization." *Architecture* 76, no. 10 (Oct. 1987): 95–98.

Greer, Nora Richter. "The Plight of Minority Architects." *Architecture* 74, no. 4 (April 1985): 58–61.

Gumperz, John J. *Discourse Strategies*. Cambridge: Cambridge University Press, 1982.

Gumperz, John and Dell Hymes, eds. *Directions in Sociolinguistics*. New York: Holt, Reinhart and Winston, 1971.

Gutman, Robert. *Architectural Practice: A Critical View*. New Jersey: Princeton Architectural Press, 1988.

Gutman, Robert. "Architecture: The Entrepreneurial Profession." *Progressive Architecture* 58, no. 5 (May 1977): 55–58.

Gutman, Robert. "Human Nature in Architectural Theory: The Example of Louis Kahn." In *Architects' People*, ed. W. R. Ellis, and D. Cuff. New York: Oxford University Press, 1989, 105–129.

Gutman, Robert and B. Westergaard. "What Architecture Schools Should Know About Their Graduates." *Journal of Architectural Education*, 31, no. 2 (1978): 2–11.

Gutman, Robert, B. Westergaard, and D. Hicks. "The Structure of Design Firms in the Construction Industry." *Environment and Planning B* 4 (1977): 3–29.

Hack, Gary and M. Canto. "Collaboration and Context in Urban Design." *Design Studies* 5, no. 3 (July 1984): 178–184.

Hamilton, E. G. "NCARB: Move to a Narrower Information Gap." *AIA Journal* (November 1973): 27–29.

Handlin, David P. *The American Home: Architecture and Society. 1815–1915.* Boston: Little, Brown, 1979.

Haviland, David, W. Coxe, D. Cuff, P. Derrington, S. Gatschet, S. M. Goldblatt, C. Grapham, R. C. Greenstreet, J. A. Seiler, G. S. Wright. "Instructor's Guide: The Architect's Handbook of Professional Practice." Washington, D.C.: AIA, 1988.

Hayden, Dolores. *The Grand Domestic Revolution.* Cambridge: MIT Press, 1981.

Hirsch, Ruth. "Management: The Market for Architects." *Progressive Architecture* 67, no. 7 (July 1986): 63–64, 66, 68.

Hosticka, Carl J. "We Don't Care About What Happened, We Only Care About What Is Going To Happen: Lawyer-Client Negotiations of Reality." *Social Problems* 26, no. 5 (June 1979): 599–610.

Houle, Cyril O. *Continuing Learning in the Professions.* San Francisco: Jossey-Bass, 1980.

Howland, Mark. "On Becoming an Architect." *Perspectives* 5, no. 1 (June 1985): 4–7.

Hoyt, Charles K. "Architects' Salaries Going Up? The New York Chapter Takes on the Cause." *Architectural Record* 170, no. 9 (July 1982): 17.

Hoyt, Donald P. "The Relationship between College Grades and Achievement. A Review of Literature." American College Testing Research Reports no. 7. Iowa City: Research and Development Division, 1965.

Hughes, E. C. *Men and Their Work.* Glencoe: The Free Press, 1958.

Illich, Ivan. *Medical Nemesis.* New York: Bantam Books, 1977.

Jamous, H. and B. Peloille. "Changes in The French University Hospital System." In *Professions and Professionalization*, ed. J. A. Jackson. Cambridge: Cambridge University Press, 1970, 111–152.

Jencks, C. and D. Riesman. *The Academic Revolution*. New York: Doubleday and Co., 1968.

Jenkins, F. *Architect and Patron*. London: Oxford University Press, 1961.

Joroff, Michael and J. A. Moore. "Case Method Teaching about Design Process Management." *Journal of Architectural Education* 38, no. 1 (Fall 1984): 14–17.

Klegon, Douglas. "The Sociology of Professions: An Emerging Perspective." *Sociology of Work and Occupations* 5, no. 3 (August 1978).

Knox, Paul, ed. *The Design Professions and the Built Environment*. London: Croom Helm, 1988.

Komendant, August. *Eighteen Years with Louis I. Kahn*. Englewood, N.J.: Aloray Publishing, 1975.

Kostof, Spiro, ed. *The Architect*. New York: Oxford University Press, 1977a.

Kostof, Spiro. "The Architect in the Middle Ages." In *The Architect*, ed. S. Kostof. New York: Oxford University Press, 1977b, 55–95.

Kostof, Spiro. "The Practice of Architecture in the Ancient World." In *The Architect*, ed. S. Kostof. New York: Oxford University Press, 1977c, 3–27.

Lapidus, Morris. *Architecture: A Profession and Business*. New York: Van Nostrand Reinhold, 1967.

Larson, Magali Sarfatti. "Emblem and Exception: The Historical Definition of the Architect's Professional Role." In *Professionals and Urban Form*, ed. Judith Blau, M. E. La Gory, and J. S. Pipkin. Albany: Statue University of New York Press, 1983, 49–86.

Larson, Magali S. *The Rise of Professionalism: A Sociological Analysis*. Berkeley: University of California Press, 1977.

Larson, Magali, G. Leon and J. Bolick. "The Professional Supply of Design: A Descriptive Study." In *Professionals and Urban Form*, ed. Judith Blau, M. E. La Gory, and J. S. Pipkin. Albany: Statue University of New York Press, 1983, 251–279.

Leiter, Kenneth. *A Primer on Ethnomethodology*. New York: Oxford University Press, 1980.

Levy, Richard Michael. "The Professionalization of American Architects and Civil Engineers, 1865–1917." Ph.D. diss., University of California, Berkeley, 1980.

Lifchez, Raymond. *Rethinking Architecture*. Berkeley: University of California Press, 1987.

Maister, David H. "Lessons in Client-Loving." *Architectural Technology* 3, no. 4 (Fall 1986): 17–19.

Maister, David H. "Industry Specialization: Essential But Hard to Manage." *Journal of Management Consulting* 2, no. 1 (Winter 1984/85): 50–55.

Marmot, Alexi and M. Symes. "The Social Context of Design: A Case Problem Approach." *Journal of Architectural Education* 38, no. 4 (Summer 1985): 27–31.

Martin, W. Mike. "A Conceptual Model for Design Education." Ph.D. diss., University of California, Berkeley, 1983.

Massachusetts Institute of Technology. *Processes in Architecture: A Documentation of Six Examples*. Special issue of *Plan* (Exhibit catalogue, Hayden Gallery) no. 10 (Spring 1979).

Mayer, Martin. *The Builders: Houses, People, Neighborhoods, Governments, Money*. New York: Norton, 1978.

Mead, Margaret. *Coming of Age in Samoa: A Psychological Study in Primitive Youth for Western Civilizations*. New York: West Marrow, 1928.

McCommons, Richard E., G. P. Haney, B. C. Ready, and J. Osborn, eds. *Architecture Schools in North America*. Princeton: Peterson's Guides, 1982.

McCommons, Richard E., ed. *Guide to Architecture Schools in North America*. Washington, D.C.: Association of Collegiate Schools of Architecture Press, 1989.

Mills, C. Wright. "Man in Middle: The Designer." In *Power, Politics and People*, ed. I. L. Horowitz. New York: Oxford University Press, 1963, 374–386.

Montgomery, Roger. "Modern Architecture Invents New People." In *Architects' People*, ed. W. R. Ellis and D. Cuff. New York: Oxford University Press, 1989, 260–281.

Murchison, Kenneth. "How Much Should an Architect Know?" *Architectural Forum* 53, no. 2 (August 1930): 225–226.

National Architectural Accrediting Board. "Criteria and Procedures." Washington, D.C.: The Board of NAAB, 1987.

National Council of Architectural Registration Boards, IDP Coordinating Committee. "IDP Training Guidelines 1987–1988." Washington, D.C.: NCARB, 1987.

National Council of Architectural Registration Boards. "Member Board Requirements." Washington, D.C.: NCARB, 1985.

Organization of Architectural and Engineering Employees. "A Survey of Architectural and Engineering Employees of California." Fourth Annual Profile Survey, 1973.

Osborne, C. Francis. "An Appeal to Caesar." *Architectural Record* 1 (1891–1892): 281–285.

Osman, M. E. "Survey of Firms Charts Decline in Employment." *AIA Journal* 64, no. 3 (September 1975): 41–42.

Peters, Tom and Nancy Austin. *A Passion for Excellence*. New York: Random House, 1985.

Peters, Thomas J. and Robert H. Waterman. *In Search of Excellence*. New York: Warner Books, 1982.

Polshek, James Stewart. "Introduction." In *The Making of an Architect, 1881–1981*, ed. Richard Oliver. New York: Rizzoli, 1981, 1–4.

Porter, William. "Notes on the Inner Logic of Designing: Two Thought-Experiments." *Design Studies* 9, no. 3 (July 1988): 169–180.

Prichard, J. Robert S. "Professional Civil Liability and Continuing Competence." In *The Professions and Public Policy*, ed. Philip Slayton and M. J. Trebilcock. Toronto: University of Toronto Press, 1978.

Progressive Architecture. "Twenty Seventh Annual Progressive Architecture Awards." Vol. 61, no. 1 (January 1980): 98.

Report and Working Papers: Graham Foundation Seminars on Architectural Education. Chicago: Graham Foundation for Advanced Studies in the Fine Arts, February 1965. [Includes "Report by the Special Committee on Education AIA, The Commission on Education," by R. F. Hastings et al. of the American Institute of Architects.]

Rittel, Horst. "Evaluating Evaluators." In *Papers Published from The Accreditation Evaluation Conference of the National Architectural Accrediting Board*. New Orleans, March 1976, 77–91.

Rittel, Horst and M. Webber. "Dilemmas in a General Theory of Planning," *Policy Sciences* 4 (1973): 155–169.

Rose, Stuart W. *Achieving Excellence in Your Design Practice*. New York: Whitney Library of Design, 1987.

Rutland, P. J. "Analysis of Architects' Work Patterns." Sydney, Australia: Research Paper 4, Architectural Research Foundation, Faculty of Architecture, University of Sydney, 1972.

Saint, Andrew. *The Image of the Architect*. New Haven: Yale, 1983.

Sawyier, Fay Horton. "A Service Model for Architects." *International Journal of Applied Sociology* 1, no. 3 (Spring 1983): 55–56.

Schluntz, R. and G. Gebert. "Tracking Study of Architectural Graduates for the Years 1967, 1972 and 1977. Final Report." Washington, D.C.: Association of Collegiate Schools of Architecture, 1980.

Schmertz, Mildred F. "A New Aquarium for Cannery Row." *Architectural Record* 173, no. 2 (February 1985): 114–123.

Schon, Donald. *The Reflective Practitioner*. New York: Basic Books, 1983.

Schon, Donald. "Designing: Rules, Types and Worlds." *Design Studies* 9, no. 3 (July 1988): 181–190.

Schutz, Alfred. *Collected Papers I: The Problem of Social Reality*. The Hague: Martinius Nijhoff, 1962.

Schutz, Alfred. *Collected Papers II: Studies in Social Theory*. The Hague: Martinius Nijhoff, 1964.

Scott-Brown, Denise. "With People in Mind." *Journal of Architectural Education* 35, no. 1 (Fall 1981): 43–45.

Scully, Vincent. *American Architecture and Urbanism*. New York: Praeger, 1969.

Stelling, Joan and Rue Bucher. "Vocabularies of Realism in Professional Socialization." *Social Science and Medicine* 7 (1973): 661–675.

Strauss, Anselm. *Negotiations: Varieties, Contexts, Processes and Social Order*. San Francisco: Jossey-Bass, 1978.

Traweek, Sharon. *Beamtimes and Lifetimes: The World of High Energy Physicists*. Cambridge: Harvard University Press, 1988.

Treib, Marc. "Of Cardboard Cities and Public Politics." *Journal of Architectural Education* 35, no. 3 (Spring 1982): 18–21.

U.S. Department of Commerce, Bureau of Census. "Census of Service Industries, 1982." Geographic Area Series SC82-A-52 and Industry Series SC82-1-5.

Van Gennep, Arnold. *The Rites of Passage*. Chicago: University of Chicago Press, 1960.

Van Rensselaer, M. "Client and Architect" [1890]. In *Roots of Contemporary American Architecture*, by L. Mumford. New York: Reinhold Publishing Corp., 1952, 202.

Vasari, Giorgio. *The Lives of the Painters, Sculptors and Architects* [1550]. Trans. A. B. Hinds. New York: Dutton Everyman's Library, 1927 (rev. ed. 1963).

Ventre, Francis. "Building in Eclipse, Architecture in Secession." *Progressive Architecture* 63, no. 12 (December 1982): 58–61.

Ventre, Francis. "Myth and Paradox in the Building Enterprise." In *The Design Professions and the Built Environment*, ed. Paul Knox. Beckenham, England: Croom Helm, 1987, 147–174.

Vickers, Geoffrey. *The Art of Judgment*. New York: Harper and Row, 1984 (2d ed.).

Vischer, Jaqueline C. & C. Cooper Marcus. "Evaluating Evaluation: Analysis of a Housing Design Awards Program." *Places* 3, no. 1 (Winter 1986): 66–85.

Vitruvius. *The Ten Books of Architecture*. Trans. M. H. Morgan. New York: Dover, 1960.

von Moos, Stanislaus. *Le Corbusier: Elements of a Synthesis* [1968]. Cambridge: MIT Press, 1979.

Vrakking, Willem J. "Revamping Organizations through Cultural Intervention." *Journal of Management Consulting* 2, no. 3 (1985): 10–16.

Walton, Thomas. *Architecture and the Corporation*. New York: Macmillan, 1988.

Wittman, Friedner. "Architectural Planning and Design of Complex Organizations." Ph.D. diss., University of California, Berkeley, 1984.

Wolff, Janet. *The Social Production of Art*. New York: New York University Press, 1984.

Wright, Frank Lloyd. *The Future of Architecture*. 1953. Reprint. New York: Mentor, 1963.

Zartman, I. W. *The Fifty Percent Solution*. New York: Anchor Press/Doubleday, 1976.

ILLUSTRATION CREDITS

1.1 Warner Brothers Archives at the University of Southern California.

1.2 Courtesy of Skidmore, Owings and Merrill, Chicago. Photo by Victor Jorgensen.

1.3 The MIT Museum.

1.4 From D. Jacobs, *Architecture* (Newsweek Books, 1974).

2.1 Courtesy of Frank O. Gehry and Associates. Photo by Kevin M. Daly.

2.2 The American Institute of Architects Archives.

2.3 Photo by Paul R. Baker. Copyright Carley P. Angell and Susan Battley.

2.4 College of Environmental Design Documents Collection, University of California, Berkeley.

2.5 Boston Athenaeum.

2.6 From the *Grandes Chroniques de Saint-Denis* (fourteenth century).

2.7 Courtesy of the Frank Lloyd Wright Archives.

2.8 The MIT Museum.

2.9 Photo by Steven Burr Williams.

2.10 Courtesy of the Chase Manhattan Archives.

3.1 Warner Brothers Archives at the University of Southern California.

3.2 Courtesy of Frank O. Gehry and Associates. Photo by Kevin M. Daly.

3.3 Courtesy of SCI–ARC Archives.

3.4 The American Institute of Architects Archives.

3.6 Courtesy of the Frank Lloyd Wright Archives.

3.7, 8 Courtesy of the School of Architecture at the University of Southern California.

3.9 American Institute of Architects.

4.1 Courtesy of Frank O. Gehry and Associates. Photo by Dana Cuff.

4.2 Courtesy of the School of Architecture at the University of Southern California.

4.3, 4 Courtesy of SCI–ARC Archives.

4.5 Courtesy of the School of Architecture at the University of Southern California.

4.6, 7 Courtesy of SCI–ARC Archives.

4.8 Esther McCoy Papers, Archives of American Art, Smithsonian Institution.

4.9 Courtesy of the School of Architecture at the University of Southern California.

4.10 Courtesy of the National Council of Architectural Registration Boards.

4.11 Special Collections, California Polytechnic State University, San Luis Obispo.

4.12 Courtesy of the Frank Lloyd Wright Archives.

4.13 Esther McCoy Papers, Archives of American Art, Smithsonian Institution.

5.1 Courtesy of Skidmore, Owings and Merrill, Chicago.

5.2 Photo by Pedro E. Guerrero.

5.3 Esther McCoy Papers, Archives of American Art, Smithsonian Institution. Photo by Willard Morgan.

5.4, 5 Courtesy of CRS-Sirrene, Inc.

5.6 Courtesy of Frank O. Gehry and Associates. Photo by Kevin M. Daly.

5.7 Avery Library, Columbia University.

5.9, 10, 11 Drawings by the office of Michael Underhill.

6.1 Photo by Tim Street Porter.

6.2, 3 Drawings by Morphosis.

6.4 Photo by Tim Street Porter.

6.5 Photo by Dana Cuff.

6.6 Drawing by Morphosis.

6.7 Photo by Paschall/Taylor.

6.8, 9 Drawings by Michael Graves, Architect.

6.10 Photo by Paschall/Taylor.

6.11 Sketches by Michael Graves.

6.12 Photo by Paschall/Taylor.

6.13 Photo by Nicholas Sapieha.

6.14, 15 Drawings by Esherick Homsey Dodge and Davis, Architects.

6.16 Photo by Jane Lidz.

6.17 Drawing by Esherick Homsey Dodge and Davis, Architects.

6.18 Photo by Peter H. Dodge.

7.1 Warner Brothers Archives at the University of Southern California.

7.2 Esther McCoy Papers, Archives of American Art, Smithsonian Institution.

7.3 Photo by Steven Burr Williams.

7.4 Courtesy of Skidmore, Owings and Merrill, Chicago.

Ideology. *See* Beliefs
Individualism, 11, 45, 73–74, 195,
    197, 241–242, 251–254
Intern Architect Development Pro-
    gram, 134, 259, 277n9, 280n9. *See
    also* Apprenticeship; Architects,
    entry-level

Jobs, architectural. *See also* Career,
    architecture as
  categories, 138–139
  first, 130–133
  mobility, 134, 164
  satisfaction, 49, 51–52
  technical, 138–139
Johnson, Herbert, 80
Jury. *See* Critique

Kahn, Louis, 153, 252
Kauffman, Edgar, Sr., 172
Knowledge. *See* Expertise
Komendant, August, 252
Kostof, Spiro, 22, 74

Labor market for architects, 130–132
Lapidus, Morris, 71, 77, 91
Larson, Magali, 33, 35, 37, 43, 45
Law. *See* Professions
Leadership, 170, 260
Le Corbusier, 13, 94, 153, 252, 274n9
Liability, 85, 100, 101, 104, 148–149,
    278n19
Licensure. *See* Registration

McKim, Charles, 23, 26
Magazines, architectural, 37, 45, 187,
    197, 258
Management, 69–72, 166, 167, 170,
    219–220, 255–258
  of architectural practice, as field of
    study, 22, 195–196, 235
  as career choice, 140, 149
  of complex process, 40
  and office size, 18, 170, 237, 244
  project, 50, 87–88, 92
Market for services, 23, 35, 149–150
Marketing, 69–70, 104–105, 149–151,
    170, 219–220
Massachusetts Institute of Technol-
    ogy (MIT), 12, 24, 28, 42

Mayne, Thom. *See* Morphosis
Medicine. *See* Professions
Meetings, 85–86, 88
  architect-client, 88, 184, 186–187
  architect-client-consultant, 188–194
  conversation in, 96–98, 185–194,
    206, 282n12
    lack of order, 185–187, 194
    sequencing, 187
    topics raised in, 190–193
    visuals in, 187–188
  studied in this research, 9
Michelangelo, 72
Miscommunication, 165, 188
Monterey Bay Aquarium, 220–232
Moonlighting, 51, 115
Morgan, Julia, 26, 144, 151
Morphosis, 199–209
Myth, 1, 4, 159, 251

National Architectural Accrediting
    Board (NAAB), 107, 279n1, 284n2,
    285n4
Negotiation, 93, 110, 230, 281n4
  between architect and client, 39,
    173, 180, 183
  design as, 10, 95–96
Neutra, Richard, 152, 161

Offices, architectural, 113, 155–157,
    234–235
  advancement within, 138–141, 145–
    146
  culture of, 111–116, 157, 165–171
    dialect, 165–166
  employees in, 18, 50–51, 130–146,
    160–161
  evolution of, 157–164
  founders, 157–160
  physical setting of, 113
  procedures, 166–169
  roles within, 169–171
  size of, 7, 21, 45–49, 155–157, 166,
    244
    large, 46–47, 53, 170, 237
    small, 18, 46, 73, 141, 170
  starting an, 141–145, 146
  success of, 162–163, 206

Theory, espoused, 20–21, 22, 43, 56,
    66, 239
Theory, in-use, 20–21, 22, 43
Transitioning, 157–158, 162
Traweek, Sharon, 116–117, 154,
    279n1

Uncertainty, in design process, 84–91,
    132, 137, 192, 241. *See also* Risk
Underhill, Michael, 178–184
Unemployment, among architects,
    130, 276n22

Values, 19, 115, 160, 166, 244
Vignettes, 93–94, 96–97
  within architectural offices, 17, 109,
    157–158, 159–160, 247
  of client meetings, 57–59, 88, 186,
    189–190
  of conversations among architects,
    132, 146
  of legend, 128
Vitruvius, 71, 84
Voice, 169

Wages. *See* Compensation
Women, in architecture, 8, 121, 128,
    273n6, 274n5, 279n4
  discrimination against, 145–146,
    279n6
Work experience. *See* Experience,
    work-related
Wright, Frank Lloyd, 38, 80, 106, 117,
    147, 152, 158, 172, 253